Leading Issues in
e-Government Research
Volume 2

For researchers, teachers and students

Edited by

Shawren Singh

and

Walter Castelnovo

Leading Issues in e-Government Volume 2

ISBN: 978-1-910810-57-6 (print)

Printed by Lightning Source POD

Published by: Academic Conferences and Publishing International Limited,
Reading, RG4 9SJ, United Kingdom, info@academic-publishing.org
Available from www.academic-bookshop.com .

Contents

About the Editors

Dr Shawren Singh, is a Senior Lecturer and researcher in the School of Computing at the University of South Africa, and has spent more than 15 years teaching and researching in the Information Systems space. His research has focused on e-Government, with particular interest in the design and development of these applications. He has developed models for understanding how e-Government applications are designed and developed. He also has an interest in usability of web-based applications. His research has been published internationally and he has presented papers at several conferences. He holds a BComm, an MSc and a PhD.

Dr Walter Castelnovo, is an Assistant Professor of Information Systems and Inter-organizational Networks at the University of Insubria (Italy). His research interests concern technological and organizational innovation in Public Administration and Inter-organizational Information Systems. He is one of the founders of the Research Center for "Knowledge and Service Management for Business Applications" of the University of Insubria and he is member of the Scientific Committee of the "Interdepartmental Center for Organizational Innovation in Public Administration" of the University of Milan. He served as member of the committee for many international conferences on e-Government and ICT evaluation. He was the General Chair of the 5th European Conference on Information Management and Evaluation (ECIME 2011) and the 13rd European Conference on e-Government (ECEG 2013). He was the Director of the first edition of the ICT for Development International School that was hosted by the University of Insubria in 2012. He is a also member of the Department of Institutional Reforms, e-Government, Cooperation and Communitarian Policies of the Association of Municipalities of the Region Lombardia (Italy).

List of Contributing Authors

Mahmoud Al-dalahmeh, University of Jordan, Amman, Jordan

Omar Al-Hujran, Princess Sumaya University for Technology, Amman, Jordan

Anas Aloudat, University of Jordan, Amman, Jordan

Leonidas Anthopoulos, Technological Education Institute (TEI) of Larissa, Larissa, Greece

Sunil Choenni, Rotterdam University –Creating 010, Rotterdam, The Netherlands

Kevin Cupido, Dept. of Information Systems, University of Cape Town, South Africa

Tony Dwi Susanto, Flinders University of South Australia, Adelaide, Australia

Alptekin Erkollar, Halic University, Istanbul, Turkey

Panos Fitsilis, Technological Education Institute (TEI) of Larissa, Larissa, Greece

Muriel Foulonneau, Luxembourg Institute of Science and Technology, Luxembourg

J. Ramon Gil-Garcia, Centro de Investigación y Docencia Económicas, Mexico

Robert Goodwin, Institute of Technology Sepuluh Nopember, Indonesia

Princely Ifinedo, Cape Breton University, Sydney, Nova Scotia, Canada

Marijn Janssen, Research and Documentation Centre – Ministry of Security and Justice, Den Haag, The Netherlands

Bert-Jaap Koops, Tilburg Institute for Law, Technology, and Society (TILT) of Tilburg University, the Netherlands

Gustav Lidén, Department of Social Sciences, Mid Sweden University, 851 70 Sundsvall, Sweden

Anna Litvinenko, *Free University of Berlin, Germany*

Luis F. Luna-Reyes, *Universidad de las Américas Puebla, Mexico*

Dolores E. Luna, *Universidad de las Américas Puebla, Mexico*

Sébastien Martin, *Université Paris 8, Vincennes-Saint-Denis, France*

Seyed Amin Mousavi, *University of East London, London, UK*

Gabriela Diaz-Murillo, *Universidad de las Américas Puebla, Mexico*

Albert Jacob Meijer, *Utrecht School of Governance in the Netherlands.*

Birgit Oberer, *Kadir Has University, Istanbul, Turkey*

Jacques Ophoff, *Dept. of Information Systems, University of Cape Town, South Africa*

Sjors Overman, *Scientific Council for Government Policy in the Netherlands*

Willem Pieterson, *Northwestern University (Evanston, Il, USA)*

Elias Pimenidis, *Department of Computer Science & Creative Technologies, Faculty of Environment & Technology, University of the West of England, Bristol, UK*

Rodrigo Sandoval-Almazan, *Universidad Autónoma del Estado de México, Mexico*

Mohini Singh, *RMIT University, Melbourne, Victoria, Australia*

Sanne ten Tije, *Twente University, The Netherlands*

Slim Turki, *Luxembourg Institute of Science and Technology, Luxembourg*

Géradine Vidou, *Luxembourg Institute of Science and Technology, Luxembourg*

Anneke Zuiderwijk, *Delft University of Technology, Delft, The Netherlands*

e-Government: A time for critical reflection and more?
An introduction to Leading Issues in e-Government Research Volume 2

For sometime now, e-Government has been a popular concept amongst policy makers, scholars, practitioners, the media and citizens. This is due to the conditional promises offered by e-Government that raise high expectations that the quality of government services to citizens in particular will be improved to being more effective and efficient. However, in pursuing these objectives governments are faced with a number of challenges due to the increase in the size of the population as well as a continuously increasing demand from citizens for more efficient and effective services (Tapscott, 2010), not to mention the persistent effects of the global financial crisis. Citizens in many parts of the world are aware that government processes and practices are still often in need of modernisation. Delays, duplication and waste, have led to increased costs, which are considered to be the hallmarks of government services (Cloete, 2012; Heerden & Rossouw, 2014). ICT, if used appropriately with organisational transformation, has been found to improve efficiency and effectiveness in the private sector and in the past this has led to a demand for the application of these technologies in the public sector as well in the form of e-Government.

e-Government systems have important implications in the lives of individuals, therefore thorough testing and understanding of the possible impacts of technologies is required, even more than those required in the private sector and also considering aspects and possible impacts that are usually neglected in the evaluation of the use of technologies in the private sector. These tests are expensive to perform and also the on-going cost of operating the e-Government systems is considerable. In short, e-Government is expensive and this represents a problem in the public sector where resources are increasingly scarce. With e-Government being one of the most rapidly growing sectors, consuming an important proportion of this sum of money (Singh & Averweg, 2015), there are problems with expenditure on e-Government, as Richard Heeks (2011) pointed out when he said:

> *'If e-Government is so great at cutting costs, how come my taxes haven't gone down?'*

Governments are consuming ever larger portions of national income and many people now believe that their contribution to the functioning of government, i.e. their taxes, should either be reduced or at least curtailed. It appears that the initial promises of e-Government have not been adequately realised, and after the first wave of enthusiasm, the general interest toward e-Government has decreased over the years. This is illustrated in Figure 1 by the decrease in the frequency relating to the search term "e-Government" on the Google search engine.

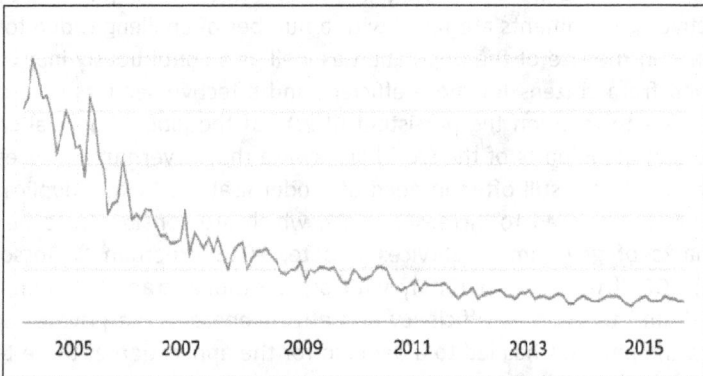

Figure 1: Search of the term "e-Government" on Google (source: Google trend)

Further, due to the evolutionary nature of ICT and a better understanding of the issues related to e-Government, what was initially covered by the umbrella term "e-Government" has developed into more specific concepts, such as "digital government", "mobile government" "ubiquitous government, "transformational government", "networked government", e-democracy", "e-participation" and, more recently, "smart government", "open government" and "government 2.0". This helps explain why the general interest in e-Government seems to have decreased, but the number of academic publications related to e-Government has increased during the past years as shown in Figure 2.

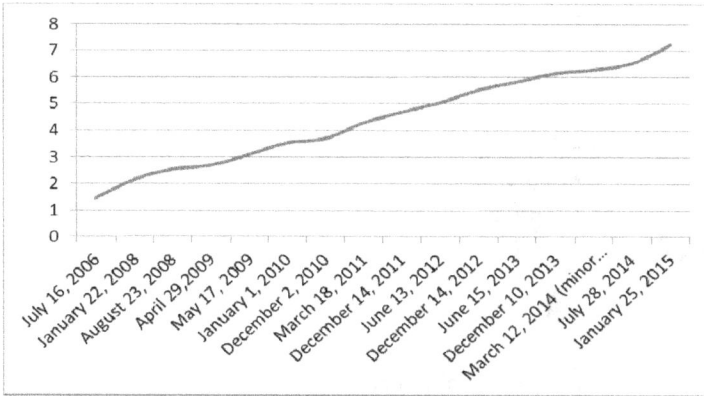

Figure 2: Number of academic publications on e-Government (source: University of Washington: e-Government Reference Library)

Whether all those new terms refer to something new, or they are simply more appealing labels to refer to the same old thing is still open to debate (it is worth remembering that the discussion on the use of "electronic" technologies in government dates back at least to the use of the Hollerith machine by the U.S. Census Bureau in 1890). Thus, for instance, Andrea di Maio, the managing vice-president for research in public sector at Gartner Research, questions the distinctions between e-Government and digital government, by identifying three possible reasons for the distinctions (Di Maio, 2013):

- The "new kids on the blocks" effect; people who are in charge of "digital" in some jurisdictions were still at college or high school during the e-Government days, and they are living this adventure as if it were all new.
- The increased pervasiveness of technology among citizens and businesses that makes much more sense today than 10 years ago.
- The recognition that e-Government has failed, or at least fell short of expectations, and must be re-branded.

Re-branding e-Government to hide past failures and scarce results does not encourage positive sentiment towards e-Government, unless a careful analysis is performed with the aim to learn from identifying why and where previous programs failed or stumbled.

The discussion on the adoption barriers and the critical success factors of e-Government is probably the area in which critical reflection is now more advanced. If we consider the papers included in the University of Washington e-Government Reference Library (Scholl, 2007; 2009; 2013), terms like "e-Government adoption", "acceptance", "success factors" and "barriers" occur quite often (87, 65, 66 and 66 times, respectively). These topics have been studied quite extensively and some critical mass has been developed (Ebrahim and Irani, 2005; Gil-Garcia, 2013, to mention just two examples).

Researchers have also began reflection on the mid and long term sustainability of e-Government solutions, especially in the context of developing countries (Klischewski and Lessa, 2013). The possible impacts of e-Government on national performance is also being researched (Srivastava and Teo, 2010) and the possible raising of an "e-Government paradox", similar to the well known productivity paradox, has been discussed and partly explained (Bertot and Jaeger, 2008; Castelnovo, 2010; Savoldelli et al., 2014).

The relationship between e-Government and the more general policies for the reform of Public Administration is currently being researched by the e-Government community (Contini and Lanzara, 2008; Ojo et al., 2009; Cordella and Bonina, 2012). The relationship between e-Government and other public sector related disciplines is being clarified by a more precise definition of the scope and the methodologies of e-Government research. Several papers have been published on these topics during the past years and also some critical analyses of the literature are now available (see, for instance, Yildiz, 2007; Charalabidis, 2011; Yusuf et al., 2014; Scholl, 2007; 2009; 2013; 2014; Bannister and Connolly, 2010).

The typical supply-push approach of the first wave of e-Government systems is now being re-evaluated (Verdegem and Verleye, 2009; Gauld et al., 2010) with a deeper understanding citizen-centric systems based on the concept of co-production (Linders, 2012), which entails a deeper involvement of citizens in public services design, delivery and evaluation. The concept of "citizen-centricity" that represented one of the fundamental characteristics of e-Government is also being re-evaluated. The thesis of neutrality of technology, which has led to the disentanglement of e-Government from political motives, social power and other contextual determinants, is again being re-evaluated. This led to critically discuss the technological determinism that appears to have dominated during the first wave of e-Government initiatives (Gil-Garcia et al., 2014).

Further, there is an emerging school of thought that e-Government as a field of academic research lacks an accepted set of theories that underpins the area. Bannister and Connolly (2015) contribute to this debate by attempting to understand what a theory of e-Government should be, and what links there could be between the theory of e-Government and other theories in the wider fields of Public Administration.

With the chapters included in this volume, we intend to contribute to the critical discussion about e-Government that is developing within the e-Government community. The topics mentioned above exemplify (without pretending to be a complete picture of what is going on within the e-Government community). Although not all the chapters in the volume directly address the critical topics listed above, selected papers describe e-Government applications, case studies and approaches but also highlight what critical aspects are involved and how they question some of the optimistic expectations reported by some e-Government contributions.

The papers we selected for this volume come from two relevant sources for the e-Government academic community: the proceedings of the European Conference on e-Government (whose 15th edition was held in 2015) and the Electronic Journal of e-Government. We have used several criteria to select the papers for this second volume of Leading Issues in e-Government Research, these criteria were:

- based on the number of times a paper was cited within the e-Government literature, or
- novel applications of e-Government, or
- new frontiers for e-Government.

The selected papers in this volume can be thematically categorised as follows: (1) papers describing new applications and problems related to their

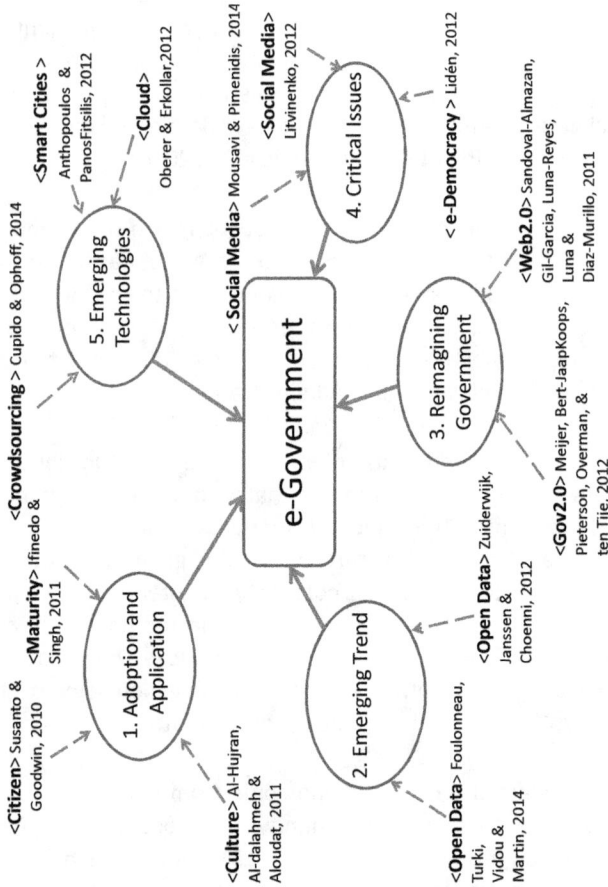

adoption, (2) papers discussing emerging trends in the e-Government literature, (3) papers concerning how new technologies can help reimagining government in the digital era, (4) papers discussing critical issues raised by the evolution of e-Government, and (5) papers concerning emerging technologies for e-Government applications. The themes covered in this volume are graphically summarized in Figure 3.

Figure 3: Themes and topics within the volume

We hope that this book will provide some important lessons of how to better understand e-Government and how to appropriately realise tangible benefits for citizens. The time has arrived to go behind the hype and to enable e-Government promises.

Dr Shawren Singh and Dr Walter Castelnovo
Editors
December 2015

References

Bannister, F. & Connolly, R. (2010). Researching e-Government: A Review of ECEG in its Tenth Year., 10th European Conference on e-Government (ECEG 2010), University of Limerick, Ireland.

Bannister, F. & Connolly, R. (2015). The great theory hunt: Does e-Government really have a   problem?. Government Information Quarterly, 32. 1–11

Bertot, J.C. & Jaeger, P.T. (2008). The e-Government paradox: Better customer service doesn't necessarily cost less. Government Information Quarterly, 25. 149–154

Castelnovo, W. (2010). Is There an e-Government Paradox?. 10th European Conference on e-Government (ECEG 2010), University of Limerick, Ireland.

Charalabidis, Y. (2011). A Roadmap for Research in Electronic Governance: The Grand Challenges Ahead. 5th International Conference on Methodologies, Technologies, and Tools Enabling e-Government (MeTTeG11), Camerino, Italy.

Cloete, F. (2012). e-Government Lessons From South Africa 2001 - 2011: Institutions, State of Progress and Measurement. *The African Journal Of Information And Communication, Issue 12*, 128-142

Contini, F. & Lanzara, G. F. (2008). ICT and innovation in the public sector. London: Palgrave

Cordella, A. & Bonina, C. M. (2012). A public value perspective for ICT enabled public sector reforms: A theoretical reflection. Government Information Quarterly, 29, 512-520.

Di Maio, A. (2013). Digital Government is little else than making e-Government work. Online: (http://blogs.gartner.com/andrea_dimaio/2013/09/18/digital-government-is-little-else-than-making-e-Government-work/)

Ebrahim, Z. & Irani, Z. (2005). e-Government adoption: architecture and barriers. Business Process Management Journal, 11. 589-611

Gauld, R., Goldfinch, S. and Horsburgh, S. (2010). Do they want it? Do they use it? The 'Demand-Side' of e-Government in Australia and New Zealand. Government Information Quarterly, 27. 177–186

Gil-Garcia, J.R. (ed.) (2013) e-Government Success Factors and Measures: Theories, Concepts, and Methodologies. Hershey PA, IGI Global.

Gil-Garcia, J.R., Vivanco, L.F, Luna-Reyes, L.F. (2014). Revisiting the Problem of Technological and Social Determinism: Reflections for Digital Government Scholars. In Janssen,M., Bannister, F., Glassey, O., Scholl, H.J., Tambouris, E., Wimmer, M., . Macintosh, A. (eds). Electronic Government and Electronic Participation (254-263). Amsterdam, IOS Press.

Heeks, R. (2011). *e-Government Benefits And Costs: Why e-Gov Raises Not Lowers Your Taxes*. Retrieved 13 September, 2013, from http://ict4dblog.wordpress.com/2011/09/29/e-Government-benefits-and-costs-why-e-gov-raises-not-lowers-your-taxes/#comments

Heerden, C. V., & Rossouw, R. (2014). Resource utilisation Efficiency: A South African Provincial Evaluation. *South African Journal of Economics, doi: 10.1111/saje.12037*

Klischewski, R. & Lessa, L. (2013). Sustainability of e-Government Success: An Integrated Research Agenda. In J. R. Gil-Garcia (Ed.), e-Government Success Factors and Measures: Theories, Concepts, and Methodologies (pp. 104-123). Hershey PA, IGI Global.

Linders, D. (2012). From e-Government to we-Government: Defining a typology for citizen coproduction in the age of social media. Government Information Quarterly, 29, 446-454.

Ojo, A., Janowski, T. & Shareef, M. (2009). Aligning Electronic Government and Public Administration Reform Programs - Process, Tool and Case Study. 9th European Conference on e-Government (ECEG 2009), London, UK.

Savoldelli, A., Codagnone, C. & Misuraca, G. (2014). Understanding the e-Government paradox: Learning from literature and practice on barriers to adoption. Government Information Quarterly, 31(S1), S63-S71.

Scholl, H. J. (2007). Discipline or interdisciplinary study domain? Challenges and Promises in Electronic Government Research. In H. Chen (Ed.), Digital Government (pp. 19-40). New York: Springer.

Scholl, H. J. (2009). Profiling the EG Research Community and its Core. In M. A. Wimmer, H. J. Scholl, M. Janssen & R. Traunmüller (Eds.), Electronic Government: Proceedings of the 8th [IFIP WG 8.5] International Conference, EGOV 2009 (Vol. 5693, pp. 1-12). Linz, Austria.

Scholl, H. J. (2013). Electronic Government Research: Topical Directions and Preferences. In M. A. Wimmer, M. Janssen & H. J. Scholl (Eds.), Electronic Government: Proceedings of the 12th IFIP WG 8.5 International Conference, EGOV 2013 (Vol. 8074, pp. 1-13). Koblenz, Germany.

Scholl, H. J. (2014). The EGOV Research Community: An Update on Where We Stand. In Janssen, M., Scholl, H.J., Wimmer, M.A. & Bannister, F. (eds.), Electronic Government: Proceedings of the 13th IFIP WG 8.5 International Conference, EGOV 2014 (Vol. 8653, pp. 1-16). Dublin, Ireland.

Singh, S., & Averweg, U. (2015). Exploring The Design And Development Of The Electronic Government (e-Government) Applications Landscape In South Africa. *Information Technology in Developing Countries, 25*(1). from

http://www.iimahd.ernet.in/egov/ifip/feb2015/dr%20shawren%20singh%20an
d%20udo%20averweg.htm

Srivastava, S.C. &Teo, T.S.H. (2010). e-Government, E-Business, and National Economic Performance. Communications of the Association for Information Systems, 26, Article 14.

Tapscott, D. (2010). Forward. In D. Lathrop & L. Ruma (Eds.), *Open Government*. Beijing: O'Reilly.

Verdegem, P. and Verleye, G. (2009). User-centered e-Government in practice: A comprehensive model for measuring user satisfaction. Government Information Quarterly, 26. 487–497

Yildiz, M. (2007). e-Government research: Reviewing the literature, limitations, and ways forward. Government Information Quarterly, 24, 646-665.

Yusuf, M., Adams, C., & Dingley, K. (2014). Research Philosophy and Methodologies of e-Government: Update From ECEG and ICEG. 14th European Conference on e-Government (ECEG 2014) (pp. 242-251). Spiru Haret University, Brasov, Romania.

The Role of National Culture on Citizen Adoption of e-Government Services: An Empirical Study

Omar Al-Hujran[1], Mahmoud Al-dalahmeh[2] and Anas Aloudat[2]

[1]Princess Sumaya University for Technology, Amman, Jordan
[2]University of Jordan, Amman, Jordan

o.hujran@psut.edu.jo
m.aldalahmeh@ju.edu.jo
aloudat@ju.edu.jo

Originally published in Electronic Journal of e-Government Volume 9 Issue 2, 2011, (pp93 – 106) http://www.ejeg.com

Editorial Commentary

ICT applications are notoriously infamous for poor adoption by end-users despite designers' and developers' best efforts to develop usable applications. e-Government applications also fall victim to low levels of adoption. Al-Hujran, Al-dalahmeh and Aloudat argue that there are gaps in the academic literature as to how national culture in developing countries affects the adoption of e-Government applications by their citizens. This paper is important because several developing counties have ambitious e-Government initiatives, and some reflection on culture is important to increase the likelihood of e-Government success.

Abstract: Increasingly governments around the world have realized the imperative of providing the public with not only improved government information and services but also improved public governance, transparency and accountability through e-Government services. However, many governments still face the problem of low level adoption of e-Government websites. It is because the issue of e-Government adoption is complex and multi-dimensional in nature. In consequence, it must be carefully addressed not only from technological perspectives but also from social, cultural, and organizational perspectives. The business case for developing sustainable successful e-Government initiatives critically depends on our knowledge and understanding of how to increase citizen adoption of e-Government websites. A review of the literature, however, shows that much of extant e-Government research has focused on e-Government adoption in developed countries. In consequence, little is known about national cultural factors that may influence e-Government adoption in developing countries. This knowledge gap Is particularly apparent in Jordan. Therefore, the objective of this paper is to examine national cultural factors that may influence citizen adoption of e-Government websites in this culturally different part of the world. We developed an integrated model by extending the technology acceptance model (TAM) with Hofstede's national culture dimensions, which is used to evaluate the impact of national culture on e-Government adoption in this paper. Based on survey data collected from a total of 197 Jordanian citizens, evidence shows that while two cultural dimensions: power distance and uncertainty avoidance had significant impacts on citizens' intention to adopt e-Government, the other three cultural dimensions: individualism, masculinity, and long-term orientation had no discernible impacts. The results also indicate that perceived usefulness, perceived ease of use, attitude are significant indicators of citizens' intention to use state government services online.

Keywords: e-Government adoption, technology acceptance model, culture, Jordan

1. Introduction

Information and communication technology (ICT) and resulting online capabilities such as the Internet provide the foundation for the transformation of the traditional government service. Over the past decade governments all over the world have realized the importance of providing government services and information via the Internet and world-wide-web to improve the efficiency, cost and quality of the government information and services provided to the public. However, although the adoption of e-Government has the potential to provide better services to citizens at lower costs, it has acceptance problems. In fact, understanding why people accept or reject new information technology (IT) has proven to be one of the most challenging issues in IT/IS research (Al-Adawi et al., 2005). The acceptance and success of e-Government is dependent upon citizen willingness to adopt this innovation (Carter and Bélanger, 2005). Yet, many governments worldwide still face the problem of low-level of citizen adoption of e-Government websites (Belanger and Carter, 2008; Choudrie and Dwivedi, 2005; Gupta et al., 2008; Kumar et al., 2007; Fu et al., 2006; Wang, 2003). e-Government adoption occurs in a turbulent social-political environment not only must be carefully addressed from a technological perspective, but also from social, political, and cultural perspectives. Without understanding what motivates the public to use e-Government services, governments will not be able to take strategic actions to increase the e-Government up-take (Gilbert et al., 2004). Hence, more empirical studies are required in the area of e-Government adoption to help governments to improve their understanding of the issues that affect citizen adoption of e-Government services and websites.

In addition, while the academic literature on e-Government adoption has mainly focused upon the adoption of e-Government websites in developed countries, relatively little attention has been given to the citizen adoption of e-Government websites in developing countries (Alhujran and Chatfield, 2008). This study, therefore, aims to fill a gap in the literature by conducting empirical field research on e-Government adoption in the Arab world, specifically in Jordan. Grounded on the Technology Acceptance Model (TAM) (Davis et al., 1989), this study develops a conceptual model by integrating the TAM with two of Hofstede's national culture dimensions - power distance, uncertainty avoidance. The extended TAM model is exploited to examine the impacts of these cultural dimensions upon citizen adoption of e-Government websites in developing countries with different national cultures and values.

Moreover, although culture is being considered as a contributing factor in the IT/IS adoption, very limited research has attempted to explore the impact of the culture on IT/IS adoption in the Arab region. Most of the previous research has only focused on economical, political, and technological factors that impact technology transfer to the Arab world (e.g. Al-Gahtani, 2004; Straub et al., 2001). Furthermore, to date, almost no prior research has considered the influence of national culture on e-Government adoption in the Arab world, in general, and Jordan, in particular.

In terms of achievements, efforts of Jordan to provide e-Government services to the public have been internationally recognized. Recently, the ministry of Information and Communication Technologies (MoICT) has introduced more than three main e-Government services to the public. Examples of these services are: police clearance, higher education admissions, and public jobs applications and tracking. However, despite some success, the e-Government services and websites in Jordan are facing the challenge of increasing the usage level of these services and websites (Al-Hujran and Shahateet, 2010). Therefore, a better understanding of the factors that influence citizen adoption of e-Government is a critically important policy issue in this country. This study provides the e-Government officials with a useful guideline for achieving better e-Government websites and increasing the citizen's adoption of these websites.

The remainder of this paper is organized as follows. Section 2 presents a background about e-Government adoption in Jordan. Section 3 presents the theoretical background and the research model. Section 4 describes the research methodology of this study. Section 5 presents the analysis and results. Finally, we present our discussions, practical implications, limitations and conclusion.

2. Background: e-Government adoption in Jordan

There is no clear definition of e-Government adoption (Kumar et al., 2007). Researchers refer to it as the 'intention' (Carter and Bélanger, 2005; Warkentin et al., 2002) or 'willingness' (Gilbert et al., 2004) to use e-Government information and services. Warkentin et al. (2002, p.159) define e-Government adoption as "the intention to 'engage in e-Government', which encompasses the intentions to receive information, to provide information, and to request e-Government services". Similarly, Kumar et al. (2007, p. 69) define it as "a simple decision of using, or not using, online [e-Government] services". For the purposes of this study, e-Government adoption refers to the intention of citizens to use e-Government websites and online services and.

Jordan is developing a strong ICT with the aim of becoming a knowledge-based country and a regional IT center. In terms of achievements, Jordan's efforts to provide e-Government services to the public have been recognized worldwide. Recently, the Jordanian Ministry of Information and Communication Technologies (MoICT) has introduced several e-Government services to the public. Examples include: police clearance, higher education admissions, and public jobs applications and tracking. However, despite some success the government is facing the challenge of increasing the low usage levels of these services and websites (Al-Hujran and Al-dalahmeh, 2011; Al-Hujran and Shahateet, 2010; Al-Jaghoub et al, 2010; Mofleh and Wanous, 2008). Specifically, Al-Jaghoub et al (2010) found that despite the government's growing investment in electronic services in Jordan, 85% of the citizens never logged in to an e-Government website.

Although the literature reported that there are several studies exploring factors that influence e-Government adoption in the developed countries (e.g. Carter and Belanger 2004; Carter and Bélanger, 2005; Gilbert et al., 2004; Fu et al. 2006; Kumar et al. 2007; Phang et al. 2005; Warkentin et al. 2002; Wang 2003), there appears to be a lack of understanding of the factors that influence the citizen intention to use e-Government services and websites in Jordan (Al-Hujran and Al-dalahmeh, 2011; Al-Hujran and Shahateet, 2010; Alomari et al, 2010). Hence, a better understanding of the factors that influence citizen adoption of e-Government is a critically important policy issue in Jordan. In this context, this study is aiming to provide the e-Government officials in Jordan with a useful guideline for achieving better e-Government websites and channeling their strategies toward increasing the citizen adoption of these websites. The results would help authorities understand the key factors that influence citizen's adoption of e-Government services and websites. Particularly, the results of this study are expected to help government agencies cultivate the positively correlating factors to enhance citizen adoption of e-Government while trying to reduce the effects of the negative factors. As mentioned earlier, the success of any e-Government is highly dependent upon the citizen willingness to use these electronic services.

3. Theoretical background and research model

The research model used to guide the study is shown in Figure 1. In the following sections, the meaning and the theories supporting the relationships are presented.

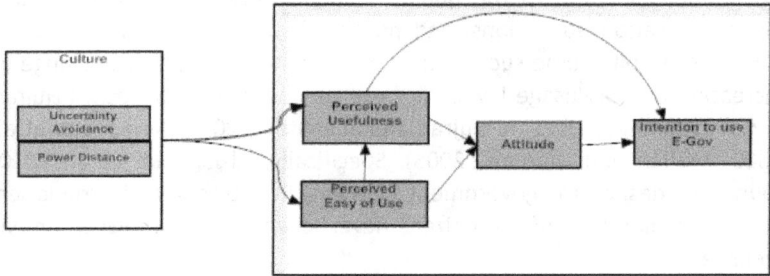

Figure 1: Research model of citizen's intention to use e-Government services and websites

3.1 Technology Acceptance Model (TAM)

The technology acceptance model (TAM) (Davis, 1989; Davis et al., 1989), is one of several models that IT/IS researchers have used to predict and explain the underlying factors that motivate users to accept and adopt new information technology systems. This model (Figure 2) is derived from the theory of reasoned action (TRA) (Fishbein and Ajzen, 1975; Ajzen and Fishbein, 1980).

According to TRA, the individual attitude and subjective norms influence the user's behavioral intention, which, in turn, influences his or her actual behavior. Building upon this, TAM was proposed to explain and predict users' acceptance of IT and IS systems by assuming that the constructs - perceived ease of use (PEOU) and perceived usefulness (PU) - are the key determinants of IT and IS acceptance behavior. Davis (1989, p.320) defined perceived usefulness as "the degree to which a person believes that using a particular system would enhance his or her job performance", and defined perceived ease of use as "the degree to which a person believes that using a particular system would be free of effort". Fishbein and Ajzen (1975, p.216) defined behavioral intention as "the strength of one's intention to perform a specified behavior". In TAM, the perceived usefulness of the system is predicted to be positively influenced by its perceived ease of use. TAM also theorizes that all other external variables are fully mediated by PU and PEOU (Heijden, 2003). Figure 2 illustrates TAM constructs and their relations. According to TAM, greater PU and PEOU of an IT/IS system would positively influence an attitude toward this system. The attitude, in turn, leads to a greater intention to use the system, which positively affects one's actual use of the system (Davis, 1989).

Several meta-analysis studies have provided sufficient data about TAM to be highly credible (King and He, 2006; Shumaila et al., 2007). It also received substantial empirical support by means of validations and replications from numerous researchers (Adams et al., 1992; Davis, 1993; Venkatesh and Davis, 2000). In addition, several studies have applied TAM to evaluate users' adoption in different settings such as e-mail, voice-mail, graphics, spreadsheet, and word processing, electronic commerce electronic learning, internet banking, and e-Government. Furthermore, TAM has reliable instruments, and is empirically sound (Pavlou, 2003). TAM has routinely explained up to 40 per cent of the behavioral intentions to use (Venkatesh and Davis, 2000). This is despite the fact that TAM is usually criticized for ignoring the social influence on technology adoption (Mathieson, 1991), but social and human factors could actually be integrated with TAM to improve its predictive powers (Venkatesh and Davis, 2000).

However, most of prior TAM research relatively focused on IT/IS adoption by employees in organizations context (Phang et al. 2005), where the use in most cases is mandatory. Therefore, researchers need to be cautious when applying the results of these studies to a different context such as e-Government, where the use of technology is voluntary. Accordingly, it is essential to study the adoption of new IT/IS with different population such as citizens.

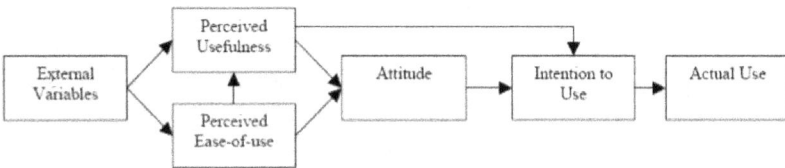

Figure 2: TAM source: Davis (1989)

Based on the above-mentioned assumptions of the original TAM, the following hypotheses are proposed in this study:

H1: There is a direct and positive relationship between perceived usefulness and attitude toward using e-Government websites.

H2: There is a direct and positive relationship between perceived ease of use and attitude toward using e-Government websites.

H3: There is a direct and positive relationship between attitude and behavioural intentions to use e-Government websites.

H4: There is a direct and positive relationship between perceived ease of use and the perceived usefulness of e-Government websites.

H5: There is a direct and positive relationship between perceived usefulness and the behavioural intentions to use e-Government websites.

3.2   e-Government adoption and TAM

Although TAM has been applied to a wide range of IS/IT settings, only a few empirical and conceptual studies have explored citizen adoption of e-Government using TAM as a theoretical framework. Table 1 summarizes the findings of these studies. Conceptual but not empirical studies are marked with a single asterisk (*).

Table 1: e-Government adoption studies using TAM

TAM core variables	Authors	Findings
Perceived usefulness(PU)	Carter and Belanger 2004; Fu et al. 2006; Kumar et al. 2007*; Phang et al. 2005; Warkentin et al. 2002*; Wang 2003	Citizens' PU is a significant predictor of their intention to use e-Government.
Perceived ease of use(PEOU)	Carter and Belanger 2004	PEOU did not have a direct effect on citizens' BI to adopt e-Government.

TAM core variables	Authors	Findings
Perceived ease of use(PEOU)	Carter and Belanger 2005; Fu et al. 2006; Kumar et al. 2007*; Phang et al. 2005; Warkentin et al. 2002*; Wang 2003	Citizens' PEOU is a significant predictor of their intention to use e-Government.
	Fu et al. 2006; Phang et al. 2005; Wang 2002	PEOU was a significant determinant of PU.
Culture	Warkentin et al. 2002*	They hypothesized that the cultural dimensions (power distance and uncertainty avoidance) were most likely associated with e-Government adoption.

3.3 National culture

The culture is not an easy concept to define (Davison and Martinsons, 2003). In addition, there is no generally accepted definition for national culture. Hofstede (1997 p.21) defines national culture as "the collective programming of the mind which distinguishes the members in one human group from another".

Although Hofstede's national culture framework has been criticized due to some methodological weaknesses (Baskerville, 2003), Leidner and Kayworth, (2006) found after an extensive literature review of national culture studies that over 60 per cent of these studies used one or more of Hofstede's cultural dimensions. In fact, Hofstede's work still has a great impact even today. According to McCoy et al (2007), most research on national culture uses Hofstede's measures and concepts, including those who disagreed with his dimensions. Therefore, as Hofstede's definition of culture and his theoretical framework are widely recognized and accepted, they have also been chosen in this research as a theoretical background to assess the impact of the national culture on e-Government adoption in Jordan.

Hofstede (1997) identified five dimensions of cultural variation. These dimensions have been conceptually defined as follows:

- Power Distance (PD): the extent to which the less powerful members of group or society accept and expect that power is unequally distributed;
- Uncertainty Avoidance (UA): the extent to which the members of group or society feel threatened by unknown situations;
- Individualism vs. Collectivism (IDV): the extent to which individuals are integrated into groups;
- Masculinity vs. Femininity (MAS): the extent to which gender roles are assigned in a culture;
- Long-Term vs. Short-Term Orientation (LTO): a society's preference to be more forward looking or future oriented.

As motioned earlier, the Arab world is considered as one of the most complex cultural and social systems in the world. Different than western countries, religion plays a significant role in determining the different aspects of social and traditional life. Religion is also considered as one of the main determinant of internet usage in these countries (Hofheinz, 2005). People in the Arab world find the internet as an approach to break up the limitations of the traditional and social life (Alomari et al, 2010). Therefore, this complex cultural system offers a different yet a rich context to study the influence of the national culture on citizen adoption of e-Government services and websites.

Figure 3 shows a comparison between the Arab world and the United States in terms of the index values of Hofstede's cultural dimensions.

The Figure demonstrates the cultural differences between the Arab world and the Western countries. While the Arab culture is high in power distance (80 vs. 40) and uncertainty avoidance (68 vs. 46), the American culture is high in individualism (91 vs. 38) and masculinity (62 vs. 53). Scores for Hofstede's fifth dimension (LTO) were not found for the Arab countries; therefore, LTO was omitted from the comparisons.

Hofstede's Cultural Dimentions

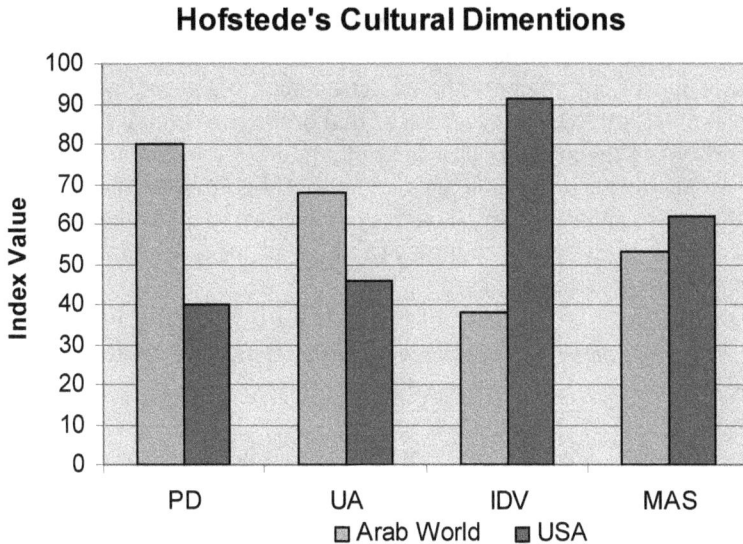

Figure 3: A comparison of Hofstede's cultural dimensions (Arab world vs. USA)

The importance of both national and organizational culture to the success of IS/IT adoption has been also widely recognized (e.g. Bagchi et al., 2003; Erumban and Jong, 2006; Leidner & Kayworth, 2006; Straub, 1994; Twati, 2006). These studies underscored the importance of the culture, and how it is linked to the success of IS/IT adoption and use. For example, Erumban and Jong (2006) found a significant relationship between cultural factors and the adoption decisions of new technologies across countries. Results of this study indicated that the power distance and uncertainty avoidance dimensions are the most significant cultural factors by which some of the differences in ICT adoption rates among countries can be explained. Countries with high scores in UA and PD, such as the Arab countries, have a lower rate of ICT adoption than countries with low UA and PD scores (Erumban and Jong, 2006). Similarly, Leidner & Kayworth (2006) stated that UA plays a significant role in determining how groups will potentially adopt and diffuse ICT. Countries high in UA are less likely to adopt frame relay technology (Leidner & Kayworth, 2006). Since ICT is inherently risky, those less comfortable with uncertainty will be less likely to adopt new technologies.

11

Researchers also explored the impact of the national culture on TAM variables (e.g. Twati, 2006; Veiga et al., 2001). Their studies concluded that the cultural dimensions influence the model variables. However, in a study by Warkentin et al. (2002), they proposed that of the five cultural dimensions, PD and UA are the most likely to differentiate e-Government adoption and use. Erumban and Jong (2006) also found that the PD and UA dimensions are the most significant cultural factors by which some of the differences in ICT adoption rates among countries can be explained. Therefore, the following hypotheses are proposed:

H6a: There is a direct and positive relationship between uncertainty avoidance and the perceived usefulness of e-Government websites.

H6b: There is a direct and positive relationship between power distance and the perceived usefulness of e-Government websites.

H7a: There is a direct and positive relationship between uncertainty avoidance and the perceived ease of use of e-Government websites.

H7b: There is a direct and positive relationship between power distance and the perceived ease of use of e-Government websites.

4. Methodology

4.1 Instrument development

The survey items were adopted from prior research. The TAM scales of PU and PEOU were measured using items adopted from Davis (1989) and Davis et al. (1989). TAM scales of ATU were adopted from Taylor and Todd (1995). BI items were adopted from Malhotra & Galletta (1999) and Pavlou (2003). Culture items were adopted from Al-Sukkar (2005). All items were measured using a five-point Likert-type scale, ranging from "strongly agree" to "strongly disagree".

Sekaran (2003) stresses the importance of choosing the questionnaire language that approximates the level of understanding of the respondents. Given that the majority of the Jordanians are communicating in Arabic language, questionnaire items of this study have been translated into Arabic language. The English version of the questionnaire has been translated into

Arabic by two independent translators. The Arabic version which has been translated by the first translator has then been translated back to English by the second translator. The same was repeated to the second translator's version. The two versions in both languages have been then compared to resolve any differences. The final version has been used for the study.

4.2 Evaluating the validity and the reliability of the instrument

Content validity is concerned with the degree to which the scale items represent the domain of the concept under study. According to Sekaran (2003), face validity is a basic index of content validity. Experts in the field can be solicited to advice on whether scale items have face validity (Straub et al., 2005). Therefore, instrument was pre-tested with three academics and one student in the field of Information Systems. An academically excellent student has been asked to fill the survey. When he finished it, he was asked to find out if there were any problems to understand the survey questions. Based on this feedback, the wording of some questions was modified to improve clarity. After this step, three academics were asked to answer the survey questions and to provide their feedback on whether the questions would accurately measure each construct, whether the questions were vague, ambiguous, difficult to understand, or contained contradictions. The instrument was then modified to reflect the feedback received from the three academics. Final survey items are found in Appendix 1.

To insure that the instrument items are measuring the same construct, Cronbach's alpha was used to evaluate the reliability of the instrument items (Cronbach, 1970). Although researchers suggest 0.7 as the accepted reliability cut-off of Cronbach's alpha test, a value more than 0.6 is regarded as a satisfactory level (Hair et al., 2006). The reliability function in the SPSS 17 was used to test the internal consistency of the items for each scale. The results are presented in Table 2. The outcomes of the statistical analysis demonstrate satisfactory reliabilities, ranging from 0.745 to 0.867 for all scales.

Table 2: Reliability statistics

Scale	No. of Items	Mean	Cronbach Alpha (α)
Perceived Usefulness (PU)	5	3.995	.798
Perceived ease of use (PEOU)	5	3.698	.831
Attitude Toward Using (ATU)	3	4.198	.745
Behavioral Intention to Use (BI)	2	4.028	.756
Culture: Uncertainty Avoidance	4	4.199	.781
Power Distance	5	2.459	.867
Total	24		

4.3   Data collection and participants

Prior research showed that the educated Jordanian citizens are the early adopters of the Internet (Al-Jaghoub and Westrup, 2003) and are likely users of e-Government services and websites in Jordan. Therefore, for this study we identify the university students and internet cafes users who are Jordanian citizens as the targeted population of this study. A face-to-face personally administered survey was the research method adopted in this study. The final survey (see Appendix 1) was distributed to a sample of 265 students drawn from different Universities and internet cafes in Jordan. A total of 208 surveys were returned, achieving a 78.4% survey response rate. Eleven incomplete surveys were exempted from the analysis. Thus, 197 of the returned surveys were usable responses.

Demographic characteristics of the overall participants are presented in Table 3. Of the surveys analyzed, 69 respondents (52.3%) were female and 128 (65.0%) were male. Most of them are between 20–30 years of age (67.0%), have a bachelor's degree (79.8%). In addition, most of the re-spondents have considerable experience in using a computer. 81.8% of the respondents had more than 3 years of computer use and around 60% of them are using the Internet in daily or weekly bases. These results indi-cated that university students in Jordan have considerable experience in using computers and the Internet. Demographic characteristics of the overall participants are presented in Table 3.

4.4   Data analyses

A set of multiple linear regressions and analyses of variance (ANOVA) were used to analyze the sample data, and to test the hypothesis associated with the research model. Multiple regression analysis is a statistical technique used to explore the relationship between a single dependent variable and several predictors (independent variables) (Hair et al, 2006). In addition, the tests of the regression assumptions were conducted. The results of testing the regression assumptions and the outcomes of the regression analyses are provided in the following sections.

4.5   Tests of multiple regression assumptions

It is important that researchers assess whether their analyses meet the underlying assumptions of multiple regression when testing the relationship between dependent and independent variables, based on a regression analysis conducted on sample data (Hair et al, 2006). These assumptions are: 'linearity', 'normality of residuals', 'multicollinearity' and 'residual independence'. In this study, there was no indication of any violation of the regression assumptions. For example, before testing hypotheses H7a and H7b, the tests of the regression assumptions were performed (same tests were repeated for the whole set of multiple linear regressions). The following subsections will provide a brief discussion on each of these assumptions.

Table 3: Demographic characteristics of participants

Characteristics		Frequency	Percent
Gender	Male	128	65.0
	Female	69	35.0
Age	Less than 20	29	14.7
	20-30	132	67.0
	31-40	25	12.7
	41-50	10	5.1
	More than 50	1	.5
Education	High school	9	4.6
	Community College	11	5.6
	Bachelor	156	79.2
	Postgraduate	21	10.7
Income	Less than 200	99	50.3
	201-500	65	33.0
	501-800	14	7.1
	More than 800	19	9.6
Occupation	Private sector employee	23	11.7
	Public sector employee	43	21.8
	Student	131	66.5

Characteristics		Frequency	Percent
Computer experience	Less than 3 years	36	18.3
	3-5	47	23.9
	More than 5 years	114	57.9
Internet usage frequencies	Once a month	39	19.8
	Several times monthly	42	21.3
	Several times weekly	55	27.9
	Once a day	20	10.2
	Several times daily	41	20.8

4.5.1 Linearity

Linearity was examined through the analysis of residuals and partial regression scatter plots. For example, by looking at the scatter plots in Figure 4, the residuals scatter plot does not exhibit any nonlinear pattern, and shows that the points are randomly and evenly dispersed throughout the scatter plot. This is an indication that the assumption of linearity and homoscedasticity for all variables has been met (Hair et al, 2006).

Dependent Variable: PEOU

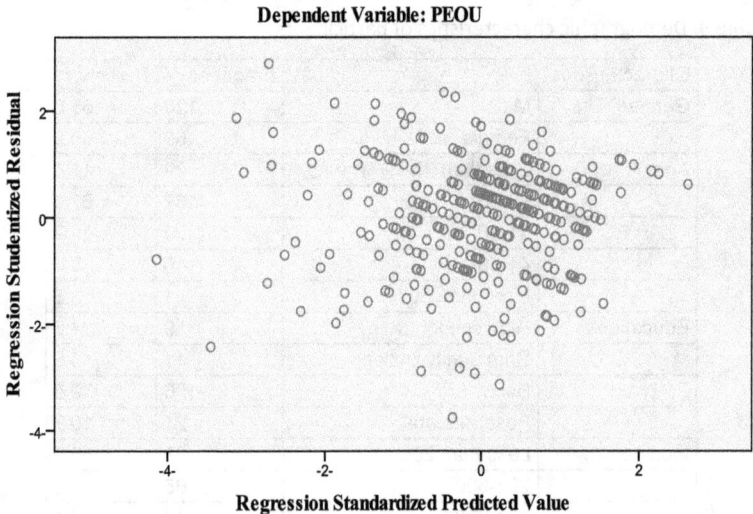

Regression Standardized Predicted Value
Figure 4: Scatter plot: Cultural dimensions (PD and AU) vs. PEOU

4.5.2   Normality of residuals

In this study, it is reasonable to assume normality in the variables since the sample size of the study is large enough (i.e. greater than 100) (StatSoft Inc, 2003).

4.5.3   Multicollinearity

Hair et al (2006) recommended examining the variable inflation factor (VIF) and tolerance level (TOL) to diagnose multicollinearity within multiple regression procedure. TOL is acceptable over 0.1 and VIF below 10 (Hair et al, 2006, Field, 2005).Table 3 shows the values of both TOL and VIF. Both of them were in the acceptable range. All the values of VIF are less than 10 and all the tolerance values are greater than 0.1. Hence, these tests confirmed that multicollinearity among the variables was not a problem.

4.5.4   Independence of residuals

The Durbin-Watson statistic was used to test whether the assumption of residual independence is acceptable or not. The Durbin-Watson statistic tests whether or not adjacent residuals are correlated (Field, 2005), and is better if the values are closer to 2 (Field, 2005). Table 3 shows that the Durbin-Watson value is 1.895. Thus, the independence of residuals assumption does not violate, because the value is very close to 2.

Table 3: Collinearity statistics: cultural dimensions vs. PEOU

Predictor Variable	Collinearity Statistics		Durbin-Watson
	Tolerance	VIF	
Uncertainty Avoidance (UA)	.816	1.531	1.895
Power distance (PD)	.717	1.487	

5. Analysis and results

Table 4 shows the results of the regression analysis based on the relationships proposed in the research model. Figure 5 is a graphical representation of the analysis results (only significant relations appear in this Figure). To investigate the research hypotheses, several multiple regression analyses were performed using SPSS 17.0 package for Windows. For example, to investigate hypotheses H6a and H6b, UA and PD were simultaneously regressed on perceived usefulness. A summary of the research hypotheses and test results are provided in Table 4 and Figure 5. The nine research

hypotheses H1, H2, H3, H4, H5, H6a, H6b, H7a, and H7b have been supported from the empirical test. In addition, the results indicated that the
research model explained around 43% of the variance in citizens' intention
to adopt and use e-Government websites (R2 = 0.433).

Table 4: Path coefficients and hypothesis testing

Analyses Type	Hypothesis		Independent Variable	Dependent Variable	Beta	Supported
Multiple Linear Regression			Cultural dimensions	PU		
		H6a	UA		0.137*	Yes
		H6b	PD		0.187*	Yes
			Cultural dimensions	PEOU		
		H7a	UA		0.223**	Yes
		H7b	PD		0.202**	Yes
	H1	-	PU	Attitude	0.236**	Yes
	H2	-	PEOU	Attitude	0.182**	Yes
	H4	-	PEOU	PU	0.505***	Yes
	H5	-	PU	BI	0.236**	Yes
	H3	-	Attitude	BI	0.534***	Yes

*** Correlation is Significant at <0.001
** Correlation is Significant at <0.01
* Correlation is Significant at <0.05

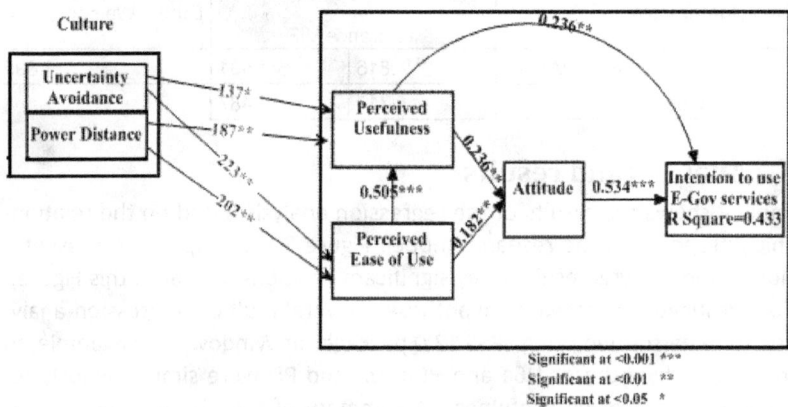

Figure 5: Significant relationships in the research model

6. Discussions

As hypothesized and consistent with TAM research, the results showed that perceived usefulness and attitude toward using e-Government websites enhanced the level of citizen intention to use e-Government websites, and together, accounted for 43.3% of the variance in the intention to use e-Government services (R^2 = 0.433). The results also indicated that perceived usefulness and perceived ease of use were significant predictors of the citizen attitude toward using e-Government services and websites, suggesting that the government should make e-Government websites more useful and usable. For example, they could achieve this by increasing the general public awareness about the usefulness of using e-Government; providing e-Government and ICT training workshops; and refining IS/IT systems selections to meet different citizens' needs. However, perceived usefulness was the strongest predictor of the citizen attitude toward using e-Government websites. This finding is in accordance with earlier TAM research that consistently found perceived usefulness a more powerful predictor than the perceived ease of use (e.g. Davis, 1989; Fu et al., 2006). This outcome yields the implication that usefulness is more interesting to some citizens than others. The possible justification may be that the effect of perceived ease of use on IS/IT usage often decreases with the familiarity of the user with the IS/IT (Venkatesh et al., 2003; Chang et al, 2005). In this study, only respondents who were familiar with e-Government services and websites were selected for the model testing. Therefore, the effect of perceived ease of use on e-Government services adoption was not as important as the perceived usefulness. Still, perceived ease of use of e-Government websites indirectly enhanced citizen attitude toward using e-Government websites through perceived usefulness. The influence of perceived ease of use on perceived usefulness was strong. This supports TAM which asserts the easier a system is to use, the more useful it can be. Hence, developing e-Government websites that are easy to use will enhance the usefulness of the services and websites and indirectly influence citizen attitude positively toward using e-Government services and websites.

This study also hypothesized there would be a positive relationship between national culture dimensions and TAM core constructs (i.e. perceived usefulness and perceived ease of use). The findings showed that only two cultural dimensions: power distance and uncertainty avoidance had a significant positive impact on perceived ease of use and perceived usefulness.

In their study, Warkentin et al. (2002) proposed that of the five cultural dimensions, power distance and uncertainty avoidance are the two dimensions that most likely differentiate e-Government adoption and use. Countries that are high in UA are less likely to adopt frame relay technology (Leidner & Kayworth, 2006). Since ICT is inherently risky, those less comfortable with uncertainty will be less likely to adopt new technologies. Similarly, cultures with high power distance are expected to have lower openness for new ideas such as e-Government as it involves decision-making on issues where there is very little information about them (Lee and Peterson, 2000).

7. Practical implications and Limitations

7.1   Practical implications

The primary objective of this study was to identify the impact of the national culture on citizen adoption of e-Government services and websites in developing countries, in particular Jordan. The study has fulfilled this objective. This research provides e-Government officials and policy makers in Jordan with a practical and communicable checklist of the cultural and technological factors, which are seamlessly integrated; and that cover the perspectives of the citizens. This checklist should be considered as the cornerstone for any current and future e-Government project. A survey on Jordanian citizens showed that the cultural dimensions - power distance and uncertainty avoidance; perceived usefulness; perceived ease of use; and the attitude - contribute significantly to the citizen adoption of e-Government services and websites in Jordan. Since Jordan and other Arab countries are facing the problem of low-level citizen adoption of e-Government services, the research outcomes are believed to assist e-Government officials and policy makers from Jordan and also from the other Arab countries, that share many similar cultural characteristics to Jordan, to better position their strategies to encourage faster and more efficient adoption of these services.

Particularly, the outcomes of this study suggested that e-Government officials need to pay attention to the dominant culture. For example, by providing the necessary training to alleviate anxiety could lead to better acceptance of IS/IT applications (Al-Gahtani, 2004), such as the e-Government. Also, government agencies should provide services that are easy to use. Carter and Belenger (2005) suggested different ways to increase the perceived ease of use. One is to provide online tutorials through the e-Government websites to illustrate how citizens can use and transact with e-Government services and websites. Government agencies should also improve help and search facilities in their websites to enable citizens to effectively find relevant information. In addition, feedback from citizens about e-Government services and websites should be encouraged, elicited and analyzed. This will enable government agencies to redesign their web-sites to present e-Government services and information in a way that is easier for citizens to use. In addition, given the dominant effect of per-ceived usefulness, it is important for the government agencies to incorpo-rate useful information and services into their websites. Also, these agen-cies should employ training and promotion approaches to develop citizens' beliefs of the usefulness and the public value of the e-Government ser-vices.

7.2   Limitations

As with all studies, this study has its limitations also. This study adopted cross-sectional design. The cross sectional study represents a slice of time and does not show how the citizen attitude and behavior may change over time. Further study employing a longitudinal design would ascertain whether or not the citizen attitude toward using e-Government services change over time. In addition, this study applied Hofstede's national cul-ture framework. Although it has been widely applied and cited, several researchers have criticized, as mentioned earlier, the framework due to some methodological weaknesses (Baskerville, 2003; Fang, 2003).

8. Conclusion

This study integrates the technology acceptance model (TAM) and Hofstede's national culture dimensions to evaluate citizen adoption of e-Government. The results of a multiple regression analysis indicate that perceived usefulness, perceived ease of use, and attitude are significant indicators of citizen intention to use state government services online. In addition, the results show that the two cultural dimensions: power dis-tance and uncertainty avoidance have significant impacts on citizens' in-tention to adopt e-Government. As government agencies continue to in-vest in e-Government services, it is very important for agencies to enhance their understanding of the factors that influence citizen adoption of e-Government websites and services.

Appendix 1: Survey items

Behavioral Intention to Use (BI)

BI1	I intend to use the e-Government portal and/or Ministry's website(s) to access government services frequently.
BI2	I predict that I should use the e-Government portal and/or Ministry's website(s) to access government services in the future.

Attitude toward Using (ATU)

ATU1	Using the e-Government portal and/or Ministry's website(s) to access government services is a good idea.
ATU2	I like the use of e-Government portal and/or Ministry's website(s) to access government services.
ATU3	Using the e-Government portal and/or Ministry's website(s) to access government services would be pleasant.

Perceived Usefulness (PU)

PU1	Using e-Government portal and/or Ministry's website(s) enable me to access government services (e.g. getting national exam result online, getting national number) more quickly.
PU2	Using e-Government portal and/or Ministry's website(s) enhances my effectiveness in accessing government services (e.g. find the most relevant information about a service).
PU3	Using e-Government portal and/or Ministry's website(s) allows me to access more government services than would otherwise possible.
PU4	Using e-Government portal and/or Ministry's website(s) to access government services increases my productivity (e.g. find information about services within shortest time frame).
PU5	Overall, I find e-Government portal and/or Ministry's website(s) useful for me to access government services.

Perceived Ease of Use (PEOU)

PEOU1	Learning how to use e-Government portal and/or Ministry's website(s) to access government services is easy for me.
PEOU2	I find it easy to use e-Government portal and/or Ministry's website(s) to find what I want.
PEOU3	My interaction with e-Government portal and/or Ministry's website(s) to access government services is clear and understandable.
PEOU4	e-Government portal and/or Ministry's website(s) is flexible to interact with.
PEOU5	Overall, I find using e-Government portal and/or Ministry's website(s) to access government services easy to use.

Uncertainty Avoidance (UA)

UA1	It is important to have job requirements and instructions spelled out in detail so that people always know what they are expected to do
UA2	Rules and regulation are important because they inform workers what the organization expects of them
UA3	Order and structure are very important in a work environment
UA4	Working in a structured environment is better than working (rules and regulations) in an unstructured work environment

Power Distance (PD)

PD1	Managers should be careful not to ask the opinions of subordinates too frequently, otherwise the manager might appear to be weak and incompetent
PD2	Manager should make most decisions without consulting subordinates
PD3	Employees should not question their manager's decisions
PD4	Manager should not ask subordinates for advice, because they might appear less powerful
PD5	Decision making power should stay with top management in the organization and not be delegated to lower level employees

References

Abu-Samaha, A. & Abdel Samad, Y. (2007) "Challenges to the Jordanian Electronic Government Initiative", Journal of Business Systems, Governance and Ethics, vol. 2, no. 3, pp 101-109.

Ajzen, I. & Fishbein, M. (1980) Understanding Attitudes and Predicting Social Behaviour, Prentice-Hall, Englewood Cliffs, NJ.

Al-Adawi, Z, Yousafza, S & Pallister, J (2005) "Conceptual Model of Citizen Adoption of e-Government", in Proceedings of the Second International Conference on Innovations in Information Technology (IIT'05), Dubai, United Arab, 26-28 September 2005, p 1-10.

Al-Gahtani, S. (2004) "Computer Technology Acceptance Success Factors In Saudi Arabia: An Exploratory Study", Journal of Global Information Technology Management, vol. 7, pp 5-29.

Al-Hujran, O. & Al-dalahmeh, M. (2011) "The Role of National Culture on Citizen Adoption of e-Government web sites ", in Proceedings of the 11th European Conference on e-Government, University of Ljubljana, Ljubljana, Slovenia 16-17 June 2011.

Alhujran, O. & Chatfield, A. (2008) "Toward a Model for e-Government Services Adoption: The Case of Jordan", in Proceedings of the 8th European Conference on e-Government, Ecole Polytechnique, Lausanne, Switzerland, 10-11 July 2008, pp 13-22.

Alhujran, O & Shahateet, M. (2010) "Citizen adoption of e-Government initiatives in developing countries: A case study of Jordan", in Proceedings of the 10th European Conference on e-Government, Limerick, Ireland.

Al-Jaghoub, S. & Westrup, C. (2003) "Jordan and ICT-led development: towards a competition state?", Information Technology & People, vol. 16, pp 93-110.

Al-Jaghoub, S., Al-Yaseen, H. & Al-Hourani, M. (2010) "Evaluation of Awareness and Acceptability of Using e-Government Services in Developing Countries: the Case of Jordan", The Electronic Journal of Information Systems Evaluation, vol. 13, no. 1, pp 1 – 8.

Alomari, M, Sandhu, K., & Woods, P. (2010) "Measuring Social Factors in e-Government Adoption in the Hashemite Kingdom of Jordan", International Journal of Digital Society (IJDS), vol. 1, no. 2, pp 78-96.

Al-Sukkar, A. (2005) "The application of Information Systems in the Jordanian Banking Sector: A study of the Acceptance of the Internet", PhD thesis, University of Wollongong, Australia.

Bagchi, K, Cerveny, R, Hart, P & Peterson, M (2003) "The Influence of National Culture in Information Technology Product Adoption", in Proceedings of the Ninth Americas Conference on Information Systems, Tampa, Florida, USA, 4-6 August 2003, pp 957-965.

Baker, E., Al-Gahtani, S. & Hubona, G. (2010) "Cultural Impacts on Acceptance and Adoption of Information Technology in a Developing Country", Journal of Global Information Management, vol. 18, no. 3, pp 35-58.

Baskerville, R (2003) "Hofstede Never Studied Culture", Accounting, Organizations and Society, vol. 28, no. 1, pp 1-14.

Carter, L. & Belanger, F. (2004) "Citizen Adoption of Electronic Government Initiatives", in the 37th Hawaii International Conference on System Sciences, Hawaii, USA.

Carter, L. & Bélanger, F. (2005) "The utilization of e-Government services: citizen trust, innovation and acceptance factors", Information Systems Journal, vol. 15, no. 1, pp 5-25.

Chatfield, A. & Alhujran, O. (2009) "A Cross-Country Comparative Analysis of e-Government Service Delivery among Arab Countries", Information Technology for Development, vol. 15, no. 3, pp 151-170.

Choudrie, J. & Dwivedi, Y. (2005) "A Survey of Citizens' Awareness and Adoption of e-Government Initiatives, The 'Government Gateway': A United Kingdom Perspective", in e-Government Workshop '05 (eGOV05), Brunel University, London, UK.

Cronbach, L. (1970) Essentials of Psychology Testing, Harper & Row, New York.

Factors Influencing Citizen Adoption of SMS-Based e-Government Services

Tony Dwi Susanto[1,2] and Robert Goodwin[1]

[1]Flinders University of South Australia, Adelaide, Australia
[2]Institute of Technology Sepuluh Nopember, Indonesia

susa0004@flinders.edu.au
Robert.goodwin@flinders.edu.au

Originally published in EJEG (2010) Volume 8, Issue , http://www.ejeg.com

Editorial Commentary

Susanto and Goodwin look at a grass-root technology, Short Messaging Service (SMS), and the challenges associated with its adoption for e-Government services. SMSs are a simpler technology that does not require any third party applications or the Internet. SMS also appear to be an easier technology to understand and use. Though citizens may perceive SMSs as an "out-dated technology with little value", SMSs can be used as a powerful low cost communication service.

Abstract: This paper identifies the factors that determine citizens' acceptance of SMS-based e-Government services. It reports on a web-based survey, paper-based questionnaires, and phone-call interviews that collected 159 responses from 25 countries. The results indicate that there are 15 perceptions toward using SMS-based e-Government services that may influence citizens to use or to reject the services: perceived ease of use; perceived efficiency in time and distance; perceived value for money; perceived usefulness; perceived responsiveness; perceived convenience; perceived relevance, quality and reliability of the information; trust in the SMS technology; perceived risk to user privacy; perceived reliability of the mobile network and the SMS-based system; trust in government and perceived quality of public services; perceived risk to money; perceived availability of device and infrastructure; perceived compatibility; and perceived self-efficacy in using SMS. Whether or not a citizen adopts an SMS-based e-Government service is influenced by these perceptions. To increase the acceptance of SMS-based e-Government services, the systems should address all of these belief factors. An intensive advertising campaign for the services in all mass media channels is critically important to make citizens aware of and to provide detailed knowledge about the services. The advertising campaign should involve people who influence individuals' decision making. These people include friends, family, teachers, experts, public figures, and government officials. This study found that Notification services are the most frequently used followed by Pull SMS, Listen, and Transaction SMS services. Notification services could be an appropriate starting point for governments who want to establish SMS-based e-Government services.

Keywords: e-Government, SMS, acceptance factors, six Level model of SMS-based e-Government, technology adoption, users' behaviour, public services

1. Introduction

Delivering public services through the Short Messaging Service (SMS) channel becoming popular in developed and developing countries. In December 2008, 54 national government agencies of the Philippines were providing SMS services to augment traditional public services; since 2006 Singapore's citizens have been able to access 150 public services through a single SMS number. In Australia, SMS is used for bushfire alerts in Victoria and notification for public transport timetables in Adelaide. In Ghana, the Philippines and Indonesia, most local authorities provide SMS-based services for listening to people's opinions. In Oman people can apply for jobs via SMS and currently the Bahrain government and the Chichester Council in the UK are developing integrated SMS systems (SMSeGov.info, 2009).

The use of Short Messaging Service (SMS) technology to enhance the access to and delivery of government services to benefit citizens, business partners, and government institutions is defined as SMS-based e-Government. SMS-based e-Government systems have enabled governments to communicate with and to provide a range of services for citizens, businesses and other government organizations through the SMS channel. Based on the service and the system complexity, Susanto and Goodwin (2008) classified SMS-based e-Government services in a Six Level model:

Listen, Notification, Pull-based Information, Communication, Transaction, and Integration levels. Current SMS-based e-Government services can deliver most of the typical Internet-based e-Government services (Susanto, Goodwin and Calder. 2008).

SMS-based e-Government has a strategic role both in developed and developing countries. It has been reported that providing public services through the SMS channel has significantly reduced time and cost; introduced a cheaper, easier and faster information-accessing channel; improved transparency, accountability, communication, and relationship between government and citizens; made the services and procedures easier for the citizens; improved the district political image; engaged more people and increased citizens participation; and promoted e-Democracy (Lallana, 2004; Rannu and Semevsky, 2005; Bremer and Prado, 2006).

For developing countries, SMS-based e-Government allows more people to access and to use e-Government services. In the Philippines, for example, people prefer to contact their government using the SMS-based channel (87%) rather than Internet (11%) (Lallana, 2004: 30). People prefer a technology channel that is more familiar, simple and easy to use, supports their native language, uses a readily available device and infrastructure and is low cost. Therefore, in order to engage more people, Susanto and Goodwin (2006) argued that SMS-based e-Government should become a frontline system for delivering e-Government services in developing countries.

For government in developed countries, SMS-based e-Government is popular as a complementary channel of existing Internet-based e-Government. The advantages of SMS are: it is simple, easy to use, extensive in coverage, reliable in delivering the message, low in cost, and can reach citizens anywhere anytime including areas with no Internet access. These are reasons why the local authorities provide this alternative channel. In developed countries SMS-based services are provided to deliver information about emergency situations, reminders, or any other business activity which needs a prompt action by the clients such as a reminder of a tax due date or warnings of extreme weather. Some of the developed countries have also provided SMS-based transaction services such as purchasing a bus ticket or a parking ticket, paying tax, and voting via SMS (MonashUniversity 2005).

Despite the high number of the initiatives and popularity of SMS-based e-Government, no study of the acceptance of the services can be found in the literature. Most existing studies on e-Government investigate Internet-based e-Government, covering PC-based as well as mobile-based implementations (Cilingir and Kushchu, 2004; Ghyasi and Kushchu, 2004). In terms of the investigated aspects, the existing studies on e-Government have covered wide-range topics including the adoption, development stage models, applications, infrastructure, and the business models (Lee and Hong, 2002; Dalziel, 2004; Choudrie and Dwivedi, 2005; Khosrowpour, 2005; Coursey and Norris, 2008). There is not a single study of the acceptance of SMS-based e-Government. Current studies found in the literature are case reports (Lallana, 2004; Rannu and Semevsky, 2005; Lallana, 2008).

A study of the factors affecting the acceptance of SMS-based e-Government is essential since in some cases the popularity of SMS itself does not guarantee the success of the SMS based e-Government service. Lallana (2004) and Alampay (2003) showed that even though SMS is very popular in the Philippines, some SMS-based e-Government applications failed to engage people due to poor replies and back-office management which led to the lack of public trust of the services. Other experiences in Denmark and Sweden also showed that the cost of each SMS-based service is another determinant which influences citizen to use or not to use the services (Westlund, 2008). Hence, it is important to understand what factors might influence citizens' intentions to engage in government services provided by SMS. For governments and e-Government practitioners, the understanding is necessary in order to devise practical methods for evaluating their existing SMS-based e-Government systems, predicting how citizens will respond to the services, improving user acceptance by altering the nature of the systems and the services, and justifying the investment in the system.

This paper aims to answer the following questions:

- What influences a citizen to use or to reject an SMS-based e-Government service?
- What should the local authorities do to ensure as many as citizens as possible use SMS-based e-Government services?

2. Methodology

In most research on technology adoption particularly technologies for public use, it seems impossible to obtain information from all users (a census). Therefore, present research on technology adoption selects from 24 up to 1,099 users as the sample and limits the conclusions to particular contexts (Rogers, 2003: 26; Carter and Belanger, 2005; Choudrie and Dwivedi, 2005; Kortemann, 2005; Titah and Barki, 2005; Hung, Chang et al, 2006; Philip, 2006; Horst, Kuttschreuter et al, 2007; Awadhi and Morris, 2008). Validations of the models are conducted afterwards by other researchers across different organizations and populations. In the end, the models which are validated and applicable to many contexts become accepted and are the prominent models, such as the Technology Acceptance Model (TAM) and the Unified Theory of Acceptance and Use of Technology (UTAUT).

Conducting a survey involving all SMS-based e-Government users around the world is impossible. Thus, to survey users from many countries with different backgrounds, this study conducted a mixed-mode design survey (Biffignandi and Toninell, 2005). In this study data was collected using a web-based survey, paper-based questionnaires and phone-call interviews and then integrated.

The web-based survey used both internal and external approaches to get respondents (Biffignandi and Toninell, 2005). The internal approach included web advertisements publishing the survey on some websites and on a social networking site (Facebook). The external approach was conducted by sending invitation emails to 31 mailing lists (the lists covered countries in Asia, Africa, America and Europe) on different topics (daily life, religion, culture, education e-Government, ICT, Human Computer Interaction, e-Government, governance, and telecommunication) as presented in Table 1.

Table 1: List of the email-groups as the sampling frame of the study

No	Name of the Mailing List	Topic	Country
1	eGov4dev	e-Government	International
2	Electronic Government	e-Government	Indonesia
3	Jatengonline	e-Government	Indonesia
4	eGov-indonesia	e-Government	Indonesia
5	E-Pemerintah	e-Government	Indonesia

No	Name of the Mailing List	Topic	Country
6	e-cilacap	e-Government	Indonesia
7	eGovINDIA	e-Government	India
8	India-egov	e-Government	India
9	E-gov_Australia	e-Government	Australia
10	Center-for-good-governance	governance	International
11	Dunia_ICT	ICT	Malaysia
12	ICT_of_Bangladesh	ICT	Bangladesh
13	Bangla_ict	ICT	Bangladesh
14	DigAfrica	ICT	Africa
15	Telematika	ICT	Indonesia
16	APWKomitel	ICT	Indonesia
17	SCSJeddah	ICT	Saudi Arabia
18	DigitalFilipino	ICT	The Philippines
19	Muslim_Its	IT	International
20	Mastel-anggota	Telecommunication	Indonesia
21	Usability matters	Computer Human Interaction	International
22	Experiencedesign	Computer Human Interaction	International
23	Nycchi	Computer Human Interaction	USA
24	Sandchi	Computer Human Interaction	USA
25	Hciidc	Computer Human Interaction	USA
26	Movement_of_Islamic_Unity	Religion	International
27	Eramuslim	Religion	Indonesia
28	Philippines_students	Education	The Philippines
29	eCulturalCenter	Culture	International
30	Iatss-alumni	Japan-Indonesia relationship	Indonesia
31	World Citizen	Daily Life	International

Technically, the users who were registered on the mailing lists were contacted via an email which provided a link directing them to the survey page and the research website http://smsegov.info. This survey page also recorded the respondents' IP addresses in order to identify any respondent who answered the questionnaires more than once. All responses to the survey were voluntary and all participants were encouraged to complete all questions in the survey.

The questionnaire used in this study contained closed questions and opened-ended questions (Appendix 1). The open-ended questions were designed to obtain qualitative information (free answers) about motivation and people who influence citizens to use or not to use SMS-based e-Government services. The questionnaire had been tested previously on a group of international students and an expert in e-Government. Since the web-survey sample does not cover other citizens who do not have access to or the skill to use the Internet, as a complement to the web-based survey, this study used phone-call interviews and paper-based questionnaires to involve people with no Internet access and skill. The same questions as in the web-based survey were asked.

3. Respondents profile

The web-based survey was run for 3 months (April–June 2009) and received 142 responses from respondents in 25 countries as shown in Table 2. Of these participants, the two largest nationalities were Indonesians and Indians (51.39 percent and 15.28 percent of the total respondents), following by Americans (6.25 percent), Bangladeshis and Tanzanians (3.47 percent each), Australians (2.08 percent), and the other 18 countries (0.6 up to 1.4 percent each).

Table 2: Respondents of the web-based survey based on countries

Countries	Percent (N=142)
Indonesia	51.39
India	15.28
United States of America	6.25
Bangladesh	3.47
Tanzania	3.47
Australia	2.08
Iran	1.39
Ireland	1.39
Nigeria	1.39
Pakistan	1.39
Spain	1.39
Austria	0.69
Bahrain	0.69
Brazil	0.69
Canada	0.69

Countries	Percent (N=142)
Gambia	0.69
Guatemala	0.69
Hongkong	0.69
Italy	0.69
Kenya	0.69
Norway	0.69
Oman	0.69
Philippines	0.69
Tokelau	0.69
Zambia	0.69
No country answer	1.39

In terms of gender, there were more male than female respondents (76.1 percent compared to 23.2 percent). In terms of age, the majority of the respondents were 31 to 40 years old (36.6 percent). Table 3 summarises the respondents by age and gender.

Table 3: Gender and age of respondents of the web-based survey (N=142)

Age	Male	Female	Null	Total	Percent
18-20	0	1	0	1	0.7
21-25	19	4	0	23	16.2
26-30	25	6	0	31	21.8
31-40	37	14	1	52	36.6
>40	27	8	0	35	24.7
Total	108	33	1	142	
Percent	76.1	23.2	0.7		100

As a complement to the web-based survey, phone-call interviews and paper-based questionnaires were conducted involving 17 Indonesians who did not have access to the Internet due to the lack of infrastructure or skill. They consisted of farmers, unemployed people, students, house wives and street vendors. The age and gender of the respondents are summarised in Table 4.

Table 4: Gender and age of respondents of the phone-call interview and paper-based questionnaire (N=17)

Age	Male	Female	Total	Percent
18-20	1	1	2	11.8
21-25	5	1	6	35.3
26-30	1	1	2	11.8
31-40	1	2	3	17.7
>40	2	2	4	23.5
Total	10	7	17	
Percent	58.8	41.2		100

In total, there were 159 respondents from 25 countries involved in this study with the gender and age compositions as shown in Table 5.

Table 5: Gender and age of all respondents, web-based survey, paper-based questionnaires, and phone-call interview (N=159)

Age	Male	Female	Null	Total	Percent
18-20	1	2	0	3	1.9
21-25	24	5	0	29	18.2
26-30	26	7	0	33	20.8
31-40	38	16	1	55	34.6
>40	29	10	0	39	24.5
Total	118	40	1	159	
Percent	74.2	25.2	0.6		100

The data indicated that the majority of the respondents in this study were from Indonesia and India, male and 31-40 years old. Overall, the survey involved respondents from Asia Pacific, America, Africa, and Middle East countries, and included respondents who have Internet access and ones who do not. The characteristics of this sample will be taken into account as a limitation in the conclusions.

4. Findings and discussion

4.1 Citizens awareness and adoption of SMS-based e-Government services

This study investigated the level of awareness and adoption of SMS-based e-Government services among respondents. It categorized the percentages of the citizens into: (i) those who used SMS-based e-Government services; (ii) those who were aware of, but did not use them; and (iii) those who were not even aware of the services. Figure 1 illustrates these findings. The results indicate that 43% of the respondents in this sample had used SMS services. Of the remaining 57% respondents, 27% stated that they were aware of but did not use the services and the remaining 30% were not even aware of SMS-based e-Government services in their countries (Figure 1).

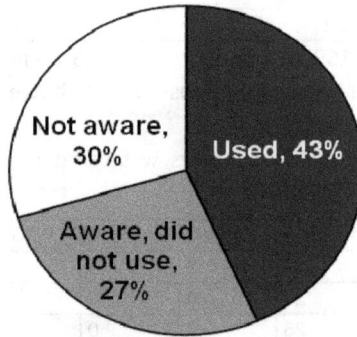

Figure 1: Awareness and adoption of SMS-based e-Government service (N=159)

Of the citizens who were aware of the services (103 people), the percentage of those who did not use the services is 33% (34 of 103 people, see Figure 2). It means that a third of the people who were aware of the services did not use the services. This figure suggests that awareness of services is not sufficient to encourage citizens to use SMS-based e-Government services; there are other factors to be considered and actions needed to encourage use of the services.

4.2 Citizens age and awareness and adoption of SMS-based e-Government services

It was found that as the citizens' age increased, there was more awareness of and adoption of SMS-based e-Government services (Figure 3). The absence of the awareness as well as adoption among the 18 to 20 age group may be because of the very small number of respondents from this age group (3 people compared to the other groups which are 29 to 55 people). While most age groups (except the 18-20 age group) have similar levels of awareness, the majority of the adopters were between the ages of 31 and 40 years: 53% (29 of 55 respondents in this group) used the service. In a further study, it will be interesting to see detail of the trends for the respondents in the 40 years and above category by breaking down this group into smaller ranges. The findings also suggest that older citizens are aware of and use SMS-based e-Government services.

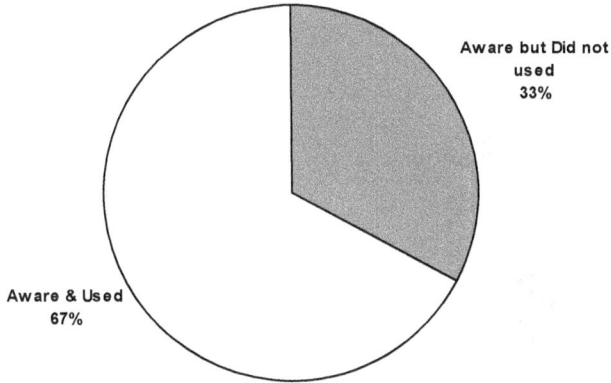

Figure 2: Adoption of SMS-based e-Government service among respondents who were aware of the services (N=103)

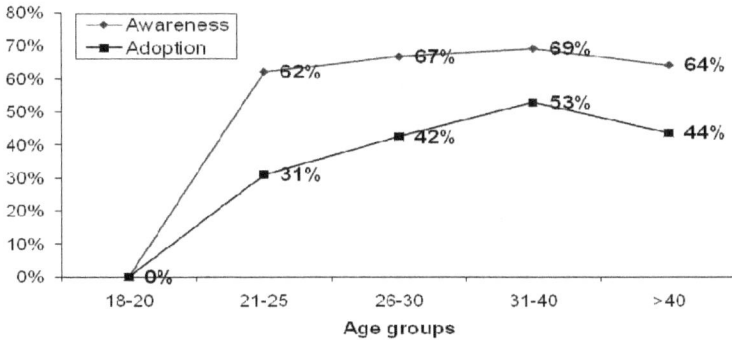

Figure 3: Awareness and adoption of SMS-based e-Government services by age group

4.3 Citizens gender and awareness and adoption of SMS-based e-Government services

Figure 4 illustrates that more males than females were aware of and used SMS e-Government services. Of the 118 male respondents, 83(70%) were aware of and 57 (48%) used the services compared to the 40 female respondents, 20 (50%) were aware of and 12 (30%) used the services. The percentage of male respondents who are aware of and adopt SMS-based e-Government services is 69% (57 of 83 people), while the percentage of females who are aware of and adopt the services is 60% (12 of 20 people). This suggests that at the initial stage of implementation of SMS-based e-Government services males are more likely to drive the adoption.

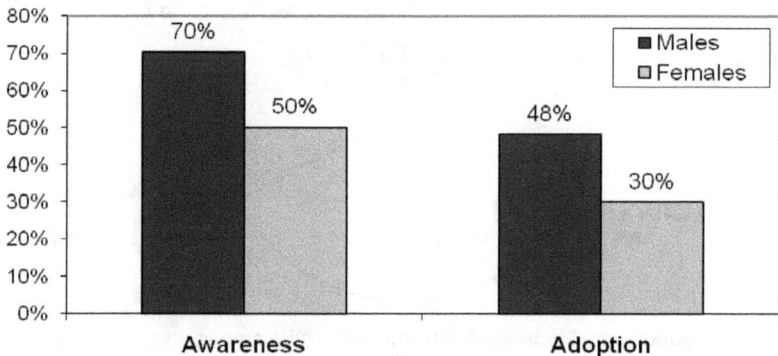

Figure 4: Comparison of awareness and adoption of SMS-based e-Government services by males and females

The findings in Section 4.2 and 4.3 suggest that the higher the awareness of the service the higher the likelihood of citizens using SMS-based e-Government services. This is congruent with most diffusion theories which suggest that awareness or individuals' knowledge about the existence and functions of an innovation is an initial step toward an adoption-decision process for the innovation (Rogers, 2003: 169).

The findings also suggest that male citizens aged 31 to 40 years are the most likely adopters of the services. While the adoption levels of the males and the females who are aware of the services are relatively similar (69% and 60%), both in awareness and adoption levels the females are fewer than the males (see Figure 4).

Accordingly, in order to increase the adoption of SMS-based e-Government services, governments should run intensive advertising campaigns about the services to make sure people are aware of the services. Since there are more female citizens who are not aware of and do not adopt the services than males, the campaigns should pay more attention to making females aware of the services. However, as suggested in Section 4.1 and referring to the Diffusion of Innovation theory, the Hierarchy-of-Effects and the Stage-of-Change models (Rogers, McGuire, and Prochaska in Rogers 2003:198), individuals' decisions toward using an SMS-based e-Government service require more stages than just awareness and each step involves variety of factors. Section 4.5 will discuss these factors.

4.4   Popular SMS-based e-Government services

For local authorities who want to develop an initial SMS-based e-Government service, recognizing what type of the SMS-based service is most likely to be used by citizens is necessary. The understanding may assist government to justify the investment in the system and to assist them in delivering the service effectively and efficiently.

Refering to the Six-Level model of SMS-based e-Government, the survey asked citizens about the kinds of SMS-based e-Government services they have used. The questions provided five answer-options: Listen, Notification, Pull SMS, Transaction, and others. Each option was explained by definition and example. The 'others' option was for respondents who had difficulty classifying the service, it was then defined using the explanation of respondent. Table 6 illustrates the findings.

Table 6: Kinds of SMS-based e-Government services used by respondents

Kinds of service	Number of people	Percent of all respondents (N=159)	Percent of all respondents who used the services (N=69)
Listen	28	17.6	40.6
Notification	49	30.8	71.0
Pull SMS	34	21.4	49.3
Transaction	22	13.8	31.9

It was found that Notification is the most popular service. Of the 159 respondents, 49 people had used Notification services. It means 30.8% of all respondents or 71% of respondents who used the SMS-based services had experience using Notification services. The Notification service is a one-way broadcast SMS service from government to citizens, such as weather warnings, changes of bus timetables, or tax due-date reminders. The popularity of this service may be because citizens can easily register for and unsubscribe from the service, and commonly the use of this service is free of charge.

The second favourite service is Pull SMS. This service enables citizens to 'pull' specific information by sending a request SMS.

The third frequently used service is a Listen service, which is an SMS channel for citizens to send report, complain, or to make suggestions to government.

Finally, the least popular is a Transaction service such as paying bills, taxes or parking fees via SMS. This may be because citizens' consider that the service usage has more consequences such as risk of money loss or risk privacy.

4.5   Thinking like citizens think: what citizens think about using an SMS-based e-Government service?

Adoption research has extended the traditional approach to technology acceptance which is studies of ergonomic or usability concerns to studies of individuals' behaviour when using technologies. The traditional approach believed that if the technology is easy to use or the intended users are able to use the technology then they must be using the technology. In reality this approach does not cover all aspects of user acceptance. Rogers (2003) and Dillon (1996) argued that while ability to use any technology is obviously necessary, it is not sufficient to ensure acceptability; many technologies that are demonstrably usable are never accepted by the target users. Technology adoption theories show that usability is just one of many factors that influence individuals to accept a technology. It is suggested that in order to be accepted, a technology should meet the mind of the target users.

Specifically for SMS-based e-Government, this study found that there are 15 beliefs which may influence citizens to use or to reject an SMS service (Table 7).

Table 7: Individual's beliefs which influence citizens to use or not use SMS-based e-Government services

No	Factors	Percent (N=159)
1	Perceived ease of use	20.8
2	Perceived efficiency in time and distance	17.6
3	Perceived value for money	12.6
4	Perceived responsiveness	12.6
5	Perceived usefulness	11.9
6	Perceived convenience	9.4
7	Trust in the SMS technology	5.7
8	Perceived relevance, quality and reliability of the information	4.4
9	Perceived risk to user privacy	3.8
10	Perceived reliability of mobile network and system performance	3.1
11	Trust of the government and perceived quality of public services	3.1
12	Perceived risk to money	3.1
13	Perceived availability of device and infrastructure	1.9
14	Perceived compatibility	1.9
15	Self-efficacy in using SMS	1.3

4.5.1 Simplicity is the main reason

The findings indicate that the main reason why citizens use SMS-based e-Government services is because they believe that the services are easy to use. The degree to which an individual perceives that an SMS-based e-Government service is free of difficulty to use is defined as perceived ease of use. Respondents said that they used the services because the services are simple, practical, less hassle, easy to access, easy to use, and the service numbers are easy to remember. The more citizens perceived that an SMS-based service is easy to use the more likely they are to use the service. Accordingly, simplicity should become a main advantage of the services. The simplicity of SMS-based e-Government services should cover the procedure to register for and to unsubscribe from the services, the information on how to use the services, the steps taken to get the information, and the reply message.

To make sure the registration for an SMS-based e-Government service is easy for all citizens, the system should enable people to register through various channels such as SMS, Internet (web-based form), phone, fax, or by coming to the office. The registration data should be simple and easy to fill in. A number of options for unsubscribing from receiving Notification services should also be available for users. Providing an easy to use unsubscribe method will encourage users to join since they know they can easily discontinue their subscription to the service.

The service should provide information on how to use the service. A respondent to the survey rejected a service because an unclear instruction meant the service could not be used. This information can be provided as a brochure, a web page, or a 'help' feature on the SMS system (users may ask assistance on how to use the service by typing and sending 'help' word).

The way in which to use the service should be simple. For the Pull-based service, for example, the text format for the request-SMS should be simple, not case sensitive, and easy to remember. The information requested by clients should be sent in one SMS (the system should not send the client other options or instructions).

Moreover, the information sent to the citizens should be concise, clear and easy to understand. If it is needed, the system may use capital letters or punctuation marks to emphasize important words.

4.5.2   *Perceived value for money: citizens are sensitive in SMS cost*
Most of the respondents had perceptions that SMS is cheap; this is one of the reasons why they used SMS-based services. People are sensitive in terms of the SMS cost. This explains why some respondents rejected services which charged users more than the standard SMS cost (premium SMS

charge). Even people who really need to use the services will weigh whether or not the benefits justify the SMS cost.

The Perceived value for money factor also relates to the perceived comparison between SMS and phone call cost. Some respondents did not use the SMS-based service if they could make a phone call at low cost for unlimited time. They expect SMS-based e-Government services to be free or cheaper than phone calls. The Diffusion of Innovation theory (Rogers, 2003) explains this service attribute as the relative advantage factor; it suggests that individuals are more likely to adopt an innovation when they perceive that it is better than the idea or product it supersedes. The degree to which an individual perceives that an SMS-based e-Government service is better value for the amount paid is defined as perceived value for money.

4.5.3   *How much time and effort could be saved by using the service?*
The third belief influencing citizens to use an SMS-based e-Government service is perceived efficiency in time and distance. It is the degree to which an individual perceives that the service will reduce the time spent and effort to go to the public service office or to use another channel. Respondents said that they prefer to use SMS-based services because they are quick, take less time and provide faster services than the traditional services and the Internet channel. Accordingly, in order to be accepted government should ensure that their SMS-based services require less time and effort compared to other e-Government channels.

4.5.4   *Perceived responsiveness: People do not want to talk with machine*
One of the advantages of SMS-based e-Government channel is that people feel that they communicate with the government person-to-person. Some respondents used the service because they perceive they communicate directly with the decision makers.

However, as a consequence of the person-to-person perception, users of SMS-based services expect a quick reply. When they do not get any replies or responses, they reject the services. Specifically for the Listen services, citizens in the survey said that they did not use the services because they were pessimistic that their SMS would be received and forwarded to the right officials, responded to quickly and satisfactorily, and they will be informed of the progress of their message. They perceived that sending a report or complain to government via SMS is like sending a letter to an empty house. The degree to which an individual believes that his or her SMS will be responded by government quickly, appropriately and satisfactorily is defined as the perceived responsiveness. The higher the perceived responsiveness toward an SMS-based service, the more likely the person will use the service. Accordingly, to encourage people to use Listen services and to build the perceived responsiveness of the services, each citizen's message should be replied to quickly and each sender should be informed that their messages have been received and read by the right officials. Senders should be informed of the response to and the progress of the message.

Additionally, in order to make messages in the Notification service seem personal for each receiver the service could add the client's name to each message. This could improve the relationship between government and citizens.

4.5.5 Perceived usefulness: Does the service really address citizens' needs?

The fifth belief is perceived usefulness, which is defined as the degree to which a citizen believes that using the SMS-based e-Government service will help them to get what they want and make their life easier. Before deciding to use a service, the survey's respondents wondered whether or not the SMS-based service provides information or functions relevant to their needs. If the service is relevant and satisfied their needs, they were likely to use the service.

4.5.6 Perceived convenience: Is the service easy to access anywhere anytime?

Another belief which influences citizens to use SMS-based e-Government services is perceived convenience. It is associated with the degree to which a citizen perceives that the services can be accessed anytime anywhere. Since SMS is a basic feature of all mobile phones and mobile networks cover a larger area than the Internet respondents in this study perceived that they could receive, send or reply the messages anywhere anytime they want to.

4.5.7 Trust in SMS technology

Respondents who used the services explained that they trusted SMS-based e-Government services since the messages are recorded by mobile phones and the SMS-based system, so they could recall the data and confirm a transaction anytime, they could not miss a message sent to them and they can check whether their messages have been delivered to the system or not. The respondents perceive that the SMS channel is concise and accurate.

On the contrary, respondents who did not use the services had perceptions that SMS is an informal channel so government would not pay serious attention to their messages, the number of characters in an SMS message is too limited to send a message, and they do not trust SMS security. The degree to which a citizen believes that using an SMS channel is safe and will not initiate any problems for him or her is one of the factors that influences citizens to use SMS-based e-Government services. This factor is defined as the trust in the SMS technology.

4.5.8 Perceived relevance, quality and reliability of the information

Relevance, quality, and reliability of the information provided by the SMS-based services are another issue for citizens. People tend to reject Notification and Pull SMS services when they find that the information is not updated, is not relevant to their needs, unclear, not precise or insufficient in detail, not accurate, and of no value. The concern with the reliability of the information is higher when using SMS-based transactions and getting information about weather forecasts and timetables. The degree to which a citizen perceives that the information is relevant for him or her, reliable and of high quality is another factor which influences citizens to use or to reject an SMS-based e-Government service.

4.5.9 Perceived risk to user privacy

In addition to the perceived trust in the SMS technology, when using SMS-based e-Government services citizens also consider the risk to their privacy due to the SMS system or the government agency. Respondents who used SMS-based services for sending complaints and reports to local authorities said that they used the services because they do not have to meet person-to-person and disclose their names or other personal information. People who did not use the services perceived that using the service might initiate and propagate repetitive SMS marketing which is irritating and infringes their privacy. They worried that the agency or the SMS service provider will sell their mobile numbers or data to other organizations and businesses or use the information for other purposes. The degree to which a citizen perceives that using SMS-based e-Government services and dealing with the government agencies may divulge his or her personal information and pose problems for his or her privacy (perceived risk to user privacy) is another determinant of service usage.

4.5.10 Perceived reliability of the mobile network and the SMS-based system

The survey also found that citizens put the performance of their mobile networks and performance of the SMS-based system as consideration factors when deciding to use or to reject SMS-based e-Government services. Some respondents did not use the services because they were not confident that mobile networks provided the coverage and good connection performance (reliability and initialization speed) needed to use SMS-based e-Government services. The performance of the SMS-based system itself also influences citizens, especially the response time and reliability of the services. The degree to which a citizen is confident that his or her mobile network is reliable when using an SMS-based e-Government service and the SMS-based system is also reliable are other determinants toward using SMS-based e-Government services.

4.5.11 Trust in the government and perceived quality of the public services

The degree to which citizens trust the government and perceive that the public services have been delivered well is another belief that influences citizens to use or to reject available SMS-based e-Government services. Some respondents of the survey did not use the service because they did not trust on the government and perceived that the quality of public services is poor. Since they found that the traditional public services were poor, they were sceptical that the electronic-services would be better. Moreover, the low accountability of the government made citizens afraid of sending reports, suggestions or even complaints. Instead of getting solutions from government, they believed that their messages might cause another problem for them.

4.5.12   Perceived risk to money

This factor refers to individuals' belief that using the service might cause financial problems. Survey respondents stopped using SMS-based e-Government services when they had the experience of receiving an unwanted SMS message for which they were charged. Also, they worried about SMS fraud and risks associated with SMS-based transactions.

4.5.13   Availability of device and infrastructure

Respondents pointed out that they used the SMS-based e-Government services because they have the device (mobile phone) and the mobile network is available for them. The degree to which an individual believes that the device and infrastructure for using SMS-based e-Government services is available for them is another determinant of the services' usage.

4.5.14   Perceived compatibility

This factor refers to the degree to which a citizen perceives that the service is consistent with the existing public service channels and the popular communication media. The respondents, particularly from the United States of America, indicated that they did not use SMS-based e-Government services because SMS is not a common or a popular communication channel for delivering public services in their country. They reject available SMS-based e-Government services simply because most people do not use SMS; they use the Internet and land-line telephone. People tend to use a new technology or service when it is consistent with the existing values and past experience of the potential users (Rogers, 2003).

4.5.15   Self-efficacy in using SMS

Whether or not a citizen uses SMS-based e-Government services is also influenced by his or her confidence in using SMS. The survey found that some respondents did not use the services simply because they had no idea of how to use SMS. The degree to which an individual perceives his or her ability to use SMS is one of the factors which influence a citizen to use or not use an SMS-based e-Government service.

Overall, this study found 15 beliefs (or perceptions) that influence citizens to use or to reject SMS-based e-Government services. In order to increase the acceptance of SMS-based e-Government services, governments take into account these factors when designing and delivering the services.

4.5.16   Communication channels and influential persons

In addition to the beliefs factor, Rogers (2003) suggests that the success of an innovation also depends on the communication channels. The communication channels are the means by which information about the innovation spreads from one individual to another. Further, Rogers (2003:18) classified the communication channels into mass media channels, interpersonal channels, and interactive communication via the Internet. The choice of communication channel may determine whether the innovation will be or will not be transmitted to and influenced the target users.

The survey found that mass media channels are the most effective means of informing and influencing citizens about the existence and benefits of SMS-based e-Government services. The majority of the respondents said that information in the mass media had made them aware of the services and influenced them to use the service.

In terms of interpersonal channels, the findings (Table 8) show that citizens were influenced to use SMS-based e-Government services by friends, family, experts, public figures, teachers, and government officials. Most of the respondents sought advice and information about SMS-based e-Government services from their friends and families.

Table 8: External factors which influenced citizens to use or reject SMS-based e-Government services

No	External factor	Percent (N=159)
1	Media	22.0
2	Friend	8.8
3	Family	4.4
4	Expert	1.3
5	Public Figure	0.6
6	Teacher	0.6
7	Government officials	0.6

Referring to the Diffusion of Innovations (DOI) theory and the Valente and Saba study (1998), these findings suggest that the mass media play a critical role in increasing awareness and detailed knowledge about available SMS-based e-Government services. Personal networks, particularly those that involve friends and family of the target users, experts, public figures, teachers, and government officials are associated with all steps to services adoption. The steps include: the awareness of, detailed knowledge about, attitude toward, and intention to use the services. Individuals who lack personal contact with users of SMS-based e-Government services may turn to the mass media for information about the services. The interactions between the mass media, personal networks, and an individual are shown in Figure 5.

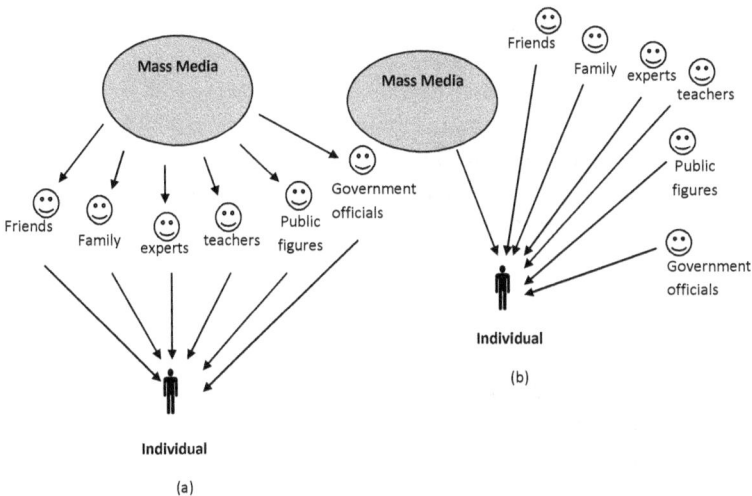

Figure 5: The interactions between mass media, personal networks, and individual: (a) The mass media reinforce interpersonal communication in influencing the use of SMS-based e-Government services, (b) the mass media substitute for interpersonal communication in influencing using the services (adapted from Valente and Saba, 1998)

This study suggests that governments should advertise services on all the mass media channels in order to make citizens aware of and to provide detailed knowledge about the services. These mass media campaigns are expected to initiate inter-personal networks influence toward using the services and to influence individuals particularly those who lack personal contact with other users of the services. To improve the effectiveness of the advertising, governments should involve families and friends of the target users and use opinion leaders such as experts, public figures, teachers and government officials. In terms of the content, the advertising should convince people that the services accommodate their perceptions, as discussed in Section 4.5, toward new SMS-based e-Government services.

5. Conclusions, limitations, and next study

To design and to deliver SMS-based e-Government services, local authorities should consider the expectations and the perceptions of citizens toward using the services. This study indicates that whether or not citizens adopt SMS-based e-Government services is influenced bythe fifteen beliefs about using SMS-based e-Government services: perceived ease of use; perceived efficiency in time and distance; perceived value for money; perceived convenience; perceived availability of device and infrastructure; perceived usefulness; perceived responsiveness; perceived relevance, quality and reliability of the information; trust in the SMS technology; perceived risk to user privacy; perceived reliability of the mobile network and the SMS-based system; trust in the government and perceived quality of public services; perceived risk to money; perceived compatibility; and self-efficacy in using SMS.

Among the factors perceived ease of use, perceived efficiency in time and distance, value for money, perceived convenience, and perceived availability of device and infrastructure are the most important in influencing the use of SMS-based e-Government services. Therefore, governments should focus on these advantage factors in promoting SMS-based e-Government services.

Common factors which discourage citizens adoption of available SMS-based e-Government services include: perceived usefulness, perceived responsiveness, perceived relevance, quality and reliability of the information, trust in the SMS technology, perceived risk to user privacy; perceived reliability of the mobile network and the SMS-based system, trust in the government and perceived quality of public services, perceived risk to money, perceived compatibility, and self-efficacy on using SMS. Hence, in order to minimize resistance to the services, government should address all of these factors. For example, to increase perceived usefulness of an SMS-based e-Government service, government should make sure that the service meets citizens' needs by conducting a preliminary survey before designing the service; to increase perceived responsiveness of a Listen SMS service, government could setup an automatic reply system and assign a group of staff to manage incoming SMS messages; to increase trust in the SMS technology, government could use encryption with each message; and to minimize perceived risk to user privacy and perceived risk to money, the government could publish a privacy statement, assure the confidence and security of the senders, and setup an easy and reliable system for verifying each transaction including a refund procedure.

In terms of popularity, the Notification service is the most frequently used SMS-based e-Government service, following by Pull SMS, Listen, and Transaction. Notification services are appropriate initial SMS-based e-Government services.

In order to increase usage of SMS-based e-Government services, governments should make people aware of and provide information about the services. Governments should run advertising campaigns on using the services in all mass media channels. The advertising should involve family and friends of the target users and be delivered by experts, public figures and teachers. In designing and delivering the services, government should address the 15 perceptions about SMS-based e-Government services. This should give citizens positive attitudes towards using the services which will lead to intention to use and actual use of SMS-based e-Government services. The relationships among the beliefs, intention to use, and actual usage of SMS-based e-Government services will be investigated further in the next study.

This study incorporates a number of features, including a mix of web-based survey, paper-based questionnaires, and phone interviews to obtain an appropriate mix of respondents from 25 different countries (the respondents include people who interact with public services, people who have Internet access and people who do not have Internet access, and citizens with a variety of occupations and levels of education); the open-ended questions enables a variety of answers from the respondents. These lend significant strength to the study. However the demographics of the respondents, the majority were from Indonesia (51.39%) and India (15.28%), male (74.2%), aged 31-40 years old (34.6%), and mainly people who have Internet access (89%) should be taken into account in any attempt to generalize the findings.

Appendix 1: Survey questionnaire

Citizens' Motivation to USE or NOT TO USE
an SMS application for public services

Part A. Demographics

1. Sex: ○ Male ○ Female
2. Age (years): ○ 18-20 ○ 21-25 ○ 26-30 ○ 31-40 ○ >40
3. Nationality: [Country Options ▾]

Part B. Motivation to Use or Not to Use an SMS application for Public Services

4. **Are you aware** of an SMS application for public services in your country? ○ YES ○ NO

[*SMS applications for public services are any public services provided by government through Short Messaging Service channel, for example sending complain/report to government via SMS, getting information about bus timetables using SMS, paying tax via SMS)

5. **Have you ever used** the SMS service? ○ YES ○ NO

6. **If YES, Which kinds of service** have you used? (*You can choose more than one*)
   ☐ Sending SMS about opinions, complains, or reports to government official/institution.
   ☐ Receiving SMS notifications, such as messages about disaster warnings, bills, or news update.
   ☐ Sending SMS in order to get some information, such as sending SMS to get information about bus timetables or weather.
   ☐ Doing transactions via SMS, such as paying bills using SMS.

   ☐ Others: _____

7. **WHY** DID or DID NOT you use the service:

8. Who is/are **person(s)** who **influenced you** to use or not to use the service?(if any):

[SUBMIT]

Thank You Very Much for Your Time and Participation

References

Alampay, E. A. (2003) Text 2920/117: Reporting Police Wrongdoing via SMS in the Philippines, mGovernment Case Study, e-Government for Development, [Online], Available: http://www.egov4dev.org/mgovernment/resources/case/text2920.shtml [19 October 2008].

Awadhi, S. A. and A. Morris (2008) 'The Use of the UTAUT Model in the Adoption of e-Government Services in Kuwait', Hawaii International Conference on System Sciences, IEEE.

Biffignandi, S. and D. Toninell (2005) FrameSampling and Inference in Web Surveys, [Online], Available:

http://www.websm.org/uploadi/editor/1133720576GUIDE_1_Sampling_and_i
nference_in_web_surveys_part1.pdf [4 December 2005].

Bremer, A. A. and L. A. L. Prado (2006) 'Municipal m-Services using SMS', Euro mgov 2006.

Carter, L. and F. Belanger (2005) 'The utilization of e-Government services', Information Systems Journal, vol. 15, pp. 5-25.

Choudrie, J. and Y. Dwivedi (2005) 'A survey of citizens' awareness and adoption of e-Government initiatives, the 'government gateway': a United Kingdom perspective', e-Government Workshop Brunel University, West London, UK, Brunel University.

Cilingir, D. and I. Kushchu (2004), e-Government and m-Government:Concurrent Leaps by Turkey, Mobile Government Lab.

Coursey, D. and D. F. Norris (2008) 'Models of e-Government: Are Th ey Correct? An Empirical Assessment', Public Administration Review, pp. 523-536.

Dalziel, D. (2004) Government Online-A multi-country Study of e-Government usage, the World Association of Research Professionals.

Dillon, A. and M. Morris, Eds. (1996). User Acceptance of New Information Technology: Theories and Models, Annual Review of Information Science and Tecnology, Medford NJ.

Ghyasi, A. F. and I. Kushchu (2004) m-Government: Cases of Developing Countries, Mobile Government Lab.

Horst, M., M. Kuttschreuter, et al. (2007) 'Perceived usefulness, personal experiences, risk perception and trust as determinants of adoption of e-Government services in The Netherlands', Computers in Human Behavior, vol. 23, no. 4, pp. 1838-1852.

Hung, S.-Y., C.-M. Chang, et al. (2006) 'Determinants of User Acceptance of the e-Government Services: The case of online tax filling and payment system', Government Information Quarterly, vol. 23, pp. 97-122.

Khosrowpour, M., Ed. (2005) An e-Government Model, Electronic Commerce, Idea Group Inc (IGI).

Kortemann, M. (2005) 'Cultural Background and Technology Acceptance: Evaluation of ICT Projects that Bridge the Digital Divide', IWIPS, Amsterdam, The Netherlands.

Lallana, E. (2008) eGovDev4Dev cases on mGovernment, e-Government for Development, [Online], Available: http://www.egov4dev.org/mgovernment/resources/index.shtml [8 May 2008].

Lallana, E. C. (2004). 'SMS, business and Government in the Philippines', a project of the Department of Science and Technology and IDRC, ICT4D.ph, [Online], Available: http://unpan1.un.org/intradoc/groups/public/documents/Other/UNPAN02483 4.pdf [July 1993].

Lee, K. J. and J.-H. Hong (2002) 'Development of An e-Government Service Model: A Business Model Approach' International Review of Public Administration 2002, vol. 7, no. 2, pp. 109-118.

MonashUniversity. (2005)'Carpark SMS', [Online], Available: http://infotech.monash.edu.au/promotion/coolcampus/projects/carparksms/index.html [14 August 2008].

Philip, F. M. (2006) 'Making a case for modifying the technology acceptance model to account for limited accessibility in developing countries', Information Technology for Development, vol. 12, no.3, pp.213-224.

Rannu, R. and M. Semevsky (2005) 'Mobile Services in Tartu', EU Interreg IIIC Programme 'Challenge of eCitizen' project, Mobi Solutions Ltd.

Rogers, E. M. (2003) Diffusion of Innovations, New York, Free Press.

SMSeGov.info (2009), [Online], Available: http://news.smsegov.info [September 2009].

Susanto, T. D. and R. Goodwin (2006) 'Opportunity and Overview of SMS-based e-Government in Developing Countries', The Internet Society II: Advances in Education, Commerce & Governance, the New Forest, UK, WIT Press, vol. 36, no. 10.

Susanto, T. D., R. Goodwin, et al. (2008) 'A Six-Level Model of SMS-based e-Government', International Conference on e-Government 2008, Melbourne, ICEG.

Taylor, S. and P. Todd (1995) 'Assessing IT Usage: The Role of Prior Experience', MIS Quarterly, vol. 19, no. 4, pp. 561.

Titah, R. and H. barki (2005)'e-Government Adoption and Acceptance: a Literature review', HEC Montreal, vol. 5, no. 3, [Online], Available: http://neumann.hec.ca/igti/cahiers de recherche/chaireIGTIcahier0503.pdf [July 2008].

Valente, T. W. and W. P. Saba (1998) 'Mass Media and Interpersonal Influences in a Reproductive Health Communication Campaign in Bolivia' Communication Research, vol. 25(1), pp. 96-124.

Westlund, O. (2008) 'Towards an understanding of the adoption and use of mobile Internet news', Roskilde Universitetscenter, [Online], Available: http://www.ruc.dk/upload/application/pdf/f51d6748/Oscar%20Westlund_%20Sweden_Paper.pdf [July 2008].

Determinants of e-Government Maturity in the Transition Economies of Central and Eastern Europe

Princely Ifinedo[1] and Mohini Singh[2]

[1]Cape Breton University, Sydney, Nova Scotia, Canada
[2]RMIT University, Melbourne, Victoria, Australia

princely_ifinedo@cbu.ca
mohini.singh@rmit.edu.au

Originally published in Electronic Journal of e-Government (2011) Volume 9 Issue 2 http://www.ejeg.com

Editorial Commentary

Ifinedo and Singh address a gap in the academic literature regarding transition economies of Central and Eastern Europe. The authors have identified issues such as: national wealth, human capital development, technological infrastructure, and rule of law that have an effect on e-Government initiatives. This is also important for developing countries as well, because a better understanding of the issues impacting e-Government maturity may also empower policy makers.

Abstract: Our research focuses on the possible determinants of e-government (E-gov) maturity in the Transition Economies of Central and Eastern Europe (TEECE). E-gov maturity, in this research, refers to the growth levels in a country's online services and its citizens' online participation in governance. Our study of the extant

53

literature indicated that few have discussed the determinants of E-gov maturity in TEECE. Studies from differing parts of the world are needed for theory development. Building on a prior framework, we used the contingency theory and the resource-based view perspective to guide our discourse. In particular, we examined the relationships between macro-environmental factors such as national wealth, technological infrastructure, rule of law, and so forth on E-gov maturity. A 5-year panel data of 16 TECEE selected from two main groupings was used for analysis in conjunction with structural equation modeling technique; the data consisted of 80 observations or data points. The data analysis underscored the relevance of such factors as technological infrastructure, rule of law, and human capital development as possible determinants of E-gov maturity in TEECE. National wealth was found to be an enabler in the research conceptualization. The implications of our study's findings for research and policy making are discussed.

Keywords: Transition Economies of Central and Eastern Europe (TECEE), e-government (E-gov), E-gov maturity, contingency theory, resource-based view, structural equation modeling

1. Introduction

The United Nations and the World Bank describe e-government (E-gov) as the utilization of the Internet and the World Wide Web for delivering government information and services to citizens and other stakeholders in a country (InfoDev, 2004; UN Public Administration Programme, 2010). E-gov allows government's services to be more effective and accessible to citizens (Fountain, 2001; Moon, 2002; West, 2004). Empirical data from international agencies, consulting organizations, and academic research shows that E-gov has become a global phenomenon with nearly all governments around the world adopting it to promote citizen engagement and empowerment (Accenture 2001; West, 2007; UN Public Administration Programme, 2010; Karunasena et al., 2011).

Despite the popularity of E-gov around the world, empirical evidence from both academic research (West, 2007; Siau & Long, 2006; Singh et al., 2007; Gupta et al., 2008; Azad et al., 2010) and international agencies' reports (InfoDev, 2004; UN Public Administration Programme, 2010) indicated that transition economies and developing countries around the world lag behind advanced countries with respect to the deployment and use of E-gov facilities. That is, more economically endowed countries often occupy the upper echelons of innovators or adopters of advanced E-gov initiatives and schemes (West, 2007; Azad et al., 2010). In part, this fact has influenced our research conceptualization. Notably, we worked with a research model indicating that economic considerations or imperatives directly or indirectly influence the advancement of E-gov schemes in emerging parts of the world.

Norris (2001) asserted that the emerging digital divide (in this case, E-gov divide) has three distinct aspects: the social digital divide, the democratic digital divide, and the global digital divide. Gascó (2005) noted that the regional digital divide is a variation of the global digital divide in the sense that it signifies the differences that exist in E-gov initiatives between countries from the same geographical region. With respect to the region of focus in this article, it can be seen that the E-gov index (i.e. an indicator of a country's electronic government adoption) for Eastern European countries averaged 0.5449 in 2010. At the same time, the scores for two countries in the region i.e. Hungary and Belarus were 0.6315 and 0.4900, respectively (UN Public Administration Programme, 2010) to indicate the existence of regional differences. In this regard, we argue that more attention needs to be paid to understanding E-gov issues at the regional level to enrich insight.

To address E-gov issues in Eastern Europe, professionals from that part of the world and elsewhere have gathered every year since 2003 on designated Eastern European E-gov days to discuss issues related to the advancement of E-gov in Central and Eastern Europe (Eastern European e-Gov Days, 2011). Knowledge transfer in the area of E-gov between advanced Western European countries and their counterparts from Central and Eastern Europe is actively encouraged. This paper adds to the growing body of knowledge in this area of interest. More precisely, more needs to be done regarding enriching the academic discourse related to the determinants of E-gov maturity in Transition Economies of Central and Eastern Europe (TECEE).

Our study's focus on TECEE is informed by two considerations. First, researchers such as Roztocki and Weistroffer (2008), Ifinedo &Davidrajuh (2005), and Ifinedo and Ifinedo (2011) have indicated that there is a lack of adequate research related to information systems and technologies (IS/IT) issues in TECEE; they called on researchers to focus on such issues in that part of Europe. Indeed, the academic literature focusing on trans-national E-gov issues in TECEE is sparse, perhaps due to the relative novelty of the subject (Katchanovski & La Porte, 2005). Moreover, research in this area of study tends to employ global E-gov data (Azad et al., 2010; Kovačić, 2005; Katchanovski & La Porte, 2005; Singh et al., 2007; Siau & Long, 2006; Moon et al., 2005) that included some TECEE rather than focus on countries from that region specifically as is the case in our own study. By not focusing on specific regions of the world, it is possible that a deeper understanding of the factors or determinants of E-gov maturity in differing parts of the world is underreported.

Second, TECEE share a common political and cultural history as most countries in the region only recently metamorphosed from centrally planned systems to free market democracies (Ifinedo & Davidrajuh, 2005; Ifinedo & Ifinedo, 2011). Thus, it is pertinent to continue to monitor progress in TE-CEE especially with regard to IS/IT use for development and governance (Levada, 2004; Alexander, 2004; EU Regional Policy; 2009). Put differently, as E-gov initiatives are implemented to reform administrative services and enhance citizen empowerment, research such as this current one could provide a useful lens through which advancement and positive changes emanating from the use of such technological innovations in governance across TECEE can be assessed or viewed. Moreover, theory development in the area is engendered by views from elsewhere other than the easily available perspectives from the developed Western countries.

With respect to the discourse of E-gov maturity around the world, our research complements the study by Singh et al. (2007) that investigated a similar theme globally by including the effects of political, economic, social, and technological factors on E-gov maturity. Nonetheless, our research differs from Singh et al.'s work in three ways: a) this current study focuses on solely on TECEE for reasons already espoused; b) it underscores the relevance of factors such as rule of law and transparency levels, which were not considered in Singh et al.'s work, c) this study seeks to contribute to the growing body of knowledge regarding the overriding impact of economic imperatives on E-gov maturity and the possible mediating influences of the others factors under focus. That is, this research does more than examining the direct impacts of selected factors on the dependent variable as is usually the case in some previous research (e.g. Kovačić, 2005; Moon et al., 2005).

Further, the focus of some prior E-gov studies in TECEE (e.g. McHenry & Borisov, 2006) was on a single country wherein the quantitative research method was favored. To some degree, comparative analyses of issues across countries can be negatively impacted through the use of such approaches. In our study, published data from reliable sources such as the United Nations (UN) and the World Bank for 16 TECEE over a 5-year period was used for analysis. Very few (e.g. Wong & Welch, 2004) have used longitudinal or time-series data to capture the development of E-gov around the world. We assert that more information could emerge when E-gov progression, over the years, in TECEE are considered and discussed with reliable data. Specifically, our research is designed to provide an answer to the following question: *Over time, what are the possible determinants of E-gov maturity in TECEE?* The resource-based view (RBV) and the contingent theory (CT) will be employed to provide the necessary conceptual underpinning for our study.

The remainder of the paper is organized as follows: First, information related to the study's underpinning theoretical frameworks and key concepts are provided. Second, the study's research model and the hypotheses are presented. Third, the research methodology and other relevant information are presented. The paper concludes by discussing its findings, implications, limitations, and avenues for further research.

2. Background information

2.1 Theoretical underpinnings

The resource-based view (RBV) is a management tool that has been used by researchers (e.g. Srivastava & Teo, 2007; 2008) to discuss E-gov issues against the background of that concept being seen as a national resource. The RBV posits that the basis for a competitive advantage of a firm lies in the application of the bundle of valuable resources at the firm's disposal (Wernerfelt, 1984, Barney, 1991). Some researchers including Mathews (2002) have extended the RBV to a "resource economy" to include the resources produced and exchanged by firms within a country. According to Srivastava & Teo (2007, p. 76), "in a resource economy, the objects of interest are not the resources existing within a particular firm, but the unique configuration of resources within the economy." In that regard, the distinctive resource configurations within an economy or state and its capability to use such resource will serve to enhance its national competitiveness. The availability of wealth or economic factors for national development has since been fundamentally recognized in the relevant literature (McClelland, 1967; Goldthorpe et al., 1968; Friedman 2005). Factors such as human resource development and other facilitating conditions such as the availability of IT resource within an economy makes it more competitive than counterparts lacking such resource (Friedman 2005; WEF, 2010). It would suffice to note that economies with requisite capabilities and endowments to effectively institute E-gov as a national resource might have benefited from the availability of such endowments (Norris, 2001; West, 2004; 2007; Srivastava & Teo, 2007).

The second relevant theoretical framework considered in this research is the contingency theory (CT), which was developed by Lawrence and Lorsch (1967). The CT has often been used at the organizational level, but it can also be extended to the national level. The CT posits that a set of independent or contingent variables are assumed to influence the dependent variable such that higher favorable outcomes result from the direct impact of the independent variables. To some degree, the CT compliments the direct measure approach (Bonoma & Johnson, 1979), which can be used to assess the direct impact of contingent variables (e.g. political rights and/or GDP per capita) on E-gov maturity. Several researchers (e.g. Moon et al., 2005; Kovačić, 2005; Katchanovski & La Porte, 2005; Singh et al., 2007; Azad et al., 2010) have framed their studies in the context of the CT. Others (e.g. Kubicek & Westholm, 2005) have built upon the CT to propose a "contingency model of E-democracy" that examines the impact of relevant socio-economic, political, and technological factors on E-gov development.

2.2   Transition economies: Definition and categorizations

In general, the term transition economy (TE) refers to an economy that is changing from a centrally planned economy to a market economy (IMF, 2000; Samoilenko & Osei-Bryson, 2008). The characteristics of TEs include rapid economic liberalization, legal and institutional reforms, restructuring and privatization, and macroeconomic stabilization (IMF, 2000). Two groups of TECEE can be found in Europe. The group of eight countries that joined the EU on 1 May 2004 (i.e. Czech Republic, Estonia, Hungary, Latvia, Lithuania, Poland, Slovakia, and Slovenia) is in fact considered as having completed the transition process. The second group comprises such countries as Romania, Russia, Moldova, Croatia, Bulgaria, Belarus, Ukraine, and

Georgia that are still transiting. The latter eight were selected from the list of TECEE in IMF (2000) for illustration purposes. It is suggested that the former and latter groups can be categorized *Leaders* and *Followers*, respectively (Samoilenko & Osei-Bryson, 2008; EU Legislation, 2010; World Bank, 2010). The inclusion of the groupings is done to ensure a fair representation of countries in this paper.

2.3   e-Government maturity

The concept of "maturity" signifies a stage of growth from lower to higher stages or phases in a process (Galliers & Sutherland, 1991; Andersen & Henriksen, 2006). In this research, E-gov maturity refers to the actual level of progress made by a country with respect to the sophistication of the features present on its government websites (Chen, 2002; Andersen & Henriksen, 2006; West, 2007; UN Public Administration Programme, 2010). Accordingly, governments' websites or web presence that have incorporated advanced functionality and features capable of providing more efficient services to their citizens are generally considered to occupy higher stages in the growth model (West, 2007). It is worth pointing out that the focus of our research is on the aspect of E-gov measures related to the extent to which each country in TECEE has advanced in that regard. It does not address "E-gov readiness" which describes how ready or able a country might be with respect to using technologies in governance (UN Public Administration Programme, 2010). E-gov readiness measures include the telecommunication infrastructure and human capital-indices, which are prerequisites for E-gov engagements; however, these measures do not show how well a country has progressed with regard to its E-gov efforts. Therefore this particular item has not been considered in this research.

Prior e-Gov maturity models and measures (e.g. Layne & Lee, 2001; UN Public Administration Programme, 2010) guide the discourse related to the development of E-gov applications and initiatives in a stage-wise manner – from immature (one-way communication) to the mature (digital democracy) stage (Andersen & Henriksen, 2006). By using a stage-wise approach it affords governments and international agencies the opportunity to assess accomplishments over time. Several of the E-gov maturity models tend to have between three to six growth phases. For example, Howard (2001) used a model comprising of three stages i.e. Publish, Interact, and Transact. Layne and Lee's (2001) model consists of four stages i.e. Cataloguing, Transaction, Vertical integration, and Horizontal integration. Chen (2002) proposes a model with the Information–Communication–Transaction continuum. The UN's e-Gov maturity model (UN Public Administration Programme, 2010) is a four-stage growth model (Figure 1).

Although there are several e-Gov maturity models, our research uses the UN's E-gov maturity model (see Table 1 for its phases and their descriptions) as it provides a global, comparative data on the Web measure/online service index measures for countries around the world. The other e-Gov models were not considered as they do not have such data. In brief, the UN's e-Gov maturity model indicates that countries that have advanced to higher growth levels on their e-Gov projects are the ones with relatively high Web measure/online service index scores.

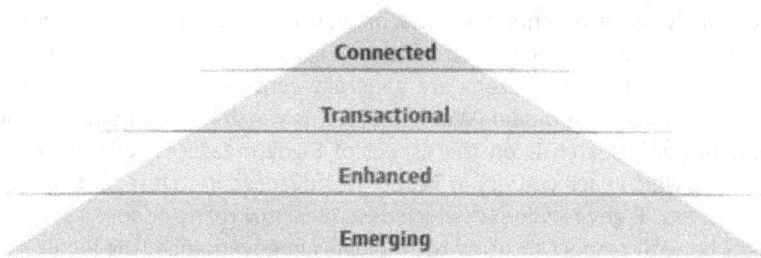

Figure 1: The UN's four stages of online services growth

Table 1: Some of the E-gov maturity models in the literature

Phase	Description	Source/proponent(s)
Phase 1: Cataloguing Phase 2: Transaction Phase 3: Vertical integration Phase 4: Horizontal integration	1. Creating web sites and making government information and services available online. 2. Supporting online transactions between governments and citizens. 3. Focusing on the integration of different systems and functionalities. 4. Focusing on the integration of government services for different functions horizontally; real one-stop center for citizens.	Layne & Lee (2001)
Phase 1: Information	1. Government "information" is creat-	Chen (2002)

Princely Ifinedo and Mohini Singh

Phase	Description	Source/prop onent(s)
Phase 2: Communica-tion Phase 3: Transaction Phase 4: Transfor-mation	ed, categorized, and indexed and delivered to its citizens through the Internet. 2. E-gov services support two-way "communication," with citizens communicating requests through web forms, email, or other Internet media. 3. "Transaction" services between citi-zens and governments are support-ed. Government branches also use the Internet for transactions among themselves. 4. An opportunity for the "transfor-mation" of government's practices and services is exploited. Applica-tion such as e-voting and e-politics that may alter the democratic and political processes are instituted.	
Stage 1: Information Stage 2: Interaction Stage 3: Transaction Stage 4: Integration	1. Government services are delivered online. One-way communication be-tween government and citizens is put in place. 2. Simple interaction between citizens and governments are supported. 3. Services enabling transactions be-tween citizens and government are supported. 4. Integration of services across the agencies and departments of gov-ernment are put in place.	Chandler & Emanuel (2002)
Phase 1: Publish Phase 2: Interact Phase 3: Transact	1. Information about government's ac-tivities is available online. 2. Enables citizens to have simple in-teractions through emails with their governments. 3. Provides citizens with full transac-tions benefits over the internet with services such as purchasing licens-es and permits.	Howard (2001)
Phase 1: Cultivation Phase 2: Extension Phase 3: Maturity Phase 4: Revolution	1. Horizontal and vertical integration within government, front-end sys-tems use, and the adoption of intra-net. 2. Extensive use of intranet, personal-ized web interface for customer pro-cesses.	Andersen & Henriksen (2006)

61

Phase	Description	Source/prop onent(s)
	3. Abandoning of intranet, accountabil-ity and transparent processes, per-sonalized web interface for custom-er processes. 4. Data mobility across organizations, application mobility across vendors, ownership of data transferred to customers.	
Phase 1: Billboard Phase 2: Partial ser-vice delivery Phase 3: Full integrat-ed service delivery Phase 4: Interactive democracy with public outreach and account-ability	1. Government's websites (usually static at this stage) are used for in-formation display. 2. Government's websites have more capabilities and functionalities to in-clude sorting and searching of in-formation. 3. One-stop centre is created with full integrated online services. 4. Government website develops into a system-wide political transfor-mation with executable and inte-grated on-line services. Customized information service is available.	West (2004)
Phase 1: Web pres-ence Phase 2: Interaction Phase 3: Transaction Phase 4: Transfor-mation	1. Government uses the web to pro-vide basic information. 2. Government provides a website equipped with search engines, doc-uments downloading capability and emails. 3. Citizens can carry out enhanced online transactions. 4. All government services and pro-cesses are integrated, unified and personalized.	Gartner's group model in Baum & Maio (2000)
Phase 1: Information publishing Phase 2: Official two-way transactions Phase 3: Multi-purpose portals Phase 4: Portal per-sonalization Phase 5: Clustering of common services Phase 6: Full integra-tion and enterprise transfor-	1. Government creates websites (stat-ic) to provide information to its citi-zens. 2. Enables customers to have elec-tronic interaction with government services such as television licenses renewal. 3. Enables customers to obtain gov-ernment services and information from a single point. 4. Government provides customers and its agencies with opportunities to customize portals according to their needs.	Deloitte & Touche (2001)

Phase	Description	Source/proponent(s)
mation	5. All government services and processes are clustered so as to provide unified and seamless services to citizens. 6. Government changes its structure to enable the provision of more sophisticated, integrated and personalized services to its citizens.	
Phase 1: Emerging Phase 2: Enhanced Phase 3: Transactional Phase 4: Connected	1. Government provides information and basic services on its web site. 2. Government websites deliver enhanced one-way or simple two-way communication between government and citizens through the use of downloadable forms. 3. Government websites uses advanced two-way communication between government and its citizens. The websites process transactions such as e-voting, filling of taxes, and licenses and certificates applications. 4. Government websites changes the way it communicates with citizens; they are proactive in requesting opinions and information from their citizens; they create and "empowered" citizens with more voice in decision making.	UN Public Administration Programme (2010)

2.4   Hypotheses formulation

The pertinence of economic imperatives (i.e. national wealth) as a possible foundation for the advancement of E-gov maturity across nations, including TECEE has been succinctly noted above. Consistent with the tenets espoused in the RBV and the CT, the research model in Figure 2 is designed to highlight the relationships between relevant factors or issues and the dependent variable i.e. E-gov maturity. The mediating influences of the other factors are also delineated in the research conceptualization. Discussions on each of the hypothesized paths are presented below.

Evidence shows that wealthier nations tend to have higher levels of human capital resource (Kiiski & Pohjola, 2002; UN Public Administration Programme, 2010; World Bank, 2011). According to the RBV, such economically endowed countries are more likely to be advantaged in providing needed resources for human capital development in their contexts (Goldthorpe et al., 1968; Barker, 2005). It is reasonable to expect that economic endowments in TEECE – as would be expected for parts of the world - will be positively related to its human capital development. We predict that:

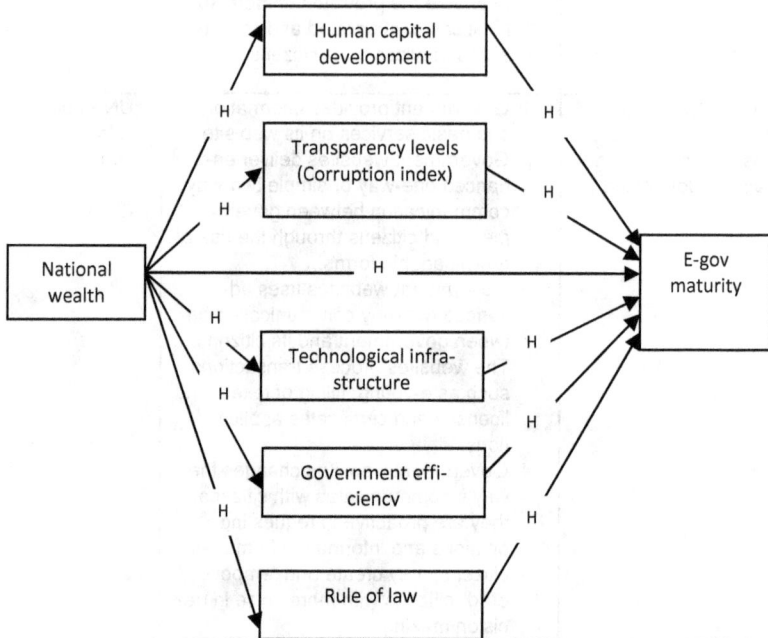

Figure 2: The research model (and highlighted hypotheses)

H1: In the context of TECEE, national wealth will be positively related to human capital development

Empirical data suggests the existence of a positive relationship between the availability of economic endowments and the perceptions of transparency levels across countries (Transparency International, 2010; WEF, 2011). The findings from past studies by Wong and Welch (2004), Torres et al. (2005), and Tolbert et al. (2008) affirm this viewpoint, to some extent. Likewise, prior research has shown that the diffusion of innovative technologies is significantly influenced by the availability of wealth (Caselli &

Coleman, 2001; Norris, 2001; Moon et al., 2005; Singh et al., 2007; WEF, 2011). More affluent countries with better financial resources than counterparts lacking in such often make more progress regarding the types and scope of quality features and services provided or seen on their government websites (Singh et al., 2007; West, 2007). We predict that:

H2: In the context of TECEE, national wealth will be positively related to transparency levels

H3: In the context of TECEE, national wealth will be positively related to E-gov maturity

Global data suggests that wealthier countries are far more likely to be advantaged in committing resources to enhancing their technological infrastructure than relatively poorer nations (Torres et al., 2005; WEF, 2011). McClelland (1967) and Goldthorpe et al. (1968) also observed the existence of a positive association between national affluence and the capability to use of technological innovations to engender social change and progress across nations. We predict that:

H4: In the context of TECEE, national wealth will be positively related to the availability of technological infrastructure

There is an association between the economic well-being of nations and their attitudes toward the national institutional variables such as government efficiency (InfoDev, 2004; Accenture, 2001; Kiiski & Pohjola, 2002; North, 1999; West, 2007; Singh et al., 2007). Such findings have implied that the efficiency of governance in countries with superior financial capability tend to be higher in comparison to those lacking in such resource (Wong & Welch, 2004; Srivastava & Teo, 2008). This is because the efficient management of governance structures, at all levels, requires substantial investments in manpower development and infrastructure acquisition (Caselli & Coleman, 2001; Kiiski & Pohjola, 2002; Norris, 2001; Singh et al., 2007; Torres et al., 2005). We predict that:

H5: In the context of TECEE, wealth will be positively related to government efficiency

Along the same line of reasoning as the preceding hypothesis, academic researchers and international agencies have also shown the existence of a positive relationship between the economic well-being of nations and the national governance variable of rule of law (InfoDev, 2004; Accenture, 2001; North, 1999; West, 2007). That is, the wealthier a country is, the more likely it is for its rule of law to be conducive for governance and business (Norris, 2001; Shih et al., 2005). We predict that:

H6: In the context of TECEE, wealth will be positively related to favorable rule of law climate

Researchers such as Norris (2001), Barker (2005), Caselli and Coleman (2001), Karunasena et al. (2011), and the WEF (2011) found that low level of educational attainment and illiteracy negatively impacts social change and the growth of an information society. The UN human capital index, which encompasses average years of schooling (across the three main levels) in populations, as well as literacy rates, captures this social measure across countries. Moon et al. (2005) and Singh et al. (2007) found the human capital index to be positively related to E-gov maturity across countries. The findings in their studies are suggesting that the capability to utilize innovation such as E-gov for development purposes is relatively high for countries with quality human capital resource. That is, top-end features on government websites may be appreciated, demanded, and supported by individuals in countries with a pool of quality human capital compared to where such are lacking. We predict that:

H7: In the context of TECEE, human capital development will be positively related to E-gov maturity

The Transparency International (2010) publishes the Corruption Perceptions Index (CPI) of countries around the world by comparing the degree "to which corruption is perceived to exist among public officials and politicians." Corruption and a lack of transparency denote abuses related to a lack of openness and abuse of entrusted power. In general, more open societies with a more enlightened public sector governance structure affording more transparency to government operations would appreciate a need to take their E-gov schemes to levels where citizen participation, engagement and empowerment are encouraged (Kovačić, 2005; Islam, 2008).

Previous studies have shown that corruption/transparency perceptions are significantly associated with E-gov progress and diffusion across nations (Azad et al., 2010; Bertort et al., 2005; Cho & Choi, 2004; Kovačić, 2005; Islam, 2008). We predict that:

H8: In the context of TECEE, transparency levels (i.e. low corruption perceptions) will be positively related to E-gov maturity

Prior researchers such as Singh et al. (2007), Norris (2001), Moon et al. (2005), and Azad et al. (2010) showed that innovative technologies spread where enabling technological infrastructure are present. In the context of the diffusion of E-gov globally, Moon et al. (2005) found that the more technologically advanced (i.e. a higher level of technological infrastructure) a country is, the more likely it is for the country to advance its E-gov projects and agenda. Likewise others, Singh et al. (2007) and Azad et al. (2010) found that the availability of technological infrastructure positively influences E-gov maturity across nations. We predict that:

H9: In the context of TECEE, the availability of technological infrastructure will be positively related to E-gov maturity

When governments adopt E-gov, they tend to do so to improve public administration efficiency (Fountain, 2001; UN Public Administration Programme, 2010; West, 2004; Wong & Welch, 2004; Srivastava & Teo, 2008). The availability of fully connected, integrated services between governments and their citizens enhance government operations as well as engender citizens' satisfaction (Fountain, 2001; Moon, 2002; UN Public Administration Programme, 2010). Srivastava and Teo (2008) and Singh et al. (2007) revealed that there is a significant association between government efficiency and E-gov development and maturity. These researchers found that efficient governments easily appreciate the need to use advanced E-gov features to improve governance in their contexts. We predict that:

H10: In the context of TECEE, government efficiency will be positively related to E-gov maturity

Rule of law refers to the sound political institutions, impartial systems, and legal protection of property rights in a country (Shih et al., 2005). Prior studies have shown that it impacts the diffusion of e-commerce and E-gov (Oxley & Yeung, 2001; Welch & Wong, 2004; Katchanovski & La Porte, 2005). It has been suggested that countries from emerging parts of the world lag behind advanced countries in technological innovations such as E-gov because of weak and or non-existent national governance institution factors such as rule of law (Azad et al., 2010). It is reasonable to expect that where favorable rule of law exists, there will be little or no problems in instituting advanced features that facilitate citizen participation and empowerment in governance. Conversely, where a serious rule of law issues exist, such progress may be curtailed; discussions on this issue have been presented in the context of some TECEE (please see for example, Alexander, 2004; Levada, 2004; Katchanovski & La Porte, 2005; McHenry & Borisov, 2006). Welch and Wong (2004) and Kovačić (2005) indicated that the authorities of countries with poorer "rule of law" may have little or no interest in providing advanced features on their websites that would encourage citizen engagement and empowerment as such enhancement may be deemed to engender dissent. We predict that:

H11: In the context of TECEE, rule of law will be positively related to E-gov maturity

3. Research method

3.1   Data sources and measures

We used data sourced from reputable world organizations such as the United Nations and the World Bank. Previous comparable research that has used data from such sources include Azad et al. (2007), Katchanovski & La Porte (2005), Kovačić (2005), Singh et al. (2007), and Siau & Long (2006). The human capital index that was obtained from the UN Public Administration Programme (2010) is derived from measures related to the educational attainment and literacy levels across the selected countries. The rule of law and government efficiency variables were obtained from Kauffman et al. (2009) who composed their data from both qualitative and quantitative sources. The rule of law and government efficiency scores ranged from +2.5 and -2.5 with higher scores indicating better values. The data for the transparency levels variable came from the Transparency International (2010) for which the scores ranged from 0 to 10 with higher numbers indicating less corruption and more transparency societies.

The GDP per capita was obtained from the World Bank's Development Index (World Bank, 2010). The GDP per capita variable was transformed and normalized with a logarithmic function. Each country's technological infrastructure level was assessed using a weighted index comprised of Internet users/1000 persons, PCs/1000 persons, telephone lines/1000 persons, online populations, mobile phones/100 persons, and TVs/1000 persons (UN Public Administration Programme, 2010). Each country's technological infrastructure level was assessed using a weighted index comprised of Internet users/1000 persons, PCs/1000 persons, telephone lines/1000 persons, online populations, mobile phones/100 persons, and TVs/1000 persons (UN Public Administration Programme, 2010). The description of the variables is provided in the Appendix.

For the dependent variable, we used two variables i.e. the Web/online services and E-participation indices from the UN Public Administration Programme (2010). We did not aggregate the aforementioned indices in operationalizing the E-gov maturity variable as was the case in Singh et al. (2007). Our use of the structural equation modeling technique is capable of handling both indices as latent constructs, in our research model. In order to have a fair representation of countries from TECEE, E-gov scores at all levels i.e. above and below scores for the region's average as well as scores close to the average were considered from the UN Public Administration Programme's data source. The selected TECEE in the research and some of the indicators used in the research are shown in Table 2.

Table 2: Selected TEECE and some of the indicators used in the study

Country	GDP per capita (2003)	GDP per capita (2010)	Web measure (WM)/Online services index (2003)	Web measure (WM)/Online services index (2010)
	Leaders TECEE			
Czech Republic	$15,300	$24,900	0.349	0.454
Estonia	$10,900	$18,500	0.642	0.502
Hungary	$13,300	$18,800	0.312	0.505
Latvia	$8,300	$14,400	0.266	0.416
Lithuania	$8,400	$15,500	0.524	0.483
Poland	$9,500	$17,900	0.541	0.387

Country	GDP per capita (2003)	GDP per capita (2010)	Web measure (WM)/Online services index (2003)	Web measure (WM)/Online services index (2010)
Slovakia	$12,200	$21,100	0.380	0.346
Slovenia	$18,000	$27,700	0.441	0.400
Mean	$11,987.50	$19,850	0.432	0.437
Standard deviation	3437.79	19850.00	0.129	0.058
	Followers TECEE			
Bulgaria	$6,600	$12,500	0.537	0.410
Romanian	$7,400	$11,500	0.419	0.416
Russian Fed.	$9,300	$15,100	0.223	0.330
Ukraine	$4,500	$6,300	0.349	0.346
Belarus	$8,200	$12,500	0.122	0.302
Croatia	$8,800	$17,500	0.424	0.422
Rep. of Moldova	$2,500	$2,300	0.070	0.295
Georgia	$3,100	$4, 400	0.048	0.248
Mean	$6,300	$10, 263	0.274	0.346
Standard deviation	2630.00	5355.89	0.184	0.065

3.2 Procedure and the estimation model

Our data was composed of items collected over a 5-year data period (2003-5, 2008, and 2010) in a span of 7 years. Accordingly, the data used for analysis is a panel data (also known as longitudinal or cross-sectional time-series data). This procedure is appropriate in capturing the development of E-gov maturity in the selected countries over time. The advantage in using a panel data lies in the fact that it accommodates variations regarding changes in used variables; a single year study (cross-sectional analysis) may not reflect such changes. For the data set of 16 countries, 80 points or observations were obtained, which is adequate for a study such as this one.

Additionally, a panel data takes the fixed-effects (FE) into consideration (Hedges & Vevea, 1998). With FE, it is assumed that each independent variable has its own individual characteristics that may or may not influence the dependent variable. Importantly, the FE removes the effect of those time-invariant characteristics from the predictor variables so that the predictors' net effect can be assessed. Thus, the pooled time series data enables precise estimates and test statistics with more power in the regression to be obtained. Having said that, this study's analysis will use the structural equation modeling technique, which is similar to the ordinary regression model (Chin, 1998). The main advantage of this technique is that it allows latent constructs to be used, and it enables the results of paths to be assessed simultaneously.

3.3   Analysis and results

The Partial Least Squares (PLS) approach of structural equation modeling technique, which utilizes a principle component-based for estimation, was used for analysis. The approach is suitable for validating predictive models (Chin, 1998). The PLS assesses the psychometric properties of the measurement model, and estimates the parameters of the structural model. The specific tool used was SmartPLS 2.0 (Ringle et al., 2005). The requisite information related to measurement model i.e. the average variance extracted (AVE) and composite reliability were not provided as the study's variables have items that were mainly operationalized by single-item variables). However, the item loadings for the two items used to represents the dependent variable were 0.907 (Web/online services) and 0.892 (E-participation) to underscore their reliability. The descriptive statistics and inter-correlations among the variables from the PLS analysis is presented in Table 3.

Table 3: Descriptive statistics and the inter-construct correlations (N = 80)

Variable	Mean	S.D.	1	2	3	4	5	6	7
1: e-Government maturity i.e. Web measures index & e-Participation index	0.34	0.15	1						
2: Human capital development	0.93	0.03	0.51	1					
3: Technological infrastructure	0.30	0.13	0.61	0.53	1				
4: Govt. efficiency	0.25	0.68	0.56	0.32	0.80	1			
5: Rule of law	0.05	0.71	0.57	0.33	0.79	0.95	1		
6:Transparency levels	3.95	1.25	0.56	0.41	0.78	0.81	0.82	1	

7: Wealth (GDP per capita $USD)	12310	6081.27	0.56	0.60	0.81	0.74	0.71	0.67	1

S.D. = Standard deviations

The structural model presents information related to path coefficients (β) and the squared R (R^2). The strength of the relationship is indicated by the β, which can be interpreted exactly like standardized regression coefficients. The R^2 shows the percentage of variance in the model to give an indication of its predictive power. The SmartPLS 2.0 results for the βs and the R^2 are shown in Figure 3. The path significance levels (t-values) are estimated by the bootstrapping method (Chin, 1998).

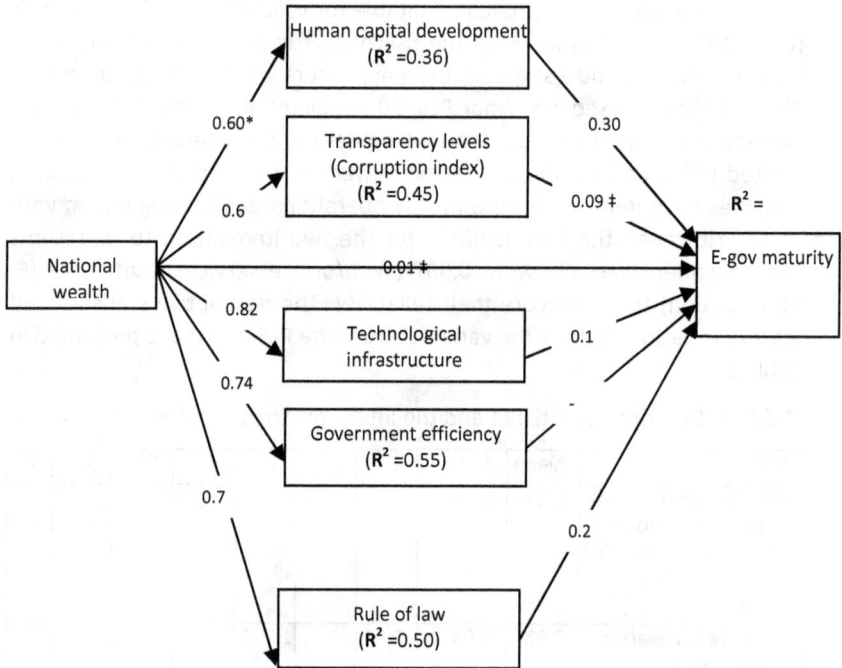

*Note: * = significant at p < 0.05; ** = significant at p < 0.01; *** = significant at p < 0.001; ‡ = not significant*

Figure 3: The hypothesized paths with results from SmartPLS 2.0

The data provided significant support for hypothesis H1, which predicted that in the context of TECEE, national wealth would be positively related to human capital development (β = 0.60). Hypothesis H2 that suggested that the national wealth of TEECE would be positively related to their transparency levels was affirmed by the data (β = 0.67). Hypothesis H3 indicating that the national wealth of TECEE would be positively related to E-gov maturity was however unsupported by the data (β = 0.01). The data showed that TECEE with higher levels of economic wealth tends to have higher technological infrastructure (β = 0.82) to support hypothesis H4. The data analysis provided support for hypothesis H5, which suggested that in the context of TECEE, national wealth would be positively related to government efficiency (β = 0.74). Hypothesis H6 was strongly supported as well to affirm the view indicating that in TEECE, national wealth was positively related to favorable rule of law climate (β = 0.71).

In the context of TECEE, human capital development will be positively related to E-gov maturity (H7), the hypothesis was confirmed by the data (β = 0.30). For TEECE, their transparency levels would be positively related to their E-gov maturity levels (H8) was unconfirmed by the path significance (β = 0.09). Support was provided for the prediction made in hypothesis H9 suggesting that in the context of TEECE, the availability of technological infrastructure would be positively related to E-gov maturity (β = 0.19). Hypothesis H10 that was formulated to ascertain the nature of the relationship between the variables of government efficiency and E-gov maturity was unsupported by the data (β = -0.01). The data provided significant support for hypothesis H11, which predicted that in the context of TECEE, rule of law would be positively related to E-gov maturity (β = 0.26).The summary of the results is presented in Table 4.

Table 4: Summary of results

Hypothesis	path coefficient (β)	Result
National wealth → Human capital development (H1)	0.60	Supported
National wealth → Transparency levels (H2)	0.67	Supported
National wealth → E-gov maturity (H3)	0.01	Not supported
National wealth → Technological infrastructure (H4)	0.82	Supported

Hypothesis	path coefficient (β)	Result
National wealth → Government efficiency (H5)	0.74	Supported
National wealth → Rule of law (H6)	0.71	Supported
Human capital development → E-gov maturity (H7)	0.30	Supported
Transparency levels → E-gov maturity (H8)	0.09	Not supported
Technological infrastructure → E-gov maturity (H9)	0.19	Supported
Government efficiency → E-gov maturity (H10)	-0.01	Not supported
Rule of law → E-gov maturity (H11)	0.26	Supported

Information related to the variances explained by the study's constructs is presented in Figure 2. It is worth noting that all the research' constructs explained 46% of the variation in the research model to indicate that the theorized conceptualization has relevance. Specifically, Chin (1998) noted that R^2 values of 0.67, 0.33, and 0.19 for the percentage of variance in a model are substantial, moderate and weak, respectively. Thus, the obtained R^2 in this study with a value of 0.46 suggests that the percentage of variance in the research model is above moderate levels.

4. Discussion

Research findings presented above present information related to the determinants of E-gov maturity in TECEE. While IS, public administration researchers, and practitioners around the world have provided relevant information related to the possible impacts of a variety of macro-environmental factors on the diffusion and adoption of E-gov initiatives globally, the review of the extant literature showed that studies discussing the determinants of E-gov maturity in TECEE are not well represented. This current research is primarily designed to fill this gap in the literature. Discussions on unconfirmed hypotheses are presented first followed by the ones that were supported. It is also important to assert that our discussions will be made in the context of the results obtained from our study. We accept that due to the limitations imposed on this study, realities across the countries in Central and Eastern Europe with regard to E-gov maturity may differ somewhat from what is being presented herein.

Our research model did not provide evidence in support of the positive, direct associations between national wealth and E-gov maturity, in the context of TEECE. Also, the transparency levels and government efficiency variables were not found to be positively related to E-gov maturity in our study. These unconfirmed hypotheses do not, in any way, affirm that such factors have no bearings on E-gov maturity issues in TECEE and elsewhere. For instance, the lack of support for the relationships between rule of law and E-gov maturity are counterintuitive propositions, which need further investigation. One plausible reason for the unconfirmed predictions in our research may be due to incomplete and missing data of some of the measures used in the research. Another explanation could be that socio-political factors of government efficiency and transparency levels may actually have little or no impact on the concept of E-gov maturity across countries complying with findings in Singh et al. (2007. It could also be possible that the variable of transparency levels may not be conceptually related to E-gov maturity (Azad et al., 2010; Kovačić, 2005; Singh et al., 2007). However, more studies are needed to debunk or re insights on the relevance of the foregoing construct on E-gov issues.

Contrary to widely held beliefs among some E-gov experts suggesting that notable progress in E-gov development, diffusion, and maturity appear to have taken place in relatively richer societies (e.g. Norris, 2001; Moon et al., 2005; West, 2007; Azad et al., 2010), the analysis with data from TEECE - with two distinct groupings being used - seem to indicate that the availability of national wealth *per se*, may not be sufficient a factor to occasion growth with respect to E-gov maturity in the region. To some degree, our result is congruent with new insights noting that remarkable progress have in fact been recorded in relatively poorer countries around the world (Accenture, 2001; InfoDev, 2004; InfoDev, 2004; UN Public Administration Programme, 2010). The data analysis seems to uphold the notion indicating that some of the determinants considered in our study mediate the relationships between national wealth and E-gov maturity.

With respect to the supported hypotheses, we offer the following comments: our research's conceptualization does not imply causation in the model. Where national economic wealth is sufficiently available, the human capital development of such societies tends to be relatively higher as the data analysis has shown. This result is consistent with the RBV. Our data confirmed that higher levels of national wealth are positively related to the pervading transparency levels in TEECE. The data confirmed the notion indicating that economic resources are likely to be vitally important to governments and their citizens in their bids to acquire requisite technological products (e.g. hardware and software) to further enhance E-gov initiatives. We found that higher levels of national wealth have positive relationships with both government efficiency and rule of law. Consistent with the CT and the RBV, higher levels of national wealth in TECEE suggest that such countries are more likely to have the capacity to develop their human capital resource, have an enabling technological infrastructure, and a favorable rule of climate in their contexts. With such foregoing resources, it is easy to argue that a platform for engendering social change and progress through E-gov advancement can be instituted.

The data showed that higher pools of quality human capital resource have positive effects on E-gov maturity. In that regard, our result in this aspect implies that quality human resource in TECEE seems to augur well for the deployment and use of advanced E-gov features in their contexts. Greater capabilities and knowledge can permit a better understanding and appreciation of advanced technological products like those present in websites with higher-end features. Prior research has shown that human capital development boded well for E-gov expansion (Norris, 2011; Wong & Welch, 2004; West, 2007). The data strongly confirmed that the selected TECEE with more technological amenities were the ones that had more favorable E-gov maturity scores. It is reasonable to believe that citizen engagement and empowerment through sophisticated technology-enhanced platforms can only thrive where the necessary, enabling infrastructure is available (Norris, 2001; Azad et al., 2010; Moon et al., 2005; West, 2007). As well, where favorable rule of law climate exists, the political institutions in such TECEE may have a belief that citizen engagement and empowerment through sophisticated technology-enhanced governance augurs well for their society (Katchanovski & La Porte, 2005; Azad et al., 2010; Kovačić, 2005; Wong & Welch, 2004).

4.1   Implications for research and practice

Our research presents some useful implications for both research and practice. With regard to research, we have attempted to answer the call for researchers to focus on E-gov development issues in emerging economies of the world, including TECEE to deepen our understanding of the phenomenon. Our paper has contributed to the theories of CT and RBV by extending their applications to E-gov maturity. Future research in the area could draw from and expand on the foregoing theoretical underpinnings and concepts in discussing comparable issues. Our findings provide support to espoused views and observations indicating the significance of factors such as national wealth, human capital, technological infrastructure, rule of law, and transparency levels on E-gov diffusion, development, and maturity in the literature (e.g. Azad et al., 2010, West, 2007, Moon, 2002; Moon et al., 2007; Singh et al., 2007; Wong & Welch, 2004; Kovačić, 2005; Katchanovski & La Porte, 2005).

We also deepen insight related to the impact of national wealth in stimulating growth in E-gov initiatives across countries. Likewise, we provided empirical analysis highlighting the roles of transparency levels and government efficiency on E-gov maturity, at least in the context of TEECE. In general, our research efforts benefit the accumulation of knowledge in this area of study. It is worth noting that previous research on E-gov issues in TECEE has used a single nation or a few countries in their analysis. By using a panel data of 16 TEECE, our effort provides a richer and robust insight into E-gov issues. Other researchers may be enticed to follow our approach in this regard, which is not entirely novel. By not focusing attention solely on the direct relationships between the independent and dependent variables in our study, we have avoided one of the commonly known mistakes in the use of CT for research studies (Ifinedo, 2007). Our work adds to Singh et al.'s (2007) model.

With regard to practice, our study also offers implications for policy makers, international agencies, and public administrators. Governments of TEECE are alerted to the salient factors that could serve as possible determinants of E-gov progress in their contexts. Accordingly, more attention may be placed on such noted factors to enhance E-gov maturity in their settings. The attention of international agencies and public administrators are drawn to the fact that national economic considerations and imperatives may not be a direct driver of E-gov maturity. Rather, such a factor constitutes an enabler in the background. In other words, if public administrators are able to properly marshal economic resources available to them in improving the quality of their human resource as well as procuring required technological infrastructural facilities; it is likely that positive outcomes on the E-gov development front will ensue. To that end, financial support from relevant sources may be called upon to accelerate investments in infrastructural acquisitions that relatively poorer nations in the region may be lacking in order to improve their E-gov capabilities.

Regarding the impacts arising from selected socio-political influences, policy makers need to know that while favorable rule of law climate may be conducive to E-gov maturity and advancement, an efficiently run government does not necessarily guarantee progress with regard to how it fares in incorporating advanced E-gov features aimed at improving citizen engagement and empowerment. Adequate focus and well-defined national IS/IT policy as well as benchmarking progress in comparable countries could be beneficial in pointing the way for policy makers (Accenture, 2001; InfoDev, 2004; UN Public Administration Programme, 2010; Eastern European e-Gov Days, 2011). Likewise, E-gov maturity does not hinge on how transparent or corrupt a country is. In fact, results in the E-gov survey of UN Public Administration Programme (2010) showed that E-gov maturity were higher in some corrupt societies than more transparent ones, which exists in TEECE as well. Policy makers and governments in comparable regions of the world such as South East Asia and elsewhere may benefit from this information.

4.2   Limitations and directions for future study

Our research has its limitations. Our research relied on secondary data sources; as such, it is difficult to ascertain with certainty the reliability and validity of items used in composing the various measures. Our dependant variable i.e. the E-gov maturity indicator largely used the assessment of efforts on governments' websites; the views of citizens are not represented. Thus, this might be limiting given that citizens' perceptions and expectations of E-gov initiatives may be dissimilar from those of their governments'. The lack of an internationally recognized 'E-gov maturity' indicator may have its drawbacks. Some of the items we used had missing entries for some of the countries and some data were not up-to-date; these might have negatively impacted the data analysis. In selecting the countries for this research we used the UN Public Administration Programme's (2010) E-gov scores to guide the selection. Notwithstanding, selection bias cannot be ruled out in our research. In fact, we caution against the generalization of our findings to all countries in Central and Eastern Europe.

The amount variation explained in our dependent variable i.e. 46% suggests that other relevant factors such as cultural norms and values, political actors' actions, citizen awareness and resistance not included in our study could be relevant. Future studies should endeavor to work with a more comprehensive framework that includes such factors. Our study was limited to a five-year observation period; it is advised that as more data become available, a much longer observation period should be considered to enhance insight. Other researchers could replicate this study in other comparable contexts such as the Middle East, South Asia, Sub-Saharan Africa, and Latin America. Accumulated body of knowledge on the possible determinants or drivers E-gov maturity across the regions of the world is welcoming to theory development. Case studies in TEECE and elsewhere could also be considered to deepen our understanding in the area.

5. Conclusion

We used the contingency theory and the resource-based view to guide our discourse of the determinants of E-gov maturity in TEECE. We employed a panel data of 16 countries in the region to provide insight. Our data analysis showed that that resources (e.g. national wealth, human capital development, technological infrastructure, and rule of law) matter in accelerating a country's the ability and willingness to advance its E-gov initiatives with features that promote citizens' participation and engagement. The confirmed hypotheses are congruent with similar prior studies and serves to enhance our understanding of the factors that could be perpetuating the progress of E-gov in selected TEECE. The unconfirmed predictions open up an opportunity for further investigations. The attention of policy makers in the region is drawn to factors or issues deserving of further attention as progress is being made in the area. The replication of this study in other emerging and developing parts of the world will be useful to improve knowledge related to the factors impacting E-gov maturity (or lack thereof) in such contexts.

References

Accenture (2001). eGovernment Leadership Rhetoric vs Reality - Closing the Gap. Retrieved May 2, 2009 from http://www.epractice.eu/files/media/media_846.pdf.

Alexander, M. (2004). The Internet and Democratization: The Development of Russian Internet Policy, Demokratizatsiya, 12, 4, 607-627.

Andersen K. V. & Henriksen H. Z. (2006). E-government maturity models: Extension of the Layne and Lee model, Government Information Quarterly, 23, 2, 236–248.

Azad, B., Faraj, S. & Goh J. F. (2010). What Shapes Global Diffusion of eGovernment: Comparing the Influence of National Governance Institutions, Journal of Global Information Management, 18, 2, 85-104.

Barker, C. (2005). Cultural Studies: Theory and Practice, London, UK: Sage.

Baum, C. & Maio, A. D. (2000). Gartner's Four Phases of E-government Model. Stamford: Gartner Group Inc.

Barney, J. B. (1991). Firm Resources and Sustained Competitive Advantage, Journal of Management, 17, 99 -120.

Bertort, J. C., Jaeger, J. T, & Grimes, J. M. (2001). Using ICTs to Create a Culture of Transparency: E-government and Social Media as Openness and Anti-corruption Tools for Societies, Government Information Quarterly, 27, 264 -271.

Bonoma, T. A. & Johnson, W. J. (1979). Decision Making Under Uncertainty: A Direct Measurement Approach, Journal of Consumer Research, 6, 177-191.

Caselli, F & Coleman, W. (2001). Cross-country Technology Diffusion: The Case of Computers, American Economic Review, 91, 2, 328 – 335.

Chandler, S. & Emanuel, S. (2002). Transformation Not Automation. In Proceedings of 2nd European Conference on EGovernment, St Catherine's College Oxford, UK, 2002, pp. 91-102.

Chen, H. (2002). Digital Government: Technologies and Practices, Decision Support Systems, 34, 223-227.

Chin, W. (1998). Issues and Opinion on Structural Equation Modeling, MIS Quarterly, 22(1), vii-xvi.

Cho, Y. H., & Choi, B. (2004). E-government to Combat Corruption: The Case of Seoul Metropolitan Government, International Journal of Public Administration, 27, 10, 719-735.

Deloitte and Touche (2001). The Citizen as Customer, CMA management, 74, 10, 58.

Eastern European e-Gov Days (2011). 9th Eastern European e-Gov Days - eGovernment in Times of Economic Challenges. Retrieved October 9, 2011 from http://eeegov2011.ocg.at/.

EU Legislation (2010). Enlargement 2004 and 2007. Retrieved October 4, 2010 from http://europa.eu/legislation_summaries/enlargement/2004_and_2007_enlargement/index_en.htm.

EU Regional Policy (2009). Working towards a New Europe: The Role and Achievements of Europe's Regional Policy, 2004-2009. Retrieved October 4, 2010 from http://ec.europa.eu/regional_policy/policy/impact/pdf/legacy_2009_en.pdf.

Fountain, J. E. (2001). Building the Virtual State: Information Technology and Institutional Change. Washington, D.C.: The Brookings Institution.

Friedman, T., (2005). The World is Flat: A Brief History of The 21st Century. New York, N.Y.: Farrar, Straus & Giroux

Gascó, M. (2005). Exploring the EGovernment Gap in South America, Intl Journal of Public Administration, 28, (7&8), 683 – 701.

Goldthorpe, J. H., Lockwood, D., Bechhofer, F. & Platt, J. (1968). The Affluent Worker: Industrial Attitudes and Behaviour. Cambridge: Cambridge University Press.

Gupta, B., Dasgupta, S., & Gupta, A. (2008). Adoption of ICT in a Government Organization in a Developing Country: An Empirical Study, Journal of Strategic Information Systems 17, 2, 140–154.

Hedges, L. V., & Vevea, J. L. (1998). Fixed and Random Effects Models in Meta Analysis, Psychological Methods, 3, 486-504.

Howard, M. (2001). E-government across the Globe: How will "e" Change Government? Government Finance Review, 17, 4, 6 - 9.

Ifinedo, P. (2007). Interactions between Organizational Size, Culture, and Structure and Some IT Factors in the Context of ERP Success Assessment: An Exploratory Investigation, Journal of Computer Information Systems, 47, 4, 28-44.

Ifinedo, P. & Davidrajuh, R. (2005). Digital Divide in Europe: Assessing and Comparing the E-readiness of a Developed and an Emerging Economy in the Nordic Region, Electronic Government: An International Journal, 2, 2, 111-133.

Ifinedo, P. & Ifinedo, A. (2011). A Snapshot of Key Information Systems (IS) Issues in Estonian Organizations for the 2000s, Baltic Journal of Management, 6, 2, 163-178.

IMF (2000). Transition Economies: An IMF Perspective on Progress and Prospects. Retrieved July 27, 2010 from http://www.imf.org/external/np/exr/ib/2000/110300.htm#I.

InfoDev (Information for Development Programme) (2004). EGovernment handbook for developing countries. Retrieved May 6, 2006 from http://www.infodev.org.

Islam, R. (2008). Does more Transparency go along with Better Governance? Economics and Politics, 18, 2, 121-167.

Karunasena, K., Deng, H. & Singh, M. (2011). Measuring the Public Value of E-government: A Case Study from Sri Lanka, Transforming Government: People, Process and Policy, 5, 1, 81 - 99.

Katchanovski, I. & La Porte, T. (2005). Cyberdemocracy or Potemkin E-Villages? Electronic Governments in OECD and Post-Communist Countries, International Journal of Public Administration, 28, 7 & 8, 665-681.

Kaufmann, D., Kraay, A. & Mastruzzi, M. (2009).Governance Matters VIII. Aggregate and Individual Governance Indicators1996–2008. Policy Research Working Paper (The World Bank). Retrieved Sept 30, 2010 from http://papers.ssrn.com/sol3/papers.cfm?abstract_id=1424591.

Kiiski, S. & Pohjola, M. (2002). Cross Country Diffusion of the Internet, Information Economics and Policy, 14, 2, 297-310.

Kovačić, Z. (2005). A Brave New eWorld? An Exploratory Analysis of Worldwide eGovernment Readiness, Level of Democracy, Corruption and Globalization, International Journal of Electronic Government Research, 1, 3, 15-32.

Kubicek, H. & Westholm, H. (2005). Scenarios for Future Use of E-Democracy Tools in Europe. International Journal of Electronic Government Research, 1, 3, 33-50.

Lawrence, P.R. & Lorsch, J.W. (1967). Organization and Environment, Division of Research, Graduate School of Business Administration, Harvard University, Boston, MA.

Layne, K. & Lee, J. (2001). Developing Fully Functional eGovernment: A Four Stage Model, Government Information Quarterly, 18, 2, 122-136.

Levada, Y. (2004). What The Polls Tell Us? Journal of Democracy, 15, 3, 43-52.

McClelland, D. C. (1961). The Achieving Society. New York, N.Y.: van Nostrand Publishers.

McHenry, W. & Borisov, A. (2006). E-government and Democracy in Russia, Communications of the Association for Information Systems, 17, 1064-1123.

Moon, J. M. (2002). The Evolution of EGovernment among Municipalities: Rhetoric or Reality? Public Administration Review, 62, 4, 424-433.

Moon, M. J., Welch, E. W. & Wong, W. (2005). What Drives Global E-governance? An Exploratory Study at a Macro level. In Proceedings of the 38th. Hawaii International Conference on System Sciences, USA.

Norris, P. (2001). Digital Divide: Civic Engagement, Information Poverty, and the Internet Worldwide. New York, N.Y.: Cambridge University Press.

Oxley, J. E. & Yeung, B. (2001). E-commerce Readiness: Institutional Environment and International Competitiveness, Journal of International Business Studies, 32, 4, 705-723.

Ringle, C.M., Wende, S., & Will, A. (2005). SmartPLS 2.0 (M3) beta, Hamburg: http://www.smartpls.de.

Robison, K. K. & Crenshaw, E.M. (2002). Post-industrial Transformations and Cyberspace: A Cross-national Analysis of Internet Development, Social Science Research, 31, 334–363.

Roztocki, N. & Weistroffer, H. R. (2008). Information Technology in Transition Economies, Journal of Global Information Technology Management, 11, 4, 2-9.

Samoilenko, S. & Osei-Bryson, K.M. (2008). Determining Strategies for Telecoms to Improve Efficiency in the Production of Revenues: An Empirical Investigation in the Context of Transition Economies, Journal of Global Information Technology Management, 11, 7, 56-75.

Shih, C-F., Dedrick, J. & Kraemer, K. L. (2005). Rule of Law and the International Diffusion of E-commerce, Communications of the ACM, 48, 11, 57-62.

Siau, K. & Long, Y. (2006). Using Social Development Lenses to Understand EGovernment Development, Journal of Global Information Management, 14, 1, 47-62.

Singh, H., Das, A. & Joseph, D. (2007). Country-Level Determinants of EGovernment Maturity, Communications of the Association for Information Systems, 40, 632-648.

Srivastava, S. C., & Teo, T. S. H. (2007). E-Government Payoffs: Evidence from Cross-Country Data, Journal of Global Information Management, 15, 4, 20-40.

Srivastava, S. C., & Teo, T. S. H. (2008). The Relationship between E-Government and National Competitiveness: The Moderating Influence of Environmental Factors, Communications of the Association for Information Systems, 23, 5, 79-94.

Tolbert, C.J., Mossberger, K. & McNeal, R. (2008). Institutions, Policy Innovation, and E-Government in the American States, Public Administration Review, 68, 3, 549-563.

Torres, L., Pina, V., Acerete, B., 2005. E-Government Developments on Delivering Public Services among EU cities, Government Information Quarterly 22, 217–238.

Transparency International (2010). Corruption Perceptions index (CPI). Retrieved October 15, 2010 from http://www.transparency.org/policy_research/surveys_indices/cpi/2009.

UN Public Administration Programme (2010). United Nations EGovernment Global Reports. Retrieved August 12, 2010 from http://www2.unpan.org/egovkb/global_reports/10report.htm.

WEF (World Economic Forum) (2010). The Global Information Technology Report 2009-2010. Retrieved October 6, 2010 from http://www.weforum.org/en/initiatives/gcp/Global%20Information%20Technology%20Report/index.htm.

Wernerfelt, B. (1984). A Resource-based View of the Firm. Strategic Management Journal, 5, 2, 171 – 180.

West, D. (2007). Global Perspectives on EGovernment. Retrieved September 2, 2010 from http://www.umass.edu/digitalcenter/events/pdfs/West_GlobalPerspectives.pdf

West, D. M. (2004). EGovernment and the Transformation of Service Delivery and Citizen Attitudes. Public Administration Review, 64, 1, 15-27.

Wong, W. & Welch, E. (2004). Does EGovernment Promote Accountability? A Comparative Analysis of Website Openness and Government Accountability. Governance: An International Journal of Policy, Administration, and Institutions, 17, 2, 275-297.

World Bank (2010). Countries & Regions. Retrieved October 3, 2010 from http://web.worldbank.org/.

Appendix : The data sources of the research

Variable	Assessment/definition	Source	Notes
E-gov maturity	The Web measures and online services index provides scores for the online services available in each country's web pages. The E-participation index assesses the extent to which ICT-supported participation in processes of governance is enabled.	UN Public Administration Programme (2010)	The Web measures online services index was added to the E-participation index. The data analysed with the two variables' average produced an analogous result to the one discussed herein.
GDP per capita	The value of all goods/services produced within a country in a given year divided by the country's population for the same year.	World Bank (2010)	Each country's data is expressed in the US dollar ($).
Technological infrastructure level	Assessed by a weighted index comprised of Internet users/1000 persons, PCs/1000 persons, telephone lines/1000 persons, online populations, mobile phones/100 persons, and TVs/1000 persons	UN Public Administration Programme (2010)	
The human capital development index	Derived from measures related to the educational attainment and literacy levels across countries	World Bank (2010)	
Rule of law	The extent to which sound political institutions as well as legal protection of property rights is permitted in a country.	Kauffman et al. (2009)	Composed by data from more than 20 sources, including qualitative and quantitative. The scores for each country ranged from +2.5 and -2.5 with higher scores indicating better values.
Government efficiency	The extent to which governments use available mechanisms to promote	Kauffman et al. (2009)	The scores for each country ranged from +2.5 and -2.5 with

Variable	Assessment/definition	Source	Notes
	and support their functions.		higher scores indicating better values.
Corruption/transparency perceptions	The degree to which corruption is perceived to exist among public officials and politicians of a country.	Transparency International (2010)	The scores ranged from 0 to 10 with 10 indicating less corruption and more transparency.

Open Data Policies: Impediments and Challenges

Anneke Zuiderwijk[1,2], Marijn Janssen[1] and Sunil Choenni[2,3]

[1]Delft University of Technology, Delft, The Netherlands
[2]Research and Documentation Centre – Ministry of Security and Justice, Den Haag, The Netherlands
[3]Rotterdam University –Creating 010, Rotterdam, The Netherlands

a.m.g.zuiderwijk-vaneijk@tudelft.nl
m.f.w.h.a.janssen@tudelft.nl
r.choenni@minvenj.nl; r.choenni@hr.nl

Originally published in the Proceedings of the European Conference on e-Government (2012) Ed. Mila Gascó, ACPIL, pp704-302.

Editorial Commentary

In their chapter, Zuiderwijk and her colleagues analyse the impediments that open data policies currently encounter, and these are classified as political, economic, technical and social impediments; data access impediments; data deposition impediments and data use impediments. All these impediments must be removed to allow the use of open data to create value, since simply publishing open data is not enough to create value. Policy directives on open data (like the EU's Public Sector Information directive) are not enough if not accompanied by the adoption of the appropriate data governance policy, methodology and practice.

Abstract: Up till now, there has been a public demand for opening up non privacy-sensitive governmental data. In 2003, the EU Public Sector Information (PSI) directive was released, which aims to enable the availability of public sector data to third parties at low prices, unrestrictive conditions and ensuring a level playing field. From that moment many countries and public agencies have started to open

their data. The open data movement is guided by PSI-directives and national policies and the definition of open data indicates that the data are accessible without
any restrictions on usage and distribution. However, the current use of open PSI is
accompanied by many impediments. Hence, in this paper the question is asked
which policy measures could be proposed to overcome the impediments that open
data policies currently encounter. Based on a literature overview and two use-
cases the impediments that open data policies currently encounter are analyzed
and categorized in four categories: 1) political, economical, technical and social
impediments, 2) data access impediments, 3) data deposition impediments and 4)
data use impediments. The impediments are categorized using a fishbone diagram.
The analysis shows that open data policies provide scant attention to the user perspective. Based on the impediment overview important challenges for open data
policies are identified. To broaden the use of open data we recommend to introduce 1) incentive policy guidelines to stimulate centralization of open data collections and to rectify the fragmentation, 2) creating access to open data to enable
the use of open data for any user, 3) creating interoperability by adding structured
metadata when making data available to ensure easy discovery and understanding
of its potential and 4) creating an infrastructure for the processing of PSI.

Keywords: open data, open data policies, impediments, challenges, open data users, user perspective

1. Introduction

For many years, there exists a public demand for opening up non privacy-
sensitive governmental data. Open governmental data can be defined as
*"all stored data of the public sector which could be made accessible by
government in the public interest without any restrictions on usage and
distribution."* (Geiger and Lucke 2011, p. 185). We adopt this definition as
it excludes the publication of data which must remain confidential, are
private or contain industrial secrets. Especially in the last years considerable attention is focused on the demand of opening up governmental data
within politics, companies, scientific communities, and citizen communi-
ties(European_Union 2010). An important event within the trends of the
last years is the release of the EU Public Sector Information (PSI)
directive,in which a common legislative framework was presented which
regulatesmaking data of public sector bodies available for re-use
(European_Commission 2003). In thisreport the European Commission
argued that a general framework "is needed in order to ensure fair,
propotionate and non-discriminatory conditions for the re-use of [PSI]" (p.
1) and that "PSI isan important primary material for digital content

products and services" (p. 1). After the launch of the EU-directive, also referred to as the PSI-directive, many directives and implementation guidelines followed. For example, in 2006 the European Commission developed a policy for the reuse of her own information sources which includes the statement that all general accessible data of the European Commission should become available for everyone, usually for free (European_Commission 2011a). Another important event with regard to the development of open data policies is the statement of the Obama Administration in 2009 that has as primary goal the establishment of an unprecedented level of openness of the Government (Obama 2009). The Obama Administration published an Open Government Directive some months afterwards (The_White_House 2009). Building on former policies, the European Commission has recently presented an Open Data Strategy for Europe, in which more evident rules on making the best use of government-held information are presented(European_Commission 2011b).

An important change of the Open Data Strategy of 2011 compared to directives and guidelines that were released by the EC before, is that "it will be made a general rule that all documents that are made accessible by public sector bodies can be re-used for any purpose, commercial or non-commercial, unless protected by third party copyright" (p. 1). Another important change is that" public bodies should not be allowed to charge more than costs triggered by the individual request for data (marginal costs)" (p. 1). The European Commission will lead by example; the EC will open its PSI for free through a new data portal with an expected launch in spring 2012 (European_Commission 2011b).

Although the open data movement is guided by PSI-directives, strategies and national policies as well as the definition of open data indicates that the data are accessible without any restrictions on usage and distribution, open data policies of organizations are accompanied by many impediments. Current open data policies seem not to facilitate the effective and successful use of open data. There are at least three main categories of impediments of current open data policies from the perspective of the user, namely data deposit impediments, data access impediments and data use impediments(FP7-ENGAGE 2011b). The first and second category of impediments has an indirect effect on the use of open data, because they refer to impediments that restrict opening up data, and therefore restrict the use of open data. The third category of impediments has a direct effect

on the use of open data. The main impediments of current open data policies are as follows.

- *Data deposit impediments* make it difficult to open up data, store
  and (re)use it(Elsevier 2011).Websites that currently provide users
  with PSI raise restrictions on data formats for depositions. Besides, they may ask users to register or to become a member
  (DataCite 2011). Van der Graaf and Waaijers(2011) show that the
  practice of depositing data is currently still limited to a minority of
  researchers and that data sharing is confined to a limited number
  of datasets.

- *Data access impediments* make it difficult to obtain data. Gaining
  access to PSI is a common problem(Boulton et al. 2011; McLaren
  and Waters 2011). PSI is published at several fragmented sources,
  which makes it hard to find certain data(Elsevier 2011; Vickery
  and Wunsch-Vincent 2006). There are only few central portals to
  access data (Judge 2010; Vickery and Wunsch-Vincent 2006). On
  some websites that pretend to provide access to PSI, the PSI cannot be found. It is also possible that the data are temporarily not
  available on the website (Veljković et al. 2011)or that the data are
  only partly available (DataCite 2011). Besides, many PSI-websites
  require taking action from the view of the scientist, for example
  registration, membership, filling a form, obtaining written permission or a fee(Blakemore and Craglia 2006; Meijer and Thaens
  2009; Murray-Rust 2008). Sometimes access to the data is restricted to a group of users (DataCite 2011). Furthermore, scientists may have to accept a variety of use agreements before they
  can get access to the original data. There is no uniform set of licensing terms for its re-use (DataCite 2011; Judge 2010; Vickery
  and Wunsch-Vincent 2006).

- *Data use impediments.*An important data use impedimentis that
  scientific users must comply with standard conditions when they
  want to use the data (Judge 2010). In addition, users may lack
  domain knowledge, which makes it difficult to compare, link and
  re-use data. This also gives problems in case that users are forced
  to employ various arbitrary data transformations to make data
  usable and comparable (FP7-ENGAGE 2011a; King et al. 2011).
  Another impedimentis that commonly there is insufficient metadata available (especially contextual metadata), so that no deci-

sions can be made about the quality of the data and the way it was gathered and measured (Hernández-Pérez et al. 2009; Schuurman et al. 2008; Xiong et al. 2011)or how measurement errors were treated (Smith 2011). The use of metadata could also make it easier to visualize data (Park et al. 2011; Zuiderwijk et al. forthcoming). Finally, it is difficult to measure the data quality from combined outputs (Smith 2011).

This literature review shows that open data policies encounter many impediments. Nevertheless, an extensive overview of essential knowledge about the impediments of current open data policies of organizations and countries is lacking(Geiger and Lucke 2011). Besides, impediments on open data are examined mainly from the view of open data providers (e.g.Geiger and Lucke 2010; Zhang, Dawes and Sarkis, 2005), excluding an examination from the view of open data users. Furthermore, there is a need for more insight into the challenges of open data policies and possible recommendations to improve these. Hence, in this paper the question is asked which policy measures could be proposed to overcome the impediments that open data policies currently encounter.

This paper is organized as follows. The next section provides a textual and visual overview of impediments that can be derived from among others two use-cases. The third section describes the consequential challenges that open data policies currently deal with. Finally, section 4 concludes the paper with some important insights and recommendations to improve open data policies.

2. User-cases

By means of two typical use-case scenarios, we analyze the problems that users encounter when using PSI. The impediments that are mentioned in the use-cases are derived from the ENGAGE-project (FP7-ENGAGE 2011b), which is a project funded by the European Commission aiming to develop an infrastructure for open, linked governmental data provision towards research communities and citizens (http://www.engage-project.eu).

The impediments mentioned in the use-cases are referred to by a number and a letter to enable tracking and tracing in figure 1 of section 2.3. The letters refer to the impediment category to which an impediment belongs.

The letter A stands for impediments in data Access, D for impediments in data Deposition and U for impediments in data Use. PEST stands for Political, Economical, Social and Technical impediments, which is a generic category with typical impediments from the perspective of the open data user(Haughey 2011).The social impediments receive less attention in this paper, because we focus on the practical impediments.

2.1 User-case 1

A researcher of a research community that concentrates on meteorological observations wants to find out how the precipitation developed in the period 1950 until 2010 in Canada. He takes a look at a website that provides data about climate and weather and sees that much of the material on the website is covered by the *Copyright Act*, by Canadian laws, policies, regulations and by international agreements *(PEST1)* and that such copyright, in specific instances, prohibits the reproduction of materials without written permission*(A1)*. The researcher needs the research data though, so he decides to ask for written permission in case he finds data and takes a look at the content of the website. The researcher sees that not all data on the website are quality controlled *(U1)*; some partner stations provide data to the website which does not undergo review processes. The researcher also notices that it is possible to get data from the year 1848 and decides that it would be even better to extend his research and find information for the years 1848 up to and including 2010. However, when he makes his selection of data, the website shows the message that the request cannot be satisfied, because the data are either-missing, invalid or subject to review*(A2)*. The researcher goes back to his original aim of examining the years 1950 up to and including 2010. Next, the website shows a very long list of weather stations that match the results. All stations display results from different months and years. It is going to take too much time for the researcher to look at all the different weather stations and because he wants to present aggregated data from all stations, he should transform the data before he can make a total out of it *(U2)*. Besides, the researcher is more interested in raw data *(A3)*.He sees that he can download a file containing daily temperature, precipitation and snow-on-the-ground data for the complete period of record for each location up to 2007. Although the data does not cover the complete research period and it requires a lot of disk space*(U3)*, the researcher decides that these data can be helpful in answering a part of his research questions. However, there is no dataset that contains data for multiple stations at once. The website states that the data user should require a customized dataset from the Climate Services office to obtain data for multiple stations at once *(A4)* and that a cost recovery service charge will apply*(PEST2)*. The researcher sees there are no other websites that provide the data he is interested in*(A5)* and decides to contact the Climate Services office and takes into account that his research will probably take longer because of the access and use impediments that were present. He also realizes that the data he is looking for may be available somewhere on the internet, but that he is not aware of it *(PEST3)*(FP7-ENGAGE 2011b).

2.2   User-case 2

A researcher who is writing a book about the development of school careersin the Netherlands wants to use some historical data seriesof significance to the local area of his research. The researcher looks up a website and notices thatit provides data about the province that he is researching for the years 1952 until 1977. The data are stored in four files with different formats. The researcher cannot make sense of two of the data files. He is unfamiliar with the data formats and the ontological categories of the data. Therefore he cannot extract the knowledge that is contained within*(U4)*. The researcher understands the data in the other two data files, but he cannot obtain the raw data from them. The researcher finds out that domain expertise is required*(U5)* and asks a colleague for help, because he sees no convenient possibility for a dialogue between the data-producing public body and himself *(PEST4)* and no tooling support or helpdesk *(U6)*. The colleague explains a lot about the dataset and provides the researcher with more insight into the historical data, but he also states that the data cannot be used in its current form. To make the data usable and comparable, the researcher is forced to employ an arbitrary data transformation*(U2)*. In addition, there are only some metadata available *(U7)*and these are not structured*(U8)*, which makes it difficult to use the data. The colleague recommends the researcher not to use these data.

2.3   Impediments from user-cases

The use-cases show impediments of websites that provide PSI and that are currently being used. Animpediment that the first use-case shows is that data on the website are covered by *copyright acts*, laws, policies, regulations, and international agreements. In specific instances this prohibits the reproduction of materials without written permission. In addition, neither information about the data quality nor about the correctness of data is provided. Furthermore, the format and the completeness of the data is unknown. Next, the available data does not include any information about the research period and the website does not provide access to all sorts of data (e.g. not all types of aggregated data) and therefore the services office must be contacted, which requires a fee(FP7-ENGAGE 2011b).

Another set of impediments of PSI-websites that are currently being used was described within the second user-case. A first impediment is that data users sometimes do not have the appropriate background to interpret data from another field of study than their own. In spite of this, websites do not always provide these data users with help to make sense of the data. The second use-case also shows that websites may provide insufficient metadata, which makes it difficult to interpret data properly. Finally, the use-case shows that only few information is given about structurally updating the data in the near future, so that it is difficult for data users to rely on this website for future work(FP7-ENGAGE 2011b).

Based on the impediments derived from the use-cases of the ENGAGE-project (FP7-ENGAGE 2011b), a brainstorm session as part of the ENGAGE-project, the literature overview that was presented in the previous section and the experiences of the authors of this paper a fish-bone diagram is created to show the important impediments of current open data policies(see figure 1).

3. Challenges for open data policies

Based on the impediments that are listed in figure 1, challenges for open data policies can be identified. Section 3.1 describes the challenges for open data policies, after which section 3.2 sketches how these challenges may be handled.

3.1   Overview of challenges

From the literature review four main challenges that concern the use of open data at this moment are identified. The challenges are related to the oversimplification of the use of open data. It is very important to realize that opening up data will not automatically result ineffective use and in value creation. In contrary, wrong conclusions can easily be drawn if the context is not clear (Kalidien et al. 2010).

Anneke Zuiderwijk, Marijn Janssen and Sunil Choenni

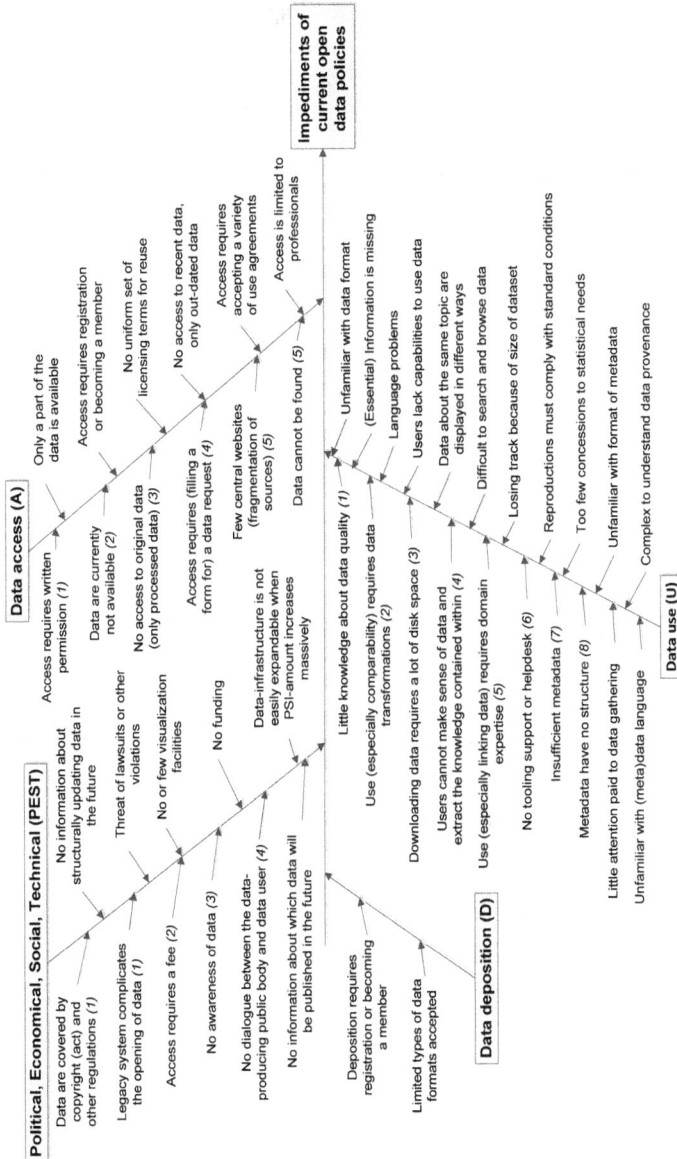

Figure 1: A fishbone diagram of impediments of open data policies

95

3.1.1 Fragmentation of open data

The first challenge is caused by the fragmentation of data(FP7-ENGAGE 2011b). PSI is placed on many different websites, and therefore it is difficult to find a comprehensive overview of PSI on a topic. Some websites present overviews of websites that provide PSI, but they are incomplete and they only refer to other websites but do not integrate the data. At this moment, there are only few central websites that provide complete overviews of data sets integrating large amounts of public sector data. The impediments that are related to the fragmentation of open data are as follows:

- Data are currently not available *(A2)*
- No access to the original data, only processed data *(A3)*
- Few central websites*(A5)*
- Data cannot be found *(A5)*
- Only a part of the data is available
- No awareness of data *(PEST 3)*

3.1.2 Lack of access to open data

The second challenge relates to obtaining access to open data(FP7-ENGAGE 2011b). There can be many types of access impediments. Most of them are related to taking steps by the potential data user. In the current situation it may very well happen that potential data users only obtain full access to data when they overcome the impedimentsas following:

- Access requires written permission *(A1)*
- Access requires (filling a form for) a data request *(A4)*
- Access requires registration or becoming a member
- No uniform set of licensing terms for reuse
- Access requires accepting a variety of use agreements
- Access is limited to a certain group of users
- Insufficient metadata *(U7)*
- Difficult to search and browse data
- Access requires a fee *(PEST2)*
- No information about which data will be published in the future
- No information about structurally updating data in the future
- Data-infrastructure is not easily expandable when the PSI-amount increases massively

3.1.3   Lack of interoperability

The third challenge refers to the lack of technical and organizational interoperability(McLaren and Waters 2011).In the current situation there is insufficient metadata (data about the data; Jeffery 2000) available to obtain an understanding of the coherence of different datasets and to see the data in connection with other data (Hernández-Pérez et al. 2009; Schuurman et al. 2008; Xiong et al. 2011; Zuiderwijk et al.forthcoming). Without creating interoperability, the following impedimentswill continue to exist:

- Data are currently not available *(A2)*
- Use (especially comparability) requires data transformations *(A2)*
- No central website (fragmentation) *(A5)*
- Data cannot be found *(A5)*
- Only a part of the data is available
- (Essential) information is missing
- Insufficient metadata to see the data in connection with other data*(U7)*
- Metadata have no structure*(U8)*
- Difficult to search and browse data because of insufficient metadata
- No dialogue between the data-producing public body and data user which makes it difficult to interpret and analyze data *(PEST4)*
- Unfamiliar with format of metadata

3.1.4   Difficulties with processing of data

Impediments concerning the processing of open data are related to the fact that governments are opening their data. Particularly for government department data, they are putting their data on a huge pile, without considering why they are doing it and for what purposes the data can be reused. Because the purpose is not considered, there is no attention for the processing of the data and for instance for the fact that metadata are required to understand the data. The following impediments make it difficult to process PSI:

- Little knowledge about data quality *(U1)*
- Users cannot make sense of data *(U4)*
- Use requires domain expertise (especially linking) *(U5)*

- No tooling support or helpdesk *(U6)*
- Insufficient metadata *(U7)*
- Metadata have no structure
- Little attention paid to data gathering
- Use (especially comparability) requires data transformations *(A2)*
- Users lack capabilities to use data
- Difficult to search and browse data
- No dialogue between the data-producing public body and data user *(PEST4)*
- Too few concessions to statistical needs
- Unfamiliar with format of metadata
- Complex to understand data provenance
- No or few visualization facilities

3.2 Discussion of policy measures to overcome the challenges

Based on the analysis of impediments, four domains of long term challenges for open data policies are identified. The challenges can be seen as directions that provide guidelines and suggestions, to be a source of inspiration. General challenges contain the provision of the following.

Rectify fragmentation by creating a single shop for PSI. A central, complete overview of data sets should be created. The pure existence of this overview is not sufficient when scientific communities are unaware of it, therefore awareness should be created by using dissemination strategies. Services should include the possibility to request access to PSI on this central website in case that special permission for the access to the PSI is needed.

Create open access for all users .Open Data as a philosophy requires that certain data are freely available, without copyright, patents or other mechanisms of control in a timely and accessible way with few or no impediments. Therefore, open data platforms should consist of free access to PSI or access on marginal costs. The access should be realised for all users of open data. When there are issues with access, for instance privacy issues, solutions may be found for these issues. Besides, there should be clear uniform use agreements that do not differ per data set. Furthermore, easy access to all web content should be created, including applications of integrated content. In addition, the future should be taken into account:

users should get information about which new data will become available in the near future and about structural updates.

Create interoperability and provide users with possibilities to analyse data .It appears to be very important that users of public sector data can obtain metadata to create interoperability; they should be able to obtain data about the data. The metadata are used for discovery, for understanding the data in context and for detailed processing of the dataset(s). These metadata should include clear descriptions of the (quality of the) data and should have an evident structure, so that interpretation issues will be reduced as much as possible. Meta-tagging can be used in order to ensure that PSI can be reused without resource-intensive and cumbersome steps that need to be taken.

Create an infrastructure for processing PSI. Data users should be able to use tools to track, (statistically) analyze and visualize the PSI they want to examine. Users should get information about the ontological categories of the data, so that they can make sense of it. The support and advice of experts in the field and other contacts will also contribute to this direction. The infrastructure should be based on a dialogue between data-producing public bodies and data users.

Governments should make a trade-off between how important they consider to elaborate the above-mentioned solution directions and the budget to spend. By implementing the strategic directions and removing the challenges open data policies can be changed. Hereby the use of open public sector data can be improved. Besides, further research should pay attention to barriers for opening up data by data producers. Some governmental organizations are willing to release datasets within the scope of open data, however, they have insufficient knowledge and there are no guidelines within these organizations to decide which datasets are eligible to be released.

4. Conclusions and discussion

Based on a literature overview and two use-cases this paper showed that despite the guidance of PSI-directives and national policies, open data policies are currentlystill accompanied by many impedimentsfrom the perspective of open data users. The impediments were categorised as 1) political, economical, technical and social impediments, 2) data access impediments, 3) data deposition impediments and 4) data use impediments. Most impediments are found in the data use category and are related to the use of open data. This suggests that opening up data will not automatically result in the effective use and in creating value out of open data. For example, wrong conclusions can easily be drawn if the context is not clear. From the overview of impediments four main challenges for the use of open data were identified, namely 1) the fragmentation of data, 2) the lack of access to data, 3) the lack of interoperability and 4) difficulties with the processing of data. These impediments can be handled by creating policies which include the following, 1) incentive policy guidelines to stimulate the centralization of open data repositories and to rectify the fragmentation, 2) creating access to open data to enable the use of open data for any user, 3) creating interoperability by adding structured metadata when making data available to ensure easy discovery and understanding of its potential and 4) creating an infrastructure for the processing of PSI. By describing these challenges and recommendations, an understanding is obtained of the improvements that can be made and the strategic directions that open data policies should follow.

Acknowledgements

This paper is related to the ENGAGE FP7 Infrastructure Project (An Infrastructure for Open, Linked Governmental Data Provision Towards Research Communities and Citizens; http://www.engage-project.eu), that started in June 2011. The authors would like to thank their colleagues of the ENGAGE project for their input for this paper although the views expressed are the views of the authors and not necessarily of the project.

References

Blakemore, M. and M. Craglia. 2006. "Access to Public-Sector Information in Europe: Policy, rights and obligations " The Information Society 22(1):13-24.

Boulton, G., M. Rawlins, P. Vallance and M. Walport. 2011. "Science as a public enterprise: the case for open data." The Lancet 377(9778):1633-1635.

Braak, S. van den, R. Choenni, R.F. Meijer and A.M.G. Zuiderwijk. Forthcoming. "Trusted third parties for secure and privacy-preserving data integration and sharing in the public sector."

DataCite. 2011. "Helping you to find access and reuse data."

Elsevier. 2011. "SciVerse." ed. SciVerse – Responding to a changing scientific landscape.

European_Commission. 2003. "Directive 2003/98/EC of the European Parliament and of the council of 17 November 2003 on the re-use of public sector information."

European_Commission. 2011a. "Communication from the Commission to the European Parliament, the Council, the European Economic and Social Committee and the Committee of the Regions. Open data. An engine for innovation, growth and transparent governance." Brussels.

European_Commission. 2011b. "Digital agenda: Turning government data into gold."

European_Union. 2010. Riding the wave. How Europe can gain from the rising tide of scientific data: Osmotica.it.

FP7-ENGAGE. 2011a. "Deliverable 4.4.1: ENGAGE Services scenario's.".

FP7-ENGAGE. 2011b. "Deliverable 8.8.1: C2.1 Baseline in Data Utilisation from Scientific Communities."

Geiger, C.P. and J. von Lucke. 2011. "Open Government Data. Free accessible data of the public sector." In Conference for E-Democracy and Open Government (CeDEM11), eds. P. Parycek, M.J. Kripp and N. Edelmann. Danube University Krems, Austria.

Graaf, M. van der and L. Waaijers. 2011. "A surfboard for riding the wave towards a four country action programme on research data." In Knowledge Exchange: Knowledge Exchange.

Haughey, D. 2011. "PEST Analysis."

Hernández-Pérez, T., D. Rodriguez-Mateos, B. Martín-Galán and M.A. García-Moreno. 2009. "Use of metadata in Spanish electronic e-Government: the challenges of interoperability." Revista Espanola de decumentacion cientifica 32(4):67-91.

Jeffery, K.G. . 2000. "Metadata: The future of information systems." In Information Systems Engineering: State of the art and research themes, ed. E. Lindencrona & A. Sølvberg J. Brinkkemper. London: Springer Verlag.

Judge, E.F. . 2010. "Enabling access and reuse of Public Sector Information in Canada: Crown commons licenses, copyright and Public Sector Information." In From "Radical Extremism" to "Balanced Copyright", Canadian Copyright and the digital agenda, ed. M. Geist: Irwin Law.

Kalidien, S., R. Choenni and R.F. Meijer. 2010. "Crime statistics online: potentials and challenges." In Proceedings of the 11th Annual International Digital Government Research Conference on Public Administration Online: Challenges and Opportunities. Puebla, Mexico: Digital Government Society of North America.

King, R.D., M. Liakata, C. Lu, S.G. Oliver and L.N. Soldatova. 2011. "On the formalization and reuse of scientific research." Journal of the Royal Society Interface 8:1440–1448.

McLaren, R. and R. Waters. 2011. "Governing Location Information in the UK." The Cartographic Journal 48(3):172–178.

Meijer, A. and M. Thaens. 2009. "Public information strategies: Making government information available to citizens." Information Polity 14:31–45.

Murray-Rust, P. 2008. "Open Data in Science." Serials Review 34(1):52-64.

Obama, B. 2009. "Memorandum for the Heads of executive Departments and Agencies: Transparency and Open Government."

Park, Y.R., H.H. Kim, H.J. Seo and J.H. Kim. 2011. "CDISC Transformer: a metadata-based transformation tool for clinical trial and research data into CDISC standards." KSII Transactions on Internet and Information Systems 5(10):1830-1840.

Schuurman, N., A. Deshpande and D.M. Allen. 2008. "Data integration across borders: A case study of the Abbotsford-Sumas Aquifer." Journal of the American Water Resources Association 44(4):921- 934.

Smith, P. 2011. "Methodological challenges in integrating data collections in business statistics. Office for National Statistics."

The_White_House. 2009. "Memorandum for the Heads of Executive Departments and Agencies: Open Government Directive." Washington, DC.

Veljković, N., S. Bogdanović-Dinić and L. Stoimenov. 2011. "Municipal Open Data Catalogues." In Conference for E-Democracy and Open Government (CeDEM11), eds. P. Parycek, M.J. Kripp and N. Edelmann. Danube University Krems, Austria.

Vickery, G. and S Wunsch-Vincent. 2006. "Digital broadband content: public sector information and content." ed. Organisation for Economic Cooperation and Development [OECD].

Xiong, J., Y. Hu, G. Li, R. Tang and Z. Fan. 2011. "Metadata Distribution and Consistency Techniques for Large-Scale Cluster File Systems." IEEE Transaction on parallel and distributed systems 22(5):803-816.

Zuiderwijk, A.M.G., K.G. Jeffery and M.F.W.H.A. Janssen. Forthcoming. "The necessity of metadata for open linked data and its contribution to policy analyses."

From Open Data to Data-Driven Services

Muriel Foulonneau[1], Slim Turki[1], Géradine Vidou[1] and Sébastien Martin[2]

[1]Luxembourg Institute of Science and Technology, Luxembourg
[2]Université Paris 8, Vincennes-Saint-Denis, France

muriel.foulonneau@list.lu
slim.turki@list.lu
geraldine.vidou@list.lu

Originally published in the Proceedings of the European Conference on e-Government (2014) Ed. Alexandru Ionas, ACPIL, pp101-108.

Editorial Commentary

What can really create value from open data are open data-based services, as pointed out in the chapter by Foulonneau and her colleagues. Data sets have to be used to implement services to have some utility. If it is not clear how to use data sets in service implementation, open data is of limited interest. In their paper, the authors suggest that one way to solve this problem is to adopt an open data policy ona service system approach that makes it clear how the data sets can be used to implement services

Abstract: The data-driven economy promises the creation of enormous amounts of economic activity and growth opportunities. However these projections lie to a large extent in the development of new services. Currently, the results in terms of service creation remain below the expectations of open data promoters. Indeed most services created are not sustainable and / or do not use the variety of datasets. They are to a wide extent relying on a limited number of very popular datasets. To increase the reuse and the value extracted by services from data, our hypothesis is that service innovation approaches can help understand the mechanisms that drive the creation of services. We therefore propose a review the current approaches to encouraging the creation of services based on data, an analysis of the creation of services from two open data platforms, in the UK and in Singapore, and a description of the roles that the data can have in the design of services based on a theoretical framework of service innovation.

Keywords: open data, service design, data-driven service, innovation

1. Introduction

The development of a data driven economy has been a major orientation of economic policies over the past few years based on (i) the wider availability of data promoted in particular by the Open Data movement (Chui et al., 2013) and (ii) the development of dedicated tools to support heterogeneous data and data in large quantities (Big data). Reports anticipate the creation of enormous amounts of economic activity and growth opportunities (e.g. Buchholtz et al., 2014). However the promise of the data-driven economy lies to a large extent in the development of new services (Deloitte, 2011). The return on investment of open data policies for instance should be evaluated from the services created based on open data sets. Open data promoters couple more and more open data initiatives with actions dedicated to the promotion of the datasets for the creation of new services (Foulonneau et al., 2014). Nevertheless the results in terms of services created remain below the expectations of open data promoters. Indeed most services created are not sustainable and / or do not use the variety of datasets. They are to a wide extent relying on a limited number of very popular datasets. In order to make the promise of the data-driven economy a reality, it is therefore necessary to increase reuse and value extracted by services from data. Our hypothesis is that service innovation approaches can help understand the mechanisms that drive the creation of services. We therefore propose to (i) review the current approaches to encouraging the creation of services based on data, to (ii) examine the creation of services from two open data platforms, in the UK and in Singapore, finally to (iii) analyse the roles that the data can have in the design of services based on a theoretical framework of service innovation.

2. Approaches to encourage the creation of services based on open data

Existing open data initiatives are often accompanied to some extent of actions dedicated to facilitating the creation of services.

In order to make datasets accessible, Open Data portals at regional, national and international level aggregate metadata on datasets. The harmonization of metadata vocabularies (Martin et al., 2013c) used to describe datasets could help the discovery of datasets.

To select the datasets to open, it is either possible to investigate which datasets are already available, whose IPR (Intellectual Property Rights) conditions would allow a publication under an open licence, and whose quality is sufficient. It is also possible to investigate what citizens and potential reusers are interested in (EC, 2013).

When data producers publish new datasets, they have to make the datasets known to potential reusers to optimize the chances that reusers will take advantage of datasets and to facilitate the creation of new services. They advertise on virtual community channels the information and reach potential reusers for their datasets.

Hackathons (i.e. organised by Paris city in France, http://goo.gl/becOH) and off–site competitions are among the initiatives organised to show the variety of services that can be created based on open datasets. They are effective at raising the awareness of developers and service creators on the potential for reuse of the open datasets.

In order to ensure the creation of sustainable services however the Singapore government organizes the co-funding of services (Calvin, 2013). All the same, the European Commission co-funds the development of services to take advantage of geographic information coming from the Galileo satellite (http://goo.gl/VGhZM7) and services that reuse open datasets (European Commission, 2013).

In order to publicize data reuse and encourage service usage, most open data portals include a section to show services and applications that use the datasets, like for example the App showroom on the Berlin Open Data portal "Anwendungen" (http://goo.gl/p6DE0), the "Apps" section (http://data.gov.uk/apps) on the data.gov.uk portal, the "Mobile Apps Gallery" (http://apps.usa.gov/) section on the data.gov portal, the "Application Showcase" on the Singapore portal (http://goo.gl/pN27Bh), or the "Application showcase" section (http://goo.gl/bNXFw) of the World Bank data portal illustrate the systematic addition of a section dedicated to services.

To lower the barrier related to intellectual property rights and reuse conditions, some platforms (like the Singapore open data platform (http://data.gov.sg)) insist on having well documented IPR on each dataset. Other platforms impose very open licences (the Europeana initiative (www.europeana.eu) has set CC0 license which all data providers have to sign in order to have their data included in the platform) to avoid to the reusers to address heterogeneous reuse conditions when reusing multiple datasets in conjunction (e.g. UK Open Government Licence, http://goo.gl/YZfzI4).

In its report for the German Open Data platform (Klessmann et al., 2012), the Fraunhofer FOKUS institute advises the creation of a platform to support reusers and help them reuse the data.

The release of open data is not sufficient to make them accessible and understandable by reusers.

In order to lower the technical barrier as well as the time required to develop a new service, certain data publishers create APIs (Cohen, 2013). Reusers therefore do not have to address format heterogeneity and the learning curve to reuse open datasets is shorter.

The World Bank platform is one of the few exceptions and provides various training services to help potential reusers how to get data and to represent data it into maps (http://goo.gl/dSzplE). The Open Knowledge Foundation offers courses on open data (http://okfn.org/training/), for stakeholders who may not have extensive technical knowledge but wish to work on the data (e.g. data journalists).

The deployment of all these strategies has enabled the creation of many services based on open datasets. In many cases, services are delivered through applications. We nevertheless use the generic term of services as "a set of deeds and acts performed by or on behalf of an agent for the benefit of a citizen, a business or another agent" as an extension of the definition provided in the Core Public Service Vocabulary ISA (2013).

In the next section, we analyse the reuse of open datasets by services.

3. Discrepancy between open datasets and created services

We observed the open datasets and the services created based on open data listed on the UK Open Data portal as well as the Singapore Open Data portal. These different cases were selected due to (i) the expressed willing of the supporting authorities to promote the creation of services based on the open data sets, and due to (ii) the availability of data concerning open datasets and developed services. In January 2014, the data.gov.uk portal lists 315 apps and the Singapore open data portal around 102.

On the UK portal, the domains of the applications (**Figure 2**) include economy (e.g., Property prize , jobmarket), environment (e.g., Use of renewable energies), transparency (e.g., Availability of governmental financial data with the famous application « Where does my money go? »), society (Criminality map), local services (e.g., best surgery services next to me, postal code where I am, fuel station search), education (e.g., geological layers where I stand), and citizen life (e.g., elections results, « UK arms export licence browser »).

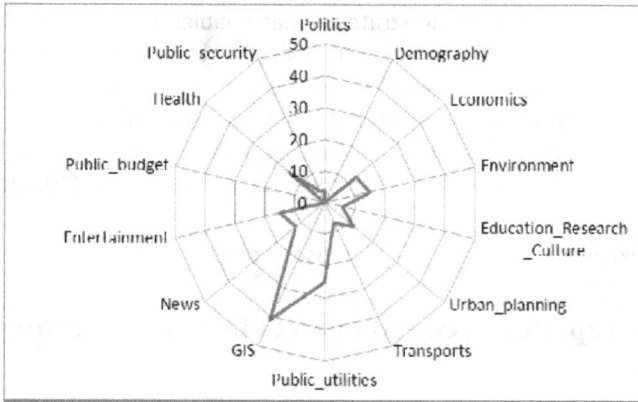

Figure 1: Thematic distribution of applications based on datasets published on data.gov.uk

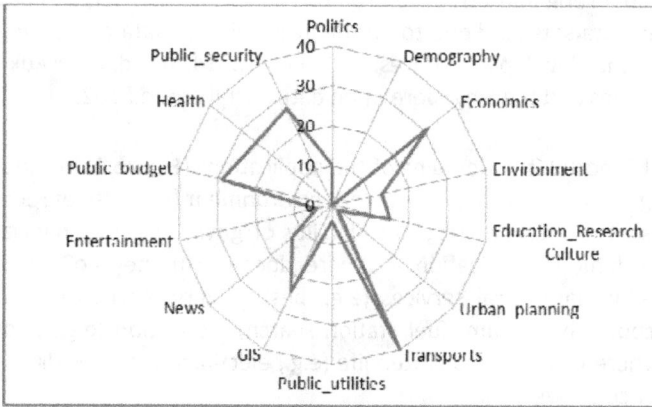

Figure 2: Thematic distribution of applications based on datasets published on data.gov.sg

106 of these applications were investigated: 78% (83) only reuse a single dataset. Sketchmap.co.uk uses 19 datasets. The most reused datasets are Code-Point® Open and the National Public Transport Access Nodes (NaP-TAN). Also, it should be noted that transportation datasets are indeed popular. **Figure 3** shows the thematic distribution of the datasets available on data.gov.uk. **Figure 4** gives the distribution of datasets used in apps on the data.gov.sg portal.

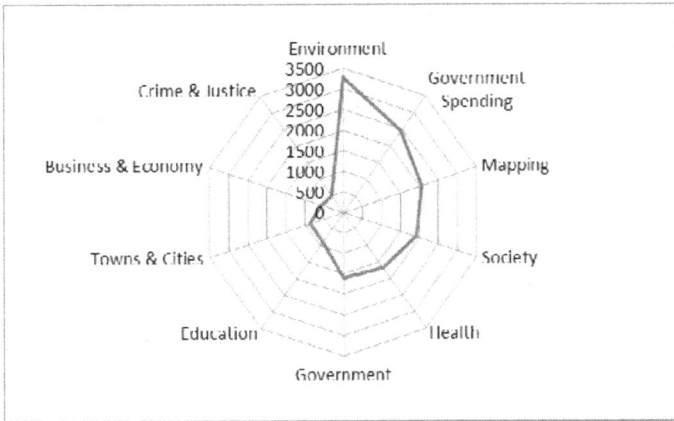

Figure 3: Distribution of datasets by topic on the data.gov.uk portal

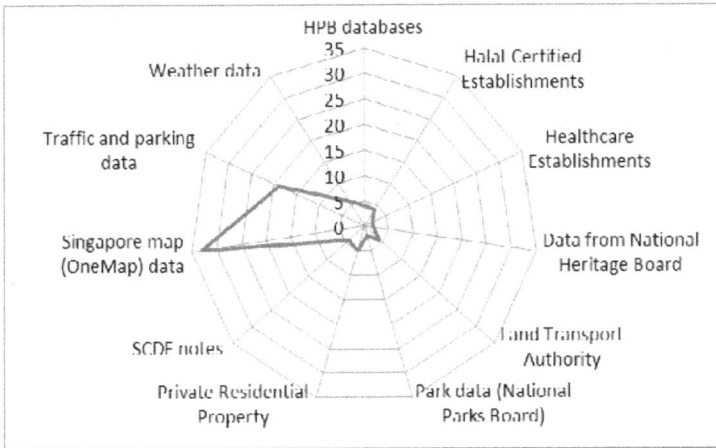

Figure 4: Distribution of datasets used in apps on the data.gov.sg portal

On the Singaporean portal, available applications concern mainly navigation and mobility (traffic, maps), Tourism, Environment, Security (Emergency contacts points), Religion (places of worship), Business (Multiple listing of companies registered in Singapore) and open jobs in public administrations.

102 applications, all of them free, are listed. Some of them available on multiple OS (iOS, Android, etc.). Only 13 apps are using more than one dataset and 89 (85%) of them use only one dataset. The most re-used data set is "Singapore map (OneMap) data" from Singapore Land Authority; used in 33 apps. Datasets related to Traffic and parking data are the second used in 19 apps.

Although categories are not exactly similar, the comparison in the both cases of UK and Singapore of both figures shows the discrepancy between the low number of geographic and transportation datasets and the very large proportion of transportation services. While transportation datasets appear to have a high reusability potential, education datasets attract less reusers in proportion of their quantity.

In Singapore, even if there are more than more than 5000 publicly-available datasets from 50 public agencies, no more than 100 of them are used by the around 100 apps. In UK, we can make the similar observation about the 17869 datasets and the 315 apps.

Although there is no direct equivalence between the domain of the dataset and the domain of the service that reuses it, this suggests the quite uneven potential of datasets for reuse.

The domain is clearly not the only element to take into consideration when assessing the reusability of a dataset.

Therefore the way in which we propose to increase data reuse and the number of services created is by understanding better the service creation process and the way in which it is possible to integrate data in this process.

4. Method / The role of the dataset in the services

Open data portals describe many datasets, available in a variety of formats and with many different access modes (Martin et al., 2013c). There are various data collection mechanisms for reusing datasets from the Web, including the open Archives Initiative Protocol for Metadata Harvesting (http://www.openarchives.org/pmh/) used for instance in the Europeana digital library, Linked Open Data (Heath et al., 2011), data dumps, and data wrappers. However, whichever the type of data and the data access mechanism, a number of similar issues are raised, in particular related to data reusability (e.g., data quality). Data producers make their data available for reuse but reuse does not always happen. It is therefore necessary to understand the service creation process and how data sources can be integrated in this process.

4.1   The service design process

The service design process is composed of multiple steps (Vidou, 2013), i.e., idea generation, maturation, and concept evaluation (**Figure 5**). It should take into consideration different aspects, including the context, the target, the synopsis, the innovativeness and sustainability, the resources, and the service system. Before it becomes an innovation, an idea has to gain its spurs: Does it have a market, technological or research potential? Is it worth investing in its development? The lifecycle of an idea is composed of 3 phases of their life: (i) birth, (ii) maturation and (iii) evaluation. This is an iterative process.

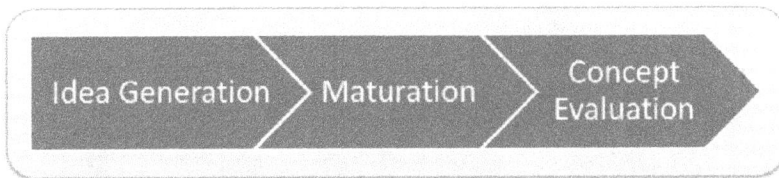

Figure 5: Service development process

The (i) ideation phase corresponds to the birth of the idea. An idea can be born spontaneously or from the systematic exploration of various fields of innovation. It can be triggered by a stimulus at the occasion of a call for ideas or an ideation contest.

The (ii) maturation phase consists in exploring the idea related issues, validate its options or not, make some investigation which other technologies and services are out there already. The idea maturation can be individual - the leader explores his idea in his personal space, with dedicated tools; shared - the leader shares his idea with specific persons, requesting specific contributions; or open - the idea is then available to all (at a department, enterprise or cluster level).

When the idea has reached a level of maturity satisfying its leader, the potential of the idea can be assessed by a group of experts who can decide to invest in its development – this is the (iii) evaluation phase.

During the idea lifecycle, some aspects of the idea should be addressed in order to avoid missing elements (Figure 6): synopsis, context, target, resources, service system, innovativeness and sustainability. The Synopsis is the minimum level of description of the service, the summary of the concept. The context dimension describes the context in which the service is delivered (time, space technological components, regulatory context: norms, standards...).

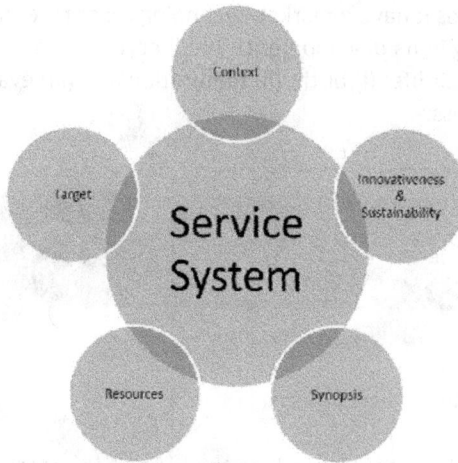

Figure 6: Dimensions of service design

The target describes the customers of the service and the reason why they would buy it.

The resource component describes the type of resources required to deliver the service (human resources: skills and competences, technological resources, process & organizational resources, norms and standards, partners, financial resources...).

The service system component describes the way in which resources are combined to deliver the service to the target in the context (key activities, key partners as stakeholders)

The innovativeness and sustainability highlights the innovative aspects of the service system through its ingredients and the expected economical, societal & environmental impacts.

For each dimension, elements can be at different levels of maturity to support the progressive maturation of the service (basics: simple description based on assumptions or insights; argued: detailed and comprehensive description, checked: detailed description, thought through, checked against literature or facts).

In innovation, there are multiple opportunities for the creation of innovative services. A demographic change, such as the increase of the elderly population can lead to opportunities for the creation of services for retired people. A technology such as indoor GPS can lead to the creation of services based on the new possibilities offered by the availability of that technology. Just like a technology and a demographic change, the availability of data can create opportunities for the creation of new services.

Data can therefore play different roles in the service design process: 1) The service is based on data, 2) the service uses data as a resource, and 3) The service is validated or enriched with data but the data is not directly used or is not directly visible in the service.

4.2   Services based on data

When the data is used as impulse to the service ideation process, it represents the core of the service concept. The objective of the ideation process is to determine with one or more datasets which services could be designed based on them.

The data producer should wonder who currently uses the data; who else could be interested by these data; and if there is any combination of these data with other data which could be of interest to a stakeholder.

The service can for instance allow visualizing the data. The Website *public-spending.net* for instance allows citizens to view budgetary data. The *nos-deputes.net* service shows the activity of French members of parliaments. The objective of these services is to provide a new didactic access point to the data and thus enable transparency. The *handimap.org* service in the French cities Rennes and Montpellier show paths through the cities for disabled citizens. By combining public and private data sources on the creation of companies in Europe, the European SPOCS project has shed a new light on the comparative ease of creating a new business in European countries (Foulonneau et al., 2013a). The Narrative science company generates texts from data so as to make it more user friendly (http://goo.gl/Cmwzf2). It is for instance possible to generate sport news articles from the raw results of local competitions which would not be covered by newspapers.

Finally, it is possible to give a new meaning to the data. *Google ngrams* (https://books.google.com/ngrams) for instance benefits from the *Google* book digitization program. In this context, Google has digitized millions of books from various countries at various times. It then applies an Optical Character Recognition process so as to enable full text search functionalities in the books. By combining the bibliographic data (including the date of publication) and the individual words used in each book, *Google ngrams* allows visualizing the evolution of the use of particular words over time (Figure 7).

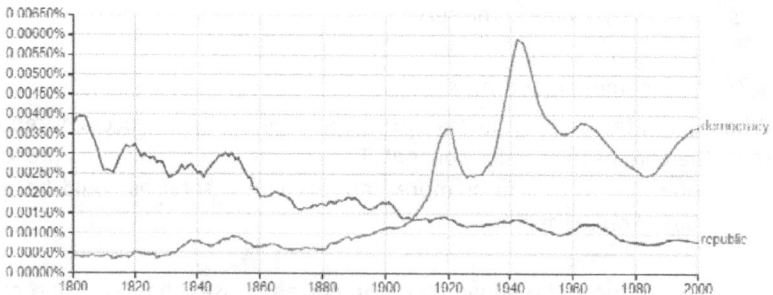

Figure 7: Google ngram viewer representation of the evolution of the words "republic" and "democracy" between 1800 and 2000

At the maturation phase, it is then necessary to analyse the characteristics of the datasets and their impact on the feasibility of the service. This includes the update frequency, the data quality, such as its reliability, completeness etc. (see Stvilia, 2007), the data source, its maintenance processes, intellectual property rights attached to the data and its conditions of use, its cost, its accessibility, including its technical accessibility (e.g., API, data dump ...) as well as its formats (e.g., RDF/XML, JSON, spread sheet), its interoperability with other datasets, typically to mix it with third party datasets, and its documentation including the documentation of its underlying semantic model in order to adequately interpret and use it.

Indeed the update frequency and the maintenance processes attached to the data may be critical and impact the quality of the service. This can jeopardize its viability. In addition, specific processes may have to be in place in order to ensure the collection of updated data for instance. The cost has a direct impact on the business model of the service, while the lack of interoperability with other datasets of interest may lead to additional costs to make aggregate them in a single service.

In this type of services, the data represents the main resource or one of the main resources. Its characteristics should therefore be analysed in detail at the occasion of the maturation phase of the service design.

4.3   Services with data as resources

In other types of services, the concept is defined at the ideation phase without any specific relation with the datasets. However when investigating the feasibility of the service at the maturation phase, the datasets have to be taken into consideration as necessary resources. Location and traffic data for instance is not the core of a delivery service concept. However they are resources that will help design the service.

Data enrichment can use for instance Wikipedia for the translation of concepts or a dataset of postcodes to automatically fill the city in an address form. In a service designed to assess the reading difficulty of educational texts (Foulonneau et al., 2013b) we used a lexical base (WordNet) to identify the relation between words in contiguous paragraphs so as to define breaks in the texts. The final system does not display the external data. It may even work without the external dataset (with simple sentence similarity metrics based on exact word matching for instance). However the external dataset increases the quality of the final system.

As for the services based on data, the datasets should be analysed in terms of intellectual property rights, reuse conditions, maintenance processes, update frequency, technical accessibility, formats, data quality, costs, interoperability with other datasets, and documentation in particular.

A major challenge for open datasets for instance is that in many cases the reuse conditions of the datasets are not clear (Martin et al., 2013a). When a service has to reuse multiple datasets, the multiplicity of reuse conditions may increase the barrier for the reusers. The *Europeana* digital library has therefore promoted the CC0 licence to ensure that all datasets would be reusable without limitation.

4.4   Service validation

Finally datasets may be used in the design phase of the service but not in the service itself. Indeed, in the concept validation phase it is possible to use external datasets only for testing a service concept or validating data which are already hold by the service designer.

Datasets can be used for validating the data already used in the service. A dataset of postcodes can be used to validate postcodes provided by users in a form. Recommendation systems are often tested against standard datasets, such as MovieLens (http://grouplens.org/datasets/movielens/) which has gathered ratings of users over many movies. Authors of new algorithms can then test their algorithm against the dataset to verify that it can accurately predict the ratings provided by users and compare its performance to the performance of the numerous other algorithms which have been tested against the MovieLens dataset and for which performance has been reported in scientific publications.

Datasets can also be used to validate a business model, through gathering economic indicators, typically from statistical institutes that publish their datasets. Simulation environments which require many datasets to recreate the context of execution of a service are often used to predict the difficulties or identify the optimal distribution of resources, for instance in traffic related services.

In these cases the external datasets do not appear in the final service. However they play a critical role to increase the quality of the service and ensure its viability.

5. Conclusion

This paper proposed a review of the current approaches to encouraging the creation of services based on data, an analysis of the creation of ser-vices from two open data platforms, in the UK and in Singapore. Also, it explored the roles that the data can have in the design of services based on a theoretical framework of service innovation. A market has emerged with companies dedicated to supporting access and the design of new ser-vices based on data (e.g., Enigma.io, Narrative Science). Even Google offers a visualization service for open data sets (http://www.google.com/publicdata/). More and more data access portal build APIs and mechanisms that lower the barrier for service designers. Dedicated software has been designed such as the Callimachus platform to reuse Linked open Data (http://callimachusproject.org). In addition, many platforms also organize competitions, such as Hackathons (http://goo.gl/cINX7L), display successful services or even co-finance the development of services based on the data (e.g., in Singapore (Calvin, 2013)). Competitions especially often focus on the first type of service for which data are the core resource. However it is important to understand the roles that the data can have in a service and most importantly that they can also help at the maturation and the validation phases of the ser-vice design. This offers new opportunities for the reuse of data and sug-gests a different approach to measuring the impact of opening datasets beyond the mere number of services created. Indeed in the future it would be necessary to ensure that the benefit of opening data can be adequately measured and that datasets reuse is not only a matter of promotion but also a matter of asset value, i.e., the characteristics of the datasets are critical to ensure their effective reuse by service designers.

References

Buchholtz S., Bukowski M., Śniegocki A., (2014). "Big & Open Data in Europe: A growth engine or a missed opportunity?" demosEUROPA & WISE Institute, ISBN: 978-83-925542-1-9, Jan 2014.

Calvin M.L. Chan (2013). "From Open Data to Open Innovation Strategies: Creating e-Services Using Open Government Data", 46th Hawaii International Conference on System Sciences.

Chui M., Farrell D., Van Kuiken S. (2013). "Generating Economic Value through Open Data". Beyond Transparency: Open Data and the Future of Civic Innovation. October 2013. ISBN-10: 0615889085.

Cohen R. (2013). "Obama Signs Open Data Executive Order: U.S. Government Data To Be Made Freely Available". Forbes, May 2013. Available at http://goo.gl/sb7cSr

Deloitte Analytics Institute (2011). "Unlocking growth: How open data creates new opportunities for the UK".

European Commission (2013). "Competitiveness and innovation framework programme (CIP)". ICT policy support programme, ICT-PSP work programme 2013.

European Commission (2013). "Results of an online consultation on the guidelines on recommended standard licences, datasets and charging for the re-use of public sector information". Final report http://ec.europa.eu/digital-agenda/en/news/results-online-survey-recommended-standard-licensing-datasets-and-charging-re-use-public-sector

Foulonneau M. et al. (2013). "SPOCS: A semantic interoperability layer to support the implementation of the service directive". Proc.of ECEG'2013, 13th European Conference on e-Government. June 2013, Como, Italy.

Foulonneau M., Martin S., Turki S. (2014). "How Open Data Are Turned into Services?", Proc. Of IESS 2014: 31-39, Exploring Services Science. Geneva, Switzerland, February 2014. Springer 2014 Lecture Notes in Business Information Processing ISBN 978-3-319-04809-3.

Foulonneau M., Ras E., Abou Zeid E., Atéchian T. (2013). "Reusing Textual Resources in Educational Assessment: Adding Text Readability Metrics to Learning Metadata". Dublin Core conference 2013, Lisbon.

Heath T., Bizer Ch (2011). "Linked data: Evolving the web into a global data space". Synthesis lectures on the semantic web: theory and technology 1.1 (2011): 1-136.

ISA (2013) Core Public Service Vocabulary 1.01, designed under the auspices of the ISA programme of the European Commission (Interoperability Solution for European Public Administrations), available at http://goo.gl/cThwGX

Klessmann et al., (2012). "Open Government Data Germany", Short Version of the Study on Open Government in Germany Commissioned by the Federal Ministry of the Interior. July 2012.

Martin et al., (2013), "Risk Analysis to Overcome Barriers to Open Data". Electronic Journal of e-Government Volume 11 Issue 1 2013, (pp348 -359), available at www.ejeg.com

Martin et al., (2013). "Open Data: Barriers, Risks, and Opportunities". Proc. Of ECEG'2013, 13th European Conference on e-Government, Como, Italy, June 2013. ISBN: 978-1-909507-22-7.

Martin, S., Foulonneau, M., Turki, S. (2013). "1-5 stars: Metadata on the Openness Level of Open Data Sets in Europe". In Metadata and Semantics Research 2013.

Communications in Computer and Information Science, Springer Verlag, Heidelberg.
Stvilia et al., (2007). "A framework for information quality assessment". Journal of the American Society for Information Science and Technology 58.12 (2007): 1720-1733.
Vidou, G. (2013). "The Service Value Pathway: the 3-6-3 tool", The XXIV ISPIM Conference, Helsinki, 2013.

The use of Web 2.0 on Mexican State Websites: A Three-Year Assessment

Rodrigo Sandoval-Almazan[1], J. Ramon Gil-Garcia[2], Luis F. Luna-Reyes[3], Dolores E. Luna[3] and Gabriela Diaz-Murillo[3]

[1]Universidad Autónoma del Estado de México, Mexico
[2]Centro de Investigación y Docencia Económicas, Mexico
[3]Universidad de las Américas Puebla, Mexico

rsandovala@uaemex.mx
joseramon.gil@cide.edu

Originally published in Electronic Journal of e-Government, Volume 9 Issue 2, (2011) http://www.ejeg.com

Editorial Commentary

The use of social media by government organizations, (which is often referred to as "government 2.0"),is an emerging trend worldwide, at the point that it could be considered as the new generation/wave of e-Government. In their chapter, Sandoval-Almazan and his colleagues analyze the relationship between electronic government, web portals and "web 2.0" on the basis of a literature review that helps to define the concept of "web 2.0" as a revolutionary way of gathering, organizing and sharing information. Although the promises of"government 2.0" are high, the paper shows how the adoption and use of "web 2.0" by governments is very slow. The data considered in the chapter dates back to 2011, but since then the situation has not changed significantly, with the exception of the use of *Twitter* and *Facebook* that, , are regarded as being among the less interactive tools in the "web 2.0" platform.

Abstract: Web 2.0 tools and applications (e.g., blogs, wikis, forums, RSS, podcasts and videocasts) as well as social markers (e.g., Del.icio.us, Technorati, Facebook and Digg) have reached government and commerce sites; however, there is still a dearth of research related to the adoption levels of such tools. The purpose of this research is to contribute toward filling this gap by assessing the impact of this trend on Mexican local government sites by asking the following question: to what extent have local e-Government websites in Mexico adopted Web 2.0 tools and applications? To answer this question, the paper starts by reviewing key concepts of Web 2.0 applications in government portals. On the basis of a longitudinal evaluation of Mexican local government sites, we found that most of the websites analyzed have increased their use of Web 2.0 tools and applications; however, we also found that not all applications are equally well-developed or used on the local websites. Web 2.0 is only in the initial stages of adoption in Mexican government websites.

Keywords: government 2.0, e-Government, social media, Twitter, Web 2.0, websites

---

1. Introduction

The use of technology in government has a long tradition. In many senses, public administrations devote great amounts of effort to generating valuable information to provide services, as well as for decision and policymaking purposes (Bozeman and Bretschneider, 1986; Rubin, 1986; Tapscott and Williams, 2006). O'Toole (1998) supports the advantages of using information technology to reduce costs and improve government efficiency. The use of Internet, and most recently Web 2.0 applications, represents an evolution in the use of information technologies in government. These advanced applications facilitate higher levels of interaction between Web content, information users and information producers. More specifically, 'Web 2.0' refers to a new collection of applications and tools based on the concept of creation of content produced and shared by the very same users of a website. In other words, consumers of information have become "prosumers" or producers of part of the information that they consume (Tapscott and Williams, 2006).

Some of these applications are the social networks, micro-formats, social labeling, RSS (content syndication), blogs, videoblogs, podcasts, wikis and forums. Examples of commercial websites that implement these applications include Technorati, Digg, Facebook, Flickr, YouTube, MySpace, Twitter and Del.icio.us, amongst others. Some government sites are also starting to include some of these applications. Web 2.0 applications may be considered the next step in Internet development technologies.

As part of this study, we evaluated the use of Web 2.0 tools on state sites. Specifically, we focus on the use of blogs, wikis, forums, RSS, APIs (such as Google Maps), podcasts, videocasts, social markers (such as Del.icio.us, Technorati, Facebook or Digg) and social networks. All of these applications, although they may appear to be very different, share certain characteristics, such as the generation and classification of information and content in a collective manner, the integration of communities, and the production and consumption of socially distributed knowledge.

These common characteristics allow them to be categorized as Web 2.0 tools and applications. These tools have proven themselves to be efficient mechanisms for developing political activism (Yang, 2009; Mesgari and Bassellier, 2011; Trechsel et al.; 2003, Krishna and Jai, 2011), perhaps the most well-known case of which is that of the Obama presidential campaign in the United States (Dochartaigh, 2001). They have also proven useful as tools for handling relationships with the media (e.g., Twitter), and as an alternative way of disseminating content in the face of social problems or political crises, such as the recent elections in Iran, the coup d'état in Honduras, and the deposition of the presidents of Egypt, Tunisia and Libya (Hewson and Laurent, 2008). Government sites that use Web 2.0 applications have the potential to generate greater interaction between different social actors (Attia et al., 2011), and as a consequence, greater citizen participation in government processes, which have recently been termed 'Government 2.0'. These applications are beginning to be used at all three levels of government and within diverse areas of public policy.

A recent study revealed that Mexicans between the ages of 18 and 28 years were dissatisfied with the level of communication established between them and political parties, and suggests that more interaction, concrete proposals and more direct messages are needed (Juarez and Marchant, 2011). Previous studies mentioned that Internet users propose that Web 2.0 tools could be an effective mechanism for opening alternative channels of communication. Although the use of these tools is developing very quickly in the relationship between government and citizens, we know little about the outcomes reached by the use of Web 2.0, and even about levels of adoption by government. Given the scarcity of research in this field, we started this research on Mexican state sites that have already worked with Web 2.0 tools. Based on measurements of these technologies taken from Mexican state sites in 2008, 2010 and 2011, this paper will show the extent to which they are currently used, and in which areas of state government these sites are used more frequently.

In this way, following this introduction, the paper is organized into four sections: Section II includes a review of the literature on electronic government, state portals and Web 2.0 as it relates to state portals; Section III is a description of the research methods; and Section IV includes the main findings, and the final section draws conclusions and discusses implications.

2. Electronic government and Web 2.0

This section of the paper constitutes a review of the relevant literature on electronic government, Web portals and Web 2.0. The first subsections include key concepts of electronic government and Web portals. The final subsection introduces the main Web 2.0 applications and their relationships with electronic government and Web portals.

2.1   Electronic government and websites

There are different definitions of 'electronic government', but all concern the use of Information and Communication Technologies (ICT) in carrying out the activities of governments (Gil-Garcia and Luna-Reyes, 2008). Some emphasize the use of ICT applications for undertaking administrative tasks, and others for providing services, and yet others for developing democracy. Government sites are just one example of these types of applications and their use is spreading, not just in Mexico, but in many countries around the world. According to the United Nations Organization, only three out of the 192 UN member states have no presence on the Internet (United Nations Public Administration Program, 2008, UNAP, 2008). In Mexico, in addition to the Federal Government's significant presence on the Internet, which is the 56th place on the last UN ranking (United Nations Public Administration Program, 2010), all state governments and a significant number of municipal governments have a presence on the Internet. Internet sites are now one of the primary means of providing information, dealing with applications and services, and interacting with different government dependencies. Web 2.0 tools have the potential to take these relationships to the next level and change interaction schemes between citizens and their participation in government processes and decision-making (Yáñez, 2009).

There is still no consensus on how best to define the term 'electronic government'. From analysis of the literature on the topic, Gil-Garcia and Luna-Reyes (2008) concluded that electronic government is or should be "the selection, implementation and use of information and communication technologies in government to provide public services, improve the effectiveness of administration and promote democratic values and mechanisms, as well as to create a legal framework that facilitates the development of intensive initiatives for the use of information resources and promote the development of the knowledge society." State government sites are just one example of the application of electronic government. The development of these applications is not only due to pressure from the public to receive the same service it receives from the private sector, but also to the government managers' perception of a multitude of potential benefits to public administration (Luna-Reyes et al., 2009). A government site is understood as "an access point integrated into a state government Internet site which provides both external entities and government personnel with a single online access point to state resources and information" (Burley-Gant et al., 2002).

2.2   Government sites as communication systems
State sites can be considered government-citizen communication systems that function via computers and Internet. This communication system is characterized by the integration of different media and their interactive potential. Multimedia extends the reach of electronic communication to every aspect of life (from home to the workplace, from schools to hospitals, from entertainment to trips) (Castells, 1998). In the mid nineties, governments and companies were searching frantically for ways to position themselves and establish this new system (Castells, 1998).

In this sense, state sites are immersed in a new multimedia system that includes and covers all expressions of culture. In this new kind of society, all types of messages work in a binary fashion of presence/absence, whereby presence enables the communicability and socialization of the message. While the function of communicability is present in all state sites, socialization is only present in some given that not all have the tools and applications needed for this socialization to take place between users and government. From a society perspective, communication based on electronic means (typographic, audiovisual or via computer) is communication (Castells, 1998). This means that the media – in this case, the site – is immersed in this multimedia universe and fulfills the role of communicating Government information. Furthermore, due to the multimodality and versatility inherent to multimedia, it is capable of covering the full range of expressions, as well as diverse interests, values and imaginations, including the expression of social conflicts.

2.3   The evolution of sites and models for communication and socialization

There are various different models that explain the processes of development and evolution of Internet sites (Layne and Lee, 2001). A few years ago, and taking these evolutionary models as a base, an evaluation of state government sites in Mexico was conducted (Almazan, Gil-Garcia, and Luna-Reyes, 2007, 2008). The stages of Information, Interaction, Transaction, Integration and Participation were proposed as complementary but not mutually exclusive components that can be used to characterize the development of government sites (Sandoval-Almazán et al., 2008). Furthermore, this reference framework can be reinterpreted from a theoretical standpoint in relation to the communication systems included in the previous section. The communication that arises from the interaction between government and citizens can take place in different ways, as explained below.

Information Stage. The characteristics of the sites that belong to the information stage are comprised by those that only display information on the activities of public administration. Examples of these characteristics include news or announcements about events, as well as services available to citizens. The communication that takes place between the government and citizens at this stage is one of sender to receiver, which is horizontal and one way. In this, as well as other levels of site development, the receiver plays both roles mentioned by Castells (1998). They can be interactors by choosing their communication path as well as deciding and selecting the topic and the knowledge that they hope to obtain, as well as the media; or they can be interacted with by users that, within their own capabilities and possibilities, select and seek out knowledge from inside a media which provides them with limited options. Nevertheless, the inherent characteristics of the information stage limit the users' capacity to interact, relegating them to the position of interacted. The interactor, in addition to being able to use the information provided on the site, will access information from other sources, such as the radio, television, and newspaper.

Interaction Stage. Characteristics inherent to sites in the interaction stage include applications that allow interaction between citizens and the government, such as forms for asking questions and making enquiries, forums, or automated applications such as virtual public servers. Communication between citizens and the government at this stage is two-way, from the sender to the receiver and vice versa, establishing channels for interaction, such as electronic mail or those mentioned previously. At this stage of two-way communication, there are more opportunities for interactors to choose their means of communication.

Transaction Stage. Characteristics of Internet sites at the transaction stage mainly include what have been topics of electronic commerce. The main difference between this and the interaction stage is the interchange of services and application processes with a well defined cycle and on many occasions, the payment of fees. Communication between the government and citizens at the transaction stage takes place from the sender to the receiver and vice versa in much the same way as in the Interaction stage. Nevertheless, since these are services with clearly defined cycles and processes, it is more common to find an interest in obtaining feedback on how they have performed. One example is online services that can be carried out by citizens.

Integration Stage. Characteristics inherent to the integration stage make reference to the capability of the site to present itself as a single window for providing services to the citizen and transparently making known which agency or agencies are in charge of delivering the services or information. At this stage, not only does communication take place between the government and citizen but also between government dependencies, which in turn communicate this information to the citizen and provide feedback from the government to the citizen, the citizen to the government and between government dependencies. For example, municipal government sites that make it easy to obtain construction permits and licenses needed

to start a business on the same site required different agencies that participate in this process to coordinate and work together. This coordination
can be achieved in different ways ranging from using an agent to process
all the applications submitted by citizens to the technical integration of
data and processes between different agencies that enabled them to offer
the service without the need for an agent.

Participation Stage. Government sites that demonstrate traits of the participation stage offer citizens the ability to socialize and in this way obtain
full interaction. At this stage, communication is most extensive, taking
place between government and citizen, between dependencies, between
citizens and providing feedback.

Communication produced through the use of Web 2.0 tools takes place
according to the type of population and media they choose to obtain information from. In the case of interactors, as mentioned by (Castells,
1998), Web 2.0 tools are useful applications for obtaining information
without needing to search for it, which simplifies the job for the user. For
example, once configured on your personal webpage or email, RSS feeds
enable information to be filtered so that you only receive the information
you want, without the need to enter the site that produces it.

As for interaction, searching for and finding information within media is
made easier by the introduction of these tools on the site; however, it is
important not only due to the type of population using the media but because Web 2.0 is implementing applications that make communication
possible between different actors within a site, in which communication
takes place in settings where citizens and government communicate with
each other.

2.4   Web 2.0 internet sites and tools

The term 'Web 2.0' has yet to be fully defined in a manner widely accepted
by experts in the field. It was coined by O'Reilly in 2005 who defines it as "a
platform that extends to all connected devices," although these devices
are not just limited to being interconnected; instead, much of their functionality rests on the fact that they use technologies that allow users to
build the content and format of sites. Table 1 shows a comparison made by
O'Reilly (2005) between Web 2.0 applications and traditional applications.

Table 1: Comparison between Web 1.0 and 2.0

Web 1.0	Web 2.0
Double click	Google AdSense
Ofoto	Flickr
Akamai	BitTorrent
mp3.com	Napster
Encyclopedia Britannica Online	Wikipedia
Personal websites	Blogging
Screen scraping	Web services
Page views	Cost per Click
Domain name speculation	Search engine optimization
Directories (taxonomy)	Tagging ('folksonomy')
Publishing	Participation
Content management systems	Wikis
Stickiness	Syndication

Source: O'Reilly, 2005

O'Reilly says that Web 2.0 is a mechanism for social cohesion and cooperation. More recent works, such as that undertaken by Tapscott and Williams
(2006) describe the phenomenon as follows: "The new Web is fundamentally different in both its architecture and applications. Instead of a digital
newspaper, it is a canvas where every splash of paint contributed by a user
enriches the tapestry; whether people are creating, sharing or socializing,
the new Web is about participating rather than passively receiving information" (p. 37).

The term Web 2.0 is still under debate, Wilson mentions that a lot of concepts have been causing confusion and ambiguity about the term. He proposes that Web 2.0 must be understood as follows: "Web 2.0 refers to the
second generation of the Web, wherein interoperable, user-centered Web
applications and services promote social connectedness, media and information sharing, user-created content, and collaboration among individuals
and organizations" (Sandoval-Almazan and Alonzo, 2011).

According to this idea Web 2.0, reveals itself as a revolutionary way of
gathering, organizing and sharing information. Some of its better-known

examples include Google, weblogs, Wikipedia, YouTube, MySpace, Twitter and Second Life. Other authors have pointed out some differences:

- Web 2.0 facilitates flexible design, creative reuse and updating;
- Offers the user an enriched and interactive interface;
- Facilitates collaboration for creating and modifying content;
- Allows new applications to be created by reusing and combining data and sources;
- Establishes social networks between people who have the same interests; and
- Supports cooperation in gathering collective intelligence. (AMIPCI, 2011)

Murugesan (2007) defines 'Web 2.0' according to its distinctive applications: blogs, RSS (Really Simple Syndication), Wiki (Web-based tool for massive collaboration in the management of content) or a system to create or manage content, tags, (keywords added to articles or blogs, and shared via social webpages), folksonomy, information taxonomies created by users as social markers. Lastly, another tool is mash-ups (websites that combine services and information from multiple sources on the network). Wilson and his colleagues (2011) gather several concepts of Web 2.0 and their authors (see Table, 1).

Table 1: Web 2.0 features and concepts

Type	Definition	Sample Reference	Examples
Mashups	The "mashing" together of two or more Web services or applications (Sutter, 2009)	(Sutter, 2009)	PadMapper.com, Flickr Maps
Information-sharing Sites	Sites whose primary purpose is the sharing of information or media, from videos to photos to articles to bookmarks/links	(Sutter, 2009)	YouTube.com, Flickr.com, del.icio.us
Social Networking	Online social networks help users keep in contact and receive updates from their friends, family, and colleagues	(Sutter, 2009)	Facebook.com, Orkut.com
Syndication	A service that tracks updates to various sites on the Web, aggregating the various "feeds" for later consumption	(Sun, He, and Leu, 2007)	RSS, Atom
Weblogs (Blogs)	A personal Web page or diary, easily updated and generally displayed in reverse chronological order	(Ip and Wagner, 2008)	HuffingtonPost.com, Engadget.com
Wikis	A website that anyone can edit	(Kane and Fichman, 2009)	Wikipedia.org, Wikihow.com

Source: Wilson (2011), p. 11.

Wamelen and Kool (2008) promote the idea of a second society built on the basis of this platform. They present a series of distinctive platform characteristics and compare them against those of Web 1.0, such as generic vs. specific, static vs. dynamic, closed vs. open, and personal vs. collective. Additionally, they present precise functions that Web 2.0 applications must fulfill, such as sharing information, mobilization, scheduling meetings, support and transaction capabilities. Lastly, Yamakami (2007) proposes that mobile content may also evolve towards mobile Web 2.0 content.

Web 2.0 is a social network platform because its content is user-generated – as if it were a collective intelligence – transforming users into co-producers of content and not just passive subjects who only receive the information. Interaction plays a vital role in this platform. This capacity for interaction is vital, and to achieve it, governments must consider this type of tool very seriously (Woods, 2007), not just as a way to enable the bureaucracy to reduce its costs and allow a greater flow of information, but also as a way of approaching citizens and making sure their participation enriches government efforts.

Although relatively new, Web 2.0 tools and applications have been used on government websites in such countries as Germany where de Kool and Van Wamelen (2008) proposed six categories for analyzing electronic government using Web 2.0, gathering case studies in their country to demonstrate the use of Web 2.0. Web 2.0 has also been suggested as a way of solving problems related to information transparency in governments. Kubicek (2008), who submitted those ticket systems used for providing services, suggested that this tool could also be employed to improve transparency and rendering of accounts, through the use of social networks (Kubicek, 2008). A number of other studies have presented different cases of electronic government and the use of Web 2.0 tools applied to public administration, such as mass collaboration, digital democracy and the use of distributed computing – cloud computing – as a means of improving attention and services both at the state and municipal level (Chenok, 2008). Lastly, Eliason and Lundberg (2006) focused their attention on investigating the specific use of Web 2.0 in designing municipal websites using gender as a tool to reduce the complexity of sites and better organize content. These researchers gathered data from seven Swiss municipalities in order to evaluate the impact of Web 2.0.

The current public administration trend of open government (o-government) or transparent government has begun to use Web 2.0 tools to interact with the citizenry and request their opinions on just how open federal government should be to its citizens. This initiative from the United States' President, Barack Obama (Memorandum of Transparency and Open Government), and the White House website, which invites citizens to participate in this initiative through discussion forums whose purpose is to establish principles (Gobierno-de-Estados-Unidos, 2009b) and come up with proposals for law reform (Gobierno-de-Estados-Unidos, 2009a) are clear examples of how these technologies can be used by government. These alternatives, which have opened up the North American government online to promoting citizen participation in specific issues and policy creation, are innovative for governments, and represent the first time that these alternatives have been used as examples of online government.

Some of the risks that may arise from the use of Web 2.0 tools and applications are data isolation, exclusion of content, privacy issues and the risk of improper use of the information (de Kool and van Wamelen, 2008). Even though the usefulness of Web 2.0 in governments is promising, the great question that prevails is whether public sector organizations are able to commit to this new way of interrelating with their citizens, and improving user-experience and their perceptions of public services (Juarez and Marchant, 2011). Recent research points in that direction, as the most frequent use of Web 2.0 features has changed the behavior and organization of the governments, adapting these kinds of technologies to their tasks (Hewson, 2008) and improving the way in which they interrelate with citizens (Wilson et al., 2011; Warkentin et al., 2002). That is why it is important to make an exploratory research and provide empirical evidence to assess the extent to which Web 2.0 has been involved in government websites, as a first approach to the field.

3. Research design and methods

This section describes the data collection methods and the procedures followed to analyze the data. Online research has become a common practice nowadays; however, very few methodologies and research models have been developed to this end. This situation creates confusion and difficulty about validity and trust in research findings that collect data online (Linders, 2011). Using innovative data collection strategies, however, does not compromise the validity of the findings; Gallupe (2007) mentions that current information systems (IS) research seems more concerned with "how" the research is conducted than "what" research is conducted and "why". Yang (2009) develops the concept of Internet-mediated research (IMR): "Internet-mediated research involves the gathering of novel, original data to be subjected to analysis in order to provide new evidence in relation to a particular research questions" (p. 58). This kind of research, though, like any other study, requires careful planning, design, and piloting. Its most obvious advantage is cost and time efficiency.

For this research on Web 2.0, the target population is comprised by the websites of the 31 Mexican states and the Federal District. Three independent observers viewed sites in three different periods of time. The first one took place during the first half of 2008; the second observation was on March and October 2010, and the third and last observation was held on March and October 2011. These last two observations focused only on collecting data from Web 2.0 features. Researchers from the 2008 observation used a guide to evaluate the state sites and record the inclusion of Web 2.0 tools, as well as the sections of the site that used these tools. Data from these observations were collected by each observer and summarized by one of them. In order to get the results related to the use and the frequency of Web 2.0, it was first determined whether the Web 2.0 tools were used, followed by their frequency. In other words, the number of times a tool was used in the sections of the different state sites.

To complement this initial measurement in 2008, two more observations were made in 2010 and 2011 that only looked at Web 2.0 tools linked to the Twitter and Facebook social networking sites in order to understand what impact this social media technology has on the web pages of state governments. We choose these two Web 2.0 tools because they are the most used nowadays with more members than any other. More specific questions include: "How do these governments currently use social media tools?" and "Which state governments use Facebook and Twitter to raise awareness?"

Once the sample from the 32 states and the two social networking platforms were chosen, the procedure was as follows: each platform was visited to determine whether the government web pages had valid accounts –

Twitter or Facebook – which were validated by entering them and verifying that they did in fact belong to the selected government and not a fictitious or erroneous name. During this validation process, data provided by the sites were noted down, such as the amount of individuals that follow in the case of Twitter and the number of "friends" in the case of Facebook. This information was collected during the months of March and October 2010 and again in 2011, using the Web browsers Firefox and Safari, and a broadband Internet connection, with an approximate time of 15-20 minutes spent on each website.

4. Findings and discussion

In this section of the paper, we introduce the main findings of the longitudinal observations of the adoption and use of Web 2.0 applications and tools in Mexican State sites. We start by showing the general trend of adoption of Web 2.0 tools and applications from 2008 to 2011. After this initial comparison, we focus more specifically on the evolution of the use of Facebook and Twitter, two of the more widely adopted Web 2.0 applications.

4.1   Web 2.0 adoption trends in Mexican State sites

The first observation was held in 2008, to identify the main features of Web 2.0 described in the first section of this paper. Table 2, presents a list of the sections where Web 2.0 tools were found. It is important to mention that many portals did not use Web 2.0 features. Regarding the frequency of use of Web 2.0 tools in the different sections of the sites, we found that tools located in the Citizens section generally received the most use, followed by those in the Government and Tourism sections. The most commonly used tool in the Citizens section was APIs, which suggests that states are interested in creating interactive applications in this section of the website. Also, the Government section demonstrates the greatest diversity of tool use, which reflects wide-ranging interest on the part of the states in terms of the type of communication they seek to create with their citizens in this section. The Tourism section showed a pattern for including multimedia information in audio and video formats. This same pattern was observed in the culture section, albeit with less frequency. It is interesting to note that only a couple of sites used content syndication services (RSS) in the press area.

Table 2: Sections where Web 2.0 tools were found in 2008

Tools/Sections	Gov-ernme nt	Citi-zen	Touri sm	Cul-ture	Applica-tions and Services	Tran spar ency	Press	Other
Podcasts	1	1	6	2	1	0	0	2
RSS	3	4	0	1	0	0	2	0
Blogs	1	0	0	0	0	0	0	0
Forums	1	1	0	0	0	0	0	0
Videocasts	1	0	4	2	0	1	1	0
Chat	1	1	0	0	1	0	0	0
API	4	17	0	0	0	0	0	0
Red Social	0	1	0	0	0	0	0	1
TOTAL	12	25	10	5	2	1	3	3

Three years later, a completely different perspective on the use of Web 2.0 features was found, as displayed in Table 3.

Table 3: Sections where Web 2.0 tools were found in 2011

Tools/Sectio ns	Gov-ernme nt	Citi-zen	Touri sm	Cul-ture	Applica-tions and Services	Tran spar ency	Press	Other
Podcasts	11	11	6	6	3	3	6	12
RSS	14	11	9	9	9	9	16	10
Blogs	4	4	1	1	0	0	2	4
Forums	2	3	3	3	3	3	2	3
Videocasts	21	23	21	19	12	12	16	21
Chat	8	7	2	2	6	3	3	6
API	9	14	9	6	14	7	1	9
Social Net-works	23	22	12	13	12	11	11	21
Social Markers	3	3	2	2	2	1	2	2
TOTAL	95	98	65	61	61	49	59	88

Clearly, there was a notable increase in the use of the different tools. Again, the Citizens sections of the local government websites have more features, followed by the Government sections. The use of social networks was the most common feature among the 32 states, and the least used were blogs and online forums. The use of podcast, videocast, and RSS were still important for most of the sample states. Finally, it is important to mention that the use of APIs is frequently found in the applications and services; for transparency purposes, social networking and videocasts were the most common for the Mexican websites.

A comparison between these two measures from 2008 and 2011 is presented in Figure 1, where the increase in the use of different tools on Web 2.0 is remarkable. Most of the features that showed growth were related to interaction – i.e., social networking, chat, videocast – and those that were reduced were one-way communication channels – blogs. This could be explained by the expansion of this kind of features among the users. In fact, potential users of government websites are interacting more and more with Web 2.0 tools and applications such as Facebook and Twitter.

As shown by Figure 2, the most commonly used tools were social networks, which rose from 6.3% in 2008 to 48.8% in 2011; almost half of all Mexican state government sites now use this tool to display dynamic content to users. The RSS and social markers maintain the same average of use. The least used mechanisms were forums, podcasts and APIS, which dramatically dropped from 2008 to 2011. According to this, it is clear that state government electronic sites focused mostly on displaying informative content in text, video and audio formats (podcasts, videocasts and RSS) in 2008; but this changed by 2011 with the use of applications that allow easy communication between public officials and citizens.

Another important comparison shown in Appendix 1 was the number of local websites with Twitter and Facebook accounts. Of the 32 states, in 2008, only 16 had both Twitter and Facebook accounts, three states (9%) had just a Facebook account, five states had just a Twitter account, and eight states have neither account. In 2011, however, 20 states have both types of accounts; only two states (Chiapas and Colima) have just a Twitter account and eight states (25%) have no account with either social networking platform.

Web 2.0 Tools in Local Sites

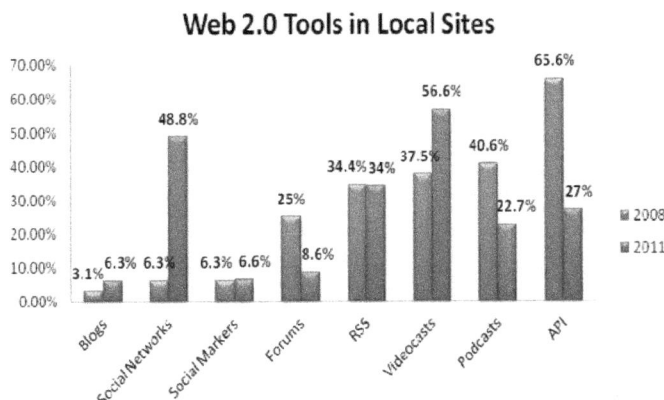

Figure 1: Percentage use of tools by state sites 2008

4.2   Facebook

The total percentage growth of the amount of friends on Facebook during 2008 to 2011 is 94.92%; however, several Mexican states show no potential growth in the number of registered friends (See Table 4).

Table 4: Evolution of Facebook Friends on state websites

GOVERMENT	MARCH 2011	OCTOBER 2011	%	GOVERMENT	MARCH 2011	OCTOBER 2011	%
Baja California Sur	0	381	N/A	Nuevo Leon	5662	8521	50.49%
Chiapas	0	0	N/A	Sinaloa	2373	3529	48.71%
Nayarit	0	0	N/A	Queretaro	9056	12238	35.14%
San Luis Potosi	0	0	N/A	Hidalgo	2770	3719	34.26%
Tabasco	0	0	N/A	Michoacan	2160	2884	33.52%
Tamaulipas	0	848	N/A	Guerrero	3094	3996	29.15%
Tlaxcala	0	617	N/A	Veracruz	8592	10960	27.56%
Yucatan	0	42717	N/A	Durango	4988	4960	-0.56%
Quintana Roo	219	835	281.28%	Morelos	4996	3208	-35.79%
Zacatecas	2470	8874	259.27%	Campeche	311	0	-100.00%
Oaxaca	530	1764	232.83%	Chihuahua	2158	0	-100.00%
State of Mexico	3893	11391	192.60%	Coahuila	313	0	-100.00%
Guanajuato	633	1402	121.48%	Colima	4053	0	-100.00%
Aguascalientes	1097	2328	112.22%	Jalisco	4451	0	-100.00%
Baja California	1978	4070	105.76%	Puebla	74	0	-100.00%
Federal District	3744	7429	98.42%	Sonora	500	0	-100.00%
TOTAL					70115	136671	94.92%

The figures for states like Colima, Sonora and Campeche, which had number of friends in some measurements, are reported as zero in the fifth column because the link was not available in the moment of the measurement. On the other hand, Queretaro, State of Mexico, and Veracruz stand out from the rest with more than ten thousand users each. States that have shown growth consistently in terms of the number of "friends" on this platform are Federal District, Guerrero, Guanajuato, Hidalgo, Michoacán, Nuevo León, Querétaro, and Morelos.

4.3   Twitter

Twitter will be analyzed in terms of its main components – followers, following, lists and tweets – for 2011. The first component of Twitter is its followers. Undoubtedly, this is one of the most interesting categories as it relates to the number of individuals or institutions that want to have a connection with government through the use of this technological tool. Table 5 presents the results of followers. As can be seen, the states of Tamaulipas, Quintana Roo and Oaxaca stand out with a growth of more than 3 times. The number of followers for the rest of the states grew significantly. Other states experiencing more modest growth included the State of Mexico, Michoacan and Zacatecas.

Table 5: Twitter - followers on Mexican local government websites

GOVERMENT	MARCH 2011	OCTOBER 2011	%	GOVERMENT	MARCH 2011	OCTOBER 2011	%
Campeche	0	0	N/A	Hidalgo	14712	33463	127.45%
Chihuahua	0	0	N/A	Colima	10881	24234	122.72%
Coahuila	0	0	N/A	Queretaro	16953	36809	117.12%
San Luis Potosi	0	0	N/A	Morelos	1441	2989	107.43%
Tabasco	0	0	N/A	Nuevo Leon	13778	28184	104.56%
Tlaxcala	0	471	N/A	Guerrero	2671	5285	97.87%
Tamaulipas	409	3077	652.32%	Federal District	27120	49680	83.19%
Quintana roo	156	871	458.33%	Baja California	2361	4299	82.08%
Oaxaca	633	3019	376.94%	State of Mexico	8550	15547	81.84%
Yucatan	13308	41783	213.97%	Michoacan	2296	3951	72.08%
Chiapas	15355	36871	140.12%	Zacatecas	1236	2082	68.45%
Veracruz	5230	12375	136.62%	Baja California Sur	9531	0	-100.00%
Sinaloa	14070	32671	132.20%	Jalisco	5659	0	-100.00%
Aguascalientes	725	1679	131.59%	Nayarit	1584	0	-100.00%
Durango	11492	26446	130.13%	Puebla	724	0	-100.00%
Guanajuato	14341	32845	129.03%	Sonora	2162	0	-100.00%
			TOTAL		197378	398631	101.96%

People following the Twitter account is another component (see Table 6). This is more meaningful in terms of website acceptance and the strategy of the government. For example, Nuevo Leon, Queretaro and Veracruz have an interesting consistent growth in the two-year sample. The State of Mexico and Guerrero show a small but consistent growth. The total percentage number of followers grows by 45.94% percent in both years.

Rodrigo Sandoval-Almazan et al

Table 6: Twitter - following by Mexican local government websites

GOVERMENT	MARCH 2011	OCTOBER 2011	%	GOVERMENT	MARCH 2011	OCTOBER 2011	%
Zacatecas	0	1170	N/A	State of Mexico	4424	7094	60.35%
Tlaxcala	0	50	N/A	Michoacan	2	3	50.00%
Baja California Sur	0	0	N/A	Queretaro	15135	21409	41.45%
Campeche	0	0	N/A	Aguascalientes	125	152	21.60%
Chihuahua	0	0	N/A	Tamaulipas	395	467	18.23%
Coahuila	0	0	N/A	Morelos	870	1002	15.17%
San Luis Potosi	0	0	N/A	Chiapas	2827	2908	2.87%
Tabasco	0	0	N/A	Federal District	1774	1778	0.23%
Guanajuato	1	10	900.00%	Quintana Roo	19	19	0.00%
Baja California	37	209	464.86%	Guerrero	1487	1482	-0.34%
Oaxaca	657	3074	367.88%	Yucatan	441	296	-32.88%
Durango	41	112	173.17%	Colima	118	54	-54.24%
Sinaloa	28	65	132.14%	Jalisco	71	0	-100.00%
Hidalgo	16	37	131.25%	Nayarit	67	0	-100.00%
Nuevo Leon	3562	6838	91.97%	Puebla	487	0	-100.00%
Veracruz	2301	4068	76.79%	Sonora	949	0	-100.00%
			TOTAL		35834	52297	45.94%

4.4 Twitter lists

The lists on Twitter is the component that makes it possible to organize followers, which could be meaningful if governments use it as a strategy to define certain profiles of people to send customized messages and pro-posals for different segments of people. In this case, according to data shown in Table 7, the behavior of the governments is very random: some states like Hidalgo, Veracruz, Colima and Morelos are increasing the number of their lists in order to have more defined profiles; others like Yucatan, Jalisco and Sonora are reducing the number of their lists; and finally some states like Nuevo Leon, Sinaloa, Durango, Queretaro, and Baja California have a consistently growing number of lists.

The percentage total growth in the lists is 37.27%, but an important number of the local websites have a growth beyond 50% in the study period.

4.5 Tweets

The most important way of communication in Web 2.0 technologies is that of microblogging as represented by Twitter. These short messages of 140 characters are used to send information and links to different media – photos, audio and video – and are shared by people with a Twitter connection. The behavior of local government sites is to increase the number of messages sent to their recipients; but more messages does not necessarily mean that users will interact with the sender. On Twitter, that is another kind of measure – the retweet – which is not analyzed in this sample.

139

Table 7: Twitter Lists on Mexican local government websites

GOVERMENT	MARCH 2011	OCTOBER 2011	%	GOVERMENT	MARCH 2011	OCTOBER 2011	%
Tlaxcala	0	19	N/A	Chiapas	226	374	65.49%
Campeche	0	0	N/A	Queretaro	311	504	62.06%
Chihuahua	0	0	N/A	Veracruz	173	262	51.45%
Coahuila	0	0	N/A	Nuevo Leon	423	635	50.12%
San Luis Potosi	0	0	N/A	Guerrero	101	151	49.50%
Tabasco	0	0	N/A	Baja California	118	168	42.37%
Oaxaca	11	60	445.45%	Michoacan	87	121	39.08%
Tamaulipas	8	43	437.50%	Distrito Federal	1216	1674	37.66%
Quintana roo	9	32	255.56%	State of Mexico	310	419	35.16%
Aguascalientes	20	48	140.00%	Zacatecas	34	40	17.65%
Colima	105	230	119.05%	Baja California Sur	68	0	-100.00%
Durango	128	256	100.00%	Jalisco	214	0	-100.00%
Guanajuato	155	302	94.84%	Nayarit	50	0	-100.00%
Sinaloa	186	338	81.72%	Puebla	19	0	-100.00%
Hidalgo	163	282	73.01%	Sonora	83	0	-100.00%
Morelos	63	105	66.67%	Yucatan	136	0	-100.00%
			TOTAL		4417	6063	37.27%

According to data presented in Table 8, the states that are more active in sending Twitter messages are Durango, Morelos, and the Federal District; those that are consistently growing in their number of messages are Zacatecas, Tlaxcala, Tamaulipas, Oaxaca, and Aguascalientes; and those that are not sending messages to their followers are Baja California Sur, Nayarit, Puebla, Sonora and Yucatan. The total percentage growth in the number of messages over the two-year sample was 82.13%.

The phenomenon related to increases in the number of followers is explained in the section on individual followers. Nevertheless, it should be added that the number of followers also depends upon the viral effect (Boynton, 2009), the replication and spreading of links among citizens and government officials who promote the page, which can lead to a significant explosion in the number of followers within just a few days.

5. Conclusions

Web 2.0 tools and applications seem to be an important alternative for governments and their websites in the not too distant future. The so-called Government 2.0 has the potential to bring governments and their citizens closer together in a simple and effective way. These types of tools will allow greater citizen participation and enable government dependencies to transmit more and better information; however, it is also clear that these tools and applications are currently receiving little use on state government sites. This evaluation reveals some preliminary data on the use of Web 2.0 by state government sites in Mexico. Given the speed at which

Web 2.0 tools change and their availability on the Internet, many sites could be using them already. Nevertheless, this initial data offers up a first look at this phenomenon and serves as the grounds for future studies on the topic.

Table 8: Amount of Tweets on Mexican local government websites

GOVERMENT	MARCH 2011	OCTOBER 2011	%	GOVERMENT	MARCH 2011	OCTOBER 2011	%
Zacatecas	0	1689	N/A	Hidalgo	1457	2989	105.15%
Tlaxcala	0	851	N/A	Nuevo Leon	3015	6072	101.39%
Campeche	0	0	N/A	Sinaloa	3916	7639	95.07%
Chihuahua	0	0	N/A	Chiapas	4181	6990	67.18%
Coahuila	0	0	N/A	Queretaro	3744	6111	63.22%
San Luis Potosi	0	0	N/A	Guerrero	3302	4827	46.18%
Tabasco	0	0	N/A	State of Mexico	5363	7748	44.47%
Tamaulipas	198	1987	903.54%	Guanajuato	720	967	34.31%
Oaxaca	415	2990	620.48%	Veracruz	1861	2171	16.66%
Aguascalientes	236	1111	370.76%	Michoacan	431	475	10.21%
Colima	1046	4638	343.40%	Baja California Sur	1	0	-100.00%
Morelos	3214	8844	175.17%	Jalisco	2699	0	-100.00%
Quintana roo	101	246	143.56%	Nayarit	4280	0	-100.00%
Durango	8844	20082	127.07%	Puebla	101	0	-100.00%
Distrito Federal	4625	9754	110.90%	Sonora	284	0	-100.00%
Baja California	964	2016	109.13%	Yucatan	17	0	-100.00%
			TOTAL		55015	100197	82.13%

In regard to the implementation of Web 2.0 tools, progress on these sites is taking place slowly. It seems that site administrators are considering the use of these applications to achieve greater interaction and integration with the citizenry through the presence and functionality of these tools, but many have yet to be implemented. From a communications approach, Web 2.0 applications fulfill their purpose of communication according to the characteristics of each tool, although some of them also allow greater socialization, through social networks or social markers, between users and the government. A next stage for the Mexican states that have begun using these tools is to hold a dialog (Boyd et al., 2010) – an exchange of Tweets and retweets – between users to bring about a citizen-government collaboration (Honeycutt and Herring, 2009) using Facebook or Twitter.

In reality, Twitter can help to both exchange information and recommend news, data or relevant information (Phelan et al., 2009). In recent research into the impact of Twitter on the government, Wigand (2010) tried to ana-lyze the participation of Twitter in the government using four theories – Diffusion of Innovation, Social Influence, Social Presence and Collective Intelligence Theories – through which social networking tools can interact with the government. In our case, we can conclude that the Mexican states we evaluated are beginning to use social networking tools in a rudimentary fashion. More research is needed to observe the level of interaction with the citizenry, their use to generate value within an organization – and that they are not simply a waste of time – as well as to determine whether these technologies are useful for improving local government practices and the relationship with citizens.

Future studies could focus on discovering users' opinions of the functionality and use of the site in order to complement and consider aspects of site functionality not included in this evaluation. This would provide a better view from a citizen's perspective of the suitability and usefulness of the communication channels at their disposal. Another line of research would be to evaluate the advantages and disadvantages for state governments of maintaining a website with Web 2.0 characteristics, due to the time and cost it may involve for some governments, in contrast to the benefits it could yield.

Finally, the use of Web 2.0 tools on electronic government sites is not just limited to posting the tool. Including tools and applications on the sites is just the first step; there needs to be a strategy and clear approach as to what these tools are expected to achieve. Government 2.0 has great potential to transform and improve relations between government, citizens, companies and other interest groups, but these tools must be combined with a clear vision and effective strategies if their effects are to be valuable and meaningful to governments and citizens alike, as well as to society as a whole. We hope that this first look at the topic proves useful and arouses greater interest in these types of applications, and leads us in the near future to Internet sites that can truly be considered shining examples of Government 2.0.

Appendix 1: Mexican States' Facebook and Twitter account addresses

Government	URL Facebook	URL Twitter	Government	URL Facebook	URL Twitter
Aguascalientes	http://www.faceboo k.com/Gobiernode Aguascalientes	http://twitter.c om/#!/GobAgs	Morelos	http://www.faceboo k.com/pages/Gobier no-Estado-de-Morelos/1124545521 27355?sk=app_1979 36773558886	http://twitter.com/#!/G obiernoMorelos
Baja California	http://www.faceboo k.com/GobiernoBC	http://twitter.c om/#!/Gobiern oBC	Nayarit		
Baja California Sur	http://www.faceboo k.com/pages/BCS-CONTIGO/194928 003877085		Nuevo León	http://www.faceboo k.com/gobiernonuev oleon	http://twitter.com/#!/n uevoleon
Campeche			Oaxaca	http://www.faceboo k.com/GobOax	http://twitter.com/#!/G obOax
Chiapas		http://twitter.c om/#!/gobierno chiapas	Puebla		
Chihuahua			Querétaro	http://www.faceboo k.com/GobQro	http://twitter.com/#!/g obqro
Coahuila			Quintana Roo	http://www.faceboo k.com/pages/Gobier no-del-Estado-de-Quintana-Roo/1321745468004 98	http://twitter.com/#!/g obedoqroo
Colima		http://twitter.c om/#!/gobierno colima	San Luis Potosí		
D. F.	http://www.faceboo k.com/GobiernoDis tritoFederal?v=wal l	http://twitter.c om/#!/Gobiern oDF	Sinaloa	http://www.faceboo k.com/gobsinaloa	http://twitter.com/#!/g obsinaloa
Durango	https://www.facebo ok.com/gobdgo	http://twitter.c om/#!/gobdgo	Sonora		
Estado de México	http://www.faceboo k.com/gobierno.edo mex	http://twitter.c om/#!/edomex	Tabasco		
Guanajuato	http://www.faceboo k.com/gobiernogua najuato	http://twitter.c om/#!/gobierno gto	Tamaulipas	http://www.faceboo k.com/pages/Gobier no-del-Estado-de-Tamaulipas/1007393 73337630	http://twitter.com/#!/g obtam/
Guerrero	http://www.faceboo k.com/portal.guerr ero	http://twitter.c om/#!/portalgu errero	Tlaxcala	http://www.faceboo k.com/Gobiernodele stadodeTlaxcala	http://twitter.com/#!/ @GobTlaxcala
Hidalgo	http://es-la.facebook.com/go bhidalgo?v=app_23 47471856	http://twitter.c om/#!/gobierno hidalgo	Veracruz	http://www.faceboo k.com/GobiernodeV eracruz	http://twitter.com/#!/ obiernover
Jalisco	http://www.faceboo k.com/GobiernoJal isco?v=wall	http://twitter.c om/#!/Gobiern oJalisco	Yucatán	http://www.faceboo k.com/pages/Ivonne-Aracelly-Ortega-Pacheco/2434880129 9	http://twitter.com/inte nt/user?screen_name= IvonneOP
Michoacán	http://www.michoa can.gob.mx/	http://twitter.c om/#!/gobmich oacan	Zacatecas	http://www.faceboo k.com/gobzac?v=pa ge_getting_started& ref=sgm	http://twitter.com/#!/g obiernozac

143

Acknowledgements

This study was partially funded by the Mexican National Council of Science and Technology (CONACYT-Mexico) though the grant number 107154. The authors want to thank Yaneileth Rojas Romero and Alfredo Lara Dotor for their valuable contributions to this research. Any mistakes or omissions are the sole responsibility of the authors.

References

AMIPCI (2011) Hábitos de Usuarios de Internet en México. . México City, AMIPCI.

Attia, A. M., Aziz, N., Friedman, B. & Elhusseiny, M. F. (2011) Comentary: The Impact Of Social Networking Tools On Political Change In Egypts "Revolution 2.0". *Electronic Commerce Research And Applications*.

Boyd, D., Golder, S. & Lotan, G. (2010) Tweet, Tweet, Retweet: Conversational Aspects Of Retweeting On Twitter. *System Sciences (Hicss), 2010 43rd Hawaii International Conference On*. Honolulu, Hi, Ieee.

Bozeman, B. & Bretschneider, S. (1986) Public Management Information Systems: Theory And Prescriptions. *Public Administration Review,* 46, 475-489.

Burley-Gant, D., Gant, J. P. & Johnson, C. L. (2002) "State Web Portals: Delivering And Financing E-Service.".

Castells, M. (1998) La Era De La Informacion (Vol.1): Economia, Sociedad Y Cultura. La Sociedad Red, Madrid, España, Alianza Editorial.

Chenok, D. (2008) e-Government: The Next Phase. *Proceedings Of The 2008 International Conference On Digital Government Research*. Montreal, Canada, Digital Government Society Of North America.

De Kool, D. & Van Wamelen, J. (2008) Web 2.0: A New Basis For e-Government? Information And Communication Technologies: From Theory To Applications, 2008. Ictta 2008. 3rd International Conference On.

Dochartaigh, N. O. (2001) The Internet Research Handbook: A Practical Guide For Students And Researchers In The Social Sciences: An Introductory Guide For The Social Sciences, Sage Publications Ltd; First Edition Edition (6 Nov 2001).

Eliason, E. & Lundberg, J. (2006) The Appropriateness Of Swedish Municipality Web Site Designs. *Proceedings Of The 4th Nordic Conference On Human-Computer Interaction: Changing Roles*. Oslo, Norway, Acm.

Gallupe, R. B. (2007) The Tyranny Of Methodologies In Information Systems Research 1. *Data Base For Advances In Information Systems,* 38, 20-28.

Gil-Garcia, J. R. & Luna-Reyes, L. F. (2008) Una Breve Introducción Al Gobierno Electrónico: Definición, Aplicaciones Y Etapas. *11th Annual International Digital Government Research Conference On Public Administration Online: Challenges And Opportunities* 49-73.

Gobierno-De-Estados-Unidos (2009a) Governance: How Do We Institutionalize Transparency Across All Government Agencies?

Gobierno-De-Estados-Unidos (2009b) Open Government Discussion Web Site

Hewson, C. (2008) Internet-Mediated Research As An Emergent Method And Its Potential Role In Facilitating Mixed Methods Research. In Hesse-Biber, Nagy, S., Leavy & Patricia (Eds.) *Handbook Of Emergent Methods*. **New York**, Guilford Press.

Hewson, C. & Laurent, D. (2008) Research Design And Tools For Internet Research. In Fielding, N., Lee, R. M. & Blank, G. (Eds.) *The Sage Handbook Of Online Research Methods* Sage.

Honeycutt, C. & Herring, S. C. (2009) Beyond Microblogging: Conversation And Collaboration Via Twitter. Hawaii.

Juarez, R. & Marchant, I. (2011) Redes Sociales En México Y Latinoamerica. 1st Ed. Mexico City, Amipci.

Krishna, C. & Jai, G. (2011) Role Of Mashups, Social Networking Platforms And Semantic In Revolutionizing Web Integration: Key Insights And Enterprise Implications. In Ais (Ed.) *Americas Conference On Information Systems*. Detroit Michigan, Ais.

Kubicek, H. (2008) Next Generation Foi Between Information Management And Web 2.0. *Proceedings Of The 2008 International Conference On Digital Government Research*. Montreal, Canada, Digital Government Society Of North America.

Layne, K. & Lee, J. (2001) Developing Fully Functional e-Government: A Four Stage Model. *Government Information Quarterly,* 18**,** 122-136.

Linders, D. (2011) We-Government: An Anatomy Of Citizen Coproduction In The Information Age. Proceedings Of The 12th Annual International Digital Government Research Conference: Digital Government Innovation In Challenging Times. College Park, Maryland, Acm.

Luna-Reyes, L. F., García, J. M. H. & Gil-García, J. R. (2009) Hacia Un Modelo De Los Determinantes De Éxito De Los Portales De Gobierno Estatal En México. *Gestión Y Política Pública,* Xviii No. 2**,** 307-341.

Mesgari, M. & Bassellier, G. (2011) How Online Social Networks Create Value For Organizations: A Resource-Based Perspective. *Amcis 2011 Proceedings*. Detroit, Michigan, Ais.

Murugesan, S. (2007) Understanding Web 2.0. *It Professional,* 9**,** 34-41.

O'rRilly, T. (2005) What Is Web 2.0 | O'reilly Media %U http://Oreilly.Com/Pub/A/Oreilly/Tim/News/2005/09/30/What-Is-Web-20.Html. O'reilly.

O'Toole Jr, L. J., Brown, M. M. & Brudney, J. L. (1998) Implementing Information Technology In Government: An Empirical Assessment Of The Role Of Local Partnerships. *Journal Of Public Administration,* 8**,** 499-525.

Phelan, O., Mccarthy, K. & Smyth, B. (2009) Using Twitter To Recommend Real-Time Topical News. 4.

Rubin, B. M. (1986) Information Systems For Public Management: Design And Implementation. *Public Administration Review,* 46**,** 540-552.

Sandoval-Almazan, R. & Alonzo, M. A. G. (2011) Empowering People Using Twitter: The Case Of Mexico Taxes. In Manoharan, A. & Holzer, M. (Eds.) *E-Governance And Civic Engagement: Factors And Determinants Of E-Democracy.* Igi-Global.

Sandoval-Almazán, R., J. Ramón, G. G. & Reyes, L. F. L. (2008) Ranking Estatal 2008 De Portales .Gob. *Politica Digital* Mexico Df, Grupo Nexos.

Tapscott, D. & Williams, A. D. (2006) *Wikinomics: How Mass Collaboration Changes Everything,* Portfolio Hardcover.

Trechsel, A. H., Kies, R., Mendez, F. & Schmitter, P. C. (2003) Evaluation Of The Use Of New Technologies In Order To Facilitate Democracy In Europe, E-Democratizing The Parliaments And Parties Of Europe. Geneva, University Of Geneva.

UNAP (2008) United Nations e-Government Survey 2008: From e-Government to Connected Governance. United Nations.

United Nations Public Administration Program, U. (2008) United Nations e-Government Survey 2010. New York, United Nations.

United Nations Public Administration Program, U. (2010) United Nations e-Government Survey 2010. New York, United Nations.

Wamelen, J. V. & Kool, D. D. (2008) Web 2.0: A Basis For The Second Society? *Proceedings Of The 2nd International Conference On Theory And Practice Of Electronic Governance.* Cairo, Egypt, Acm.

Warkentin, M., Gefen, D., Pavlou, P. A. & Rose, G. M. (2002) Encouraging Citizen Adoption Of e-Government By Building Trust Electronic Markets 12, 157-162.

Wigand, F. D. L. (2010) Twitter In Government: Building Relationships One Tweet At A Time. *Information Technology: New Generations (Itng), 2010 Seventh International Conference On.*

Wilson, D. W., Lin, X., Longstreet, P. & Sarker, S. (2011) Web 2.0: A Definition, Literature Review, And Directions For Future Research. *Americas Conference On Information Systems.* Detroit Michigan, Ais.

Woods, E. (2007) Web 2.0 And The Public Sector - Public Sector - Breaking Business And Technology Silicon.Com Driving Business Through Technology.

Yamakami, T. (2007) Mobileweb 2.0: Lessons From Web 2.0 And Past Mobile Internet Development. *Multimedia And Ubiquitous Engineering, 2007. Mue '07. International Conference On.* Ieee.

Yang, G. (2009) Online Activism. *Journal Of Democracy,* Volume 20, 3.

Yáñez, A. (2009) El Gobierno Y La Generación Y La Revolución De Su Relación. Deloitte.

Government 2.0: Key Challenges to Its Realization

Albert Jacob Meijer[1], Bert-Jaap Koops[2], Willem Pieterson[3,5], Sjors Overman[4], Sanne ten Tije[5]

[1]Utrecht School of Governance in the Netherlands.
[2]Tilburg Institute for Law, Technology, and Society (TILT) of Tilburg University, the Netherlands
[3]Northwestern University (Evanston, II, USA)
[4]Scientific Council for Government Policy in the Netherlands.
[5]Twente University, The Netherlands.

a.j.meijer@uu.nl

Originally published in the Elecectronic Journal of e-Gvernment, Volume 10 Issue 1 (2012) http://www.ejeg.com

---

Editorial Commentary

The difficulties and challenges for an effective use of "web 2.0" tools by governments identified in the chapter are still real, as is also shown in the chapter by Meijer and colleagues. In their chapter they show how to realize the expected (and claimed) benefits of, and critical challenges to "government 2.0", should be solved in order not to replicate the mistakes of technological determinism that affected many approaches to e-Government in the past years. The authors argue for a socio-technical approach to "government 2.0" that helps identifying and accounting for the key success factors for the adoption of "government 2.0." Transforming government toward a less vertical and hierarchical structure,fostering citizens' interests and carefully managing trust and identity in the virtual contexts, are the main challenges that should be faced for a successful "government 2.0 initiative", behind the overly optimistic and simplified ideas that too often have guided the design and implementation of "government 2.0" initiatives.

Abstract: Government 2.0 is often presented as a means to reinforce the relation between state and citizens in an information age. The promise of Government 2.0 is impressive but its potential has not or hardly been realized yet in practice. This paper uses insights from various disciplines to understand Government 2.0 as an institutional transformation. It focuses on three key issues - leadership in government, incentives for citizens and mutual trust - and our analysis shows that Government 2.0 efforts are too often guided by overly optimistic and simplified ideas about these issues. Our discussion suggests that there are no easy, one-size-fits-all ways to address challenges of leadership, citizen incentives and trust: a contextual approach and hard work is needed to tackle these challenges. Realizing Government 2.0 means looking beyond the technology and understanding its potential in a specific situation.

Keywords: Government 2.0, Leadership, Incentives, Trust.

1. Introduction

Government 2.0 – a more open, social, communicative, interactive and user-centered version of e-Government – has the potential to reshape the relationship between government and citizens, in a sense that services, control and policy formulation are designed through a cooperation of citizens, governments and civil society. These networks of cooperation hold an enormous potential to enhance the effectiveness and legitimacy of government and, therefore, Government 2.0 is presented as the appropriate reaction to changes in society. In practice, however, the use of the Government 2.0 potential is still limited (see, for example, Mergel, Schweik and Fountain 2009). The question remains why? Is the potential overestimated by enthusiasts? Or is it underused by skeptics? In enthusiastic and promising publications on Government 2.0 (e.g. Tapscott, Williams and Herman 2008), there is an insufficient awareness of the fact that a Government 2.0 requires more than just a good idea: realizing Government 2.0 is a difficult job. It requires a fundamental transformation in relations between government and citizens (Borins 2010).

The expectations of the benefits brought about by Web 2.0 technologies for government are exceedingly high. The use of new technologies is supposed to strengthen government legitimacy as well as to boost the efficiency and effectiveness of government policies (Eggers 2005). Governments are able to tap into the intelligence of the crowd through using Web 2.0 technologies. New interactions are expected to enhance citizens' trust in government as well as to enable them to make a contribution to public policies. Yet, one could question whether, and to what extent, these expectations are realistic. Countering the promising Web 2.0 stories of gurus, Norris (2010) argues that, despite all technological developments, a greater degree of interactivity or more e-participation or democracy cannot be expected (see also Coursey & Norris, 2008). One might even argue that these stories are dangerous, since they present these new technologies as value free and inevitable. Utopian stories about new technologies may, therefore, hamper public debate about the benefits and drawbacks (Meijer, Boersma and Wagenaar 2009).

A wide variety of contextual factors has been identified in the literature on e-Government and innovation to explain patterns of adoption and diffusion such as size of government, population characteristics (income, e-readiness), form of government, technological infrastructure, political climate, etc. (see Grimmelikhuijsen, 2008 for a discussion of these factors). These contextual factors help to understand why Government 2.0 is developed in certain situations but they do not enhance our understanding of the transformational process. In order to understand Government 2.0 as an institutional transformation (Meijer and Zouridis 2006), three sets of factors need to be studied more extensively:

- *Leadership*. The first set of factors relates to government itself. Government 2.0 will only be developed if there is a government that uses technology to improve relations with citizens. How are governments enticed to change these relations? What kind of leadership is needed to realize Government 2.0?
- *Citizen incentives*. The second set of factors relates to citizens. Citizens need to be willing and able to connect to government: Government 2.0 without citizen participation is empty. Why do citizens participate in public matters? What kind of incentives need to be created to get citizens engaged in Government 2.0?
- *Trust*. The third set of factors relates to the relation between government and citizens: technologies need to be used to develop trusting relations between government and citizens. What are conditions for fruitful relations to develop? What kinds of precon-

ditions are needed for substantive and ongoing interactions between Government 2.0 and citizens?

This paper presents an exploration of these three, interconnected factors
to enhance our understanding of key challenges to the realization of Government 2.0.

2. A socio-technological perspective on Government 2.0

For a realistic assessment of Government 2.0 and a public debate about
technologically induced transformations of government, we will need to
define Government 2.0. Government 2.0 is the next generation of e-
Government: while traditional e-Government strongly focused on internal
and supply-driven technological changes, Government 2.0 reshifts our focus to citizens as not only users but active contributors to e-Government.
In a general sense, one could describe Government 2.0 as a government
that uses Web 2.0. There are many definitions of Web 2.0 and several de-
nominations (e.g. the social web, social software, social media, participative web, user-generated web) due to the different disciplines in which the
term Web 2.0 is used, like informatics, communication science or business
administration. According to Osimo (2008), Web 2.0 is composed of a set
of technologies (e.g. AJAX, XML), applications (e.g. blogs, wikis, social networks) and values (e.g. collective intelligence, produsage, perpetual beta).
Frissen *et al.* (2008, p. 62) more specifically indicate that Web 2.0 consists
of new platforms for interactions with extensive input from users, integration of knowledge and user participation in the production of web services.
The applications or platforms of Web 2.0 are often called social media,
since they give the opportunity for individuals to be active participants in
creating, organizing, editing, combining, sharing, commenting, and rating
web content as well as to form a social network by interacting and linking
one another (Chun *et al.* 2010). The term 2.0 is used in a metaphorical
sense: the 'old' Web, Web 1.0, is being replaced by a new and better version. A similar argument is applied to government: the 'old' government is
to be replaced by a new and better version. The newer version is supposed
to be better because it is increasingly open (in terms of access to information as well as acceptance of new ideas), increasingly social (in terms of
networks within and between government) and user-centered (in terms of
content and technology).

Albert Jacob Meijer et al.

In a more fundamental sense, we would like to define Government 2.0 as a government that uses interactive communication technologies to trans- form connections between government and citizens into increasingly open, social and user-centered relations. The idea of a fundamental impact of new technologies originating in their ability to create new connections is based upon the seminal work of Sproull and Kiesler (1991) on e-mail and organizations. The same changes, in terms of creating new connections, can take place in the domain of government (Tapscott, Williams and Her- man 2008). Traditionally, there are connections between the representa- tives of citizen groups such as trade unions and environmental groups and citizen employees. Interactions are channeled through these formal con- nections. The new media enable direct connections between individual citizens and government employees. Individuals are no longer tied to for- mal structures but create their own networks.

The realization of Government 2.0 should not be understood as a techno- deterministic process but as a socio-technological process. Structuration Theory (Orlikowski 1992; Orlikowski *et al.* 1995; Orlikowski, 2000) poses that the introduction of new technologies in organizations have to be stud- ied as an interaction between technology and the existing social system and this theory can also be used to study the relation between technology and government (Heinze & Hu, 2005). Technologies have certain proper- ties which, in turn, are enacted by governments using these technologies in a specific institutional context. Governments will adapt their use of Web 2.0 to their existing communication patterns but, at the same time, these existing patterns are influenced by the new technologies. The adaptation of new technologies is a process of both reinforcement of institutional structures and institutional change.

In sum, the new networks between government and citizens are facilitated by new technologies and they build upon existing structures as well as they radically alter these structures. The process of structuration should be un- derstood as an interaction between new technologies, government (em- ployees) and citizens. This complicated process needs to be analyzed from different angles to enhance our understanding of the new, emerging struc- tures. We will start our analysis from a government perspective, followed by a citizen perspective, and, finally, we will analyze the relations between government and citizens. The three perspectives will provide different,

151

sometimes slightly overlapping, insights in the complicated process of socio-technological change.

3. Challenge 1: Transformational Leadership

Why do processes of institutional innovation only take place in certain organizations? Legal constraints, financial resources, technological capacity and political climate play a role (Grimmelikhuijsen 2008) but all these factors are framed and mediated by leadership. Leadership should not be confused with management. Selznick (1957) emphasizes that leadership is crucial when it comes to critical decisions, whereas management is about routine decisions. More specifically, transformational leadership is about building something new but also reforming a preexisting situation (Boin & 't Hart, 2011; Wright & Pandey, 2010; Moynihan, Pandey &. Wright, 2012). Innovations in government generally demand the government organization to change routines and organizational structures and (transformational) leadership is needed to guide these changes (Selznick 1957, p. 10).

How can we apply these general notions about transformational leadership to issues of Government 2.0? Information technology (IT) projects often have a highly complex nature, which sometimes leads to a slowly muddling through (Ciborra 2002). The development and use of technological systems has an impact on (public) organizations and their relations with their environments and, therefore, the introduction of technology will always meet resistance. When it comes to innovation, we should focus on leaders as institution builders and reformers. This role of leadership certainly applies to the introduction of Government 2.0 since these new technologies have far reaching consequences for existing structures and routines (Luk, 2008; Noveck 2009). The introduction of Web 2.0 applications in public services requires, among others ideas, support from different actors, and a successful implementation. Meanwhile, innovations can be constrained by the institutional environment, consisting of rules, laws and regularities. Considering all these barriers, one could wonder how innovation can still occur. Strong leadership is a key factor: it is pushes these complex processes of socio-technological change forward (Ke & Wei, 2004).

While much of the literature about leadership focuses on executive leadership a broader variety of leadership roles can be identified. Selznick (1957, p. 82) defines a role as a way of behaving associated with a defined position in a social system. The first role identified in the literature is facilitating leadership; formal leaders can create and enhance an organizational culture in which employees are encouraged to come up with new ideas and try out new innovations (Jung *et al.* 2003). A culture in which new ideas can be implemented is a prerequisite for Government 2.0 projects, while such a culture can be influenced by leadership. This form of leadership is often referred to as *entrepreneurial leadership*. The second level is *hands-on leadership*. This form of leadership involves the ability to act and change. The question, therefore, is: who drives the car? The attention is focused on the leadership roles and styles that are required for a successful realization of Government 2.0. How do these levels interrelate? Entrepreneurial leaders may be successful in selecting and training the leaders that are needed to move an idea forward and, conversely, leaders who move an idea forward may be able to stimulate entrepreneurial leadership.

For Government 2.0, the traditional roles of entrepreneurial and hands-on leaders may carry an additional component: both roles need to be considered within the context of an open, interactive environment. Entrepreneurial leadership needs to support an innovative culture means to support processes of open innovation (Chesbrough 2003). Leadership is not only about supporting experimenting and learning within the organization but also in relation with the environment. Forging new alliances with knowledge partners outside the organization is crucial to this form of leadership. Connecting and crowd sourcing can be expected to be crucial to this form of leadership: leaders need to create incentives for outsiders to contribute to Government 2.0. Entrepreneurial leaders need to be able to pick up signals from distributed communities and transfer these signals to others. Bringing together various communities becomes crucial to the work of the new policy entrepreneurs.

Hands-on leadership of Government 2.0 is about being able to lead dispersed and fragmented teams of technology developers. Increasingly, project members will be spatially and organizationally dispersed. A project team may consist of individuals in various organizations or even loosely connected to the project. The classic image of an innovator is someone sitting in his attic and developing a great idea. This image needs to be revised: the innovator of Government 2.0 is someone who develops an idea within digital communities and who uses these communities to develop the innovation. Technology developers may be able to not only use resources within their own organization to develop the technologies but also man power outside the organizations. Crowd sourcing is an important venue for technology development. Linux is the key example of technology development 2.0. Linus Torvald managed to motivate people worldwide to contribute to the development of Linux. Tapping into this type of dynamic to improve government through new technologies is both a promising and a challenging task. Bringing the efforts of these distributed individuals together in the development of Government 2.0 is a challenging task for project leaders.

Overall, one could also suggest that Government 2.0 does not require a single leader, but rather a form of collective leadership, a group of individuals who complement each other and fulfill a comprehensive set of leadership roles. Leadership needs to be exerted both bottom-up and top-down: leaders that move an idea forward need support from the top and the leaders that support an innovative culture need individuals who use the opportunities to develop ideas. Leadership for Government 2.0 is not a matter of individual great leaders but rather an issue of 'collective leadership' (Boin and 't Hart 2011; Alvarez and Svejenova 2005). Government organizations need to develop forms of Collective Leadership 2.0 to be able to effectively use the potential of Web 2.0 technologies. The need for new forms of collective leadership may count as a reason why Government 2.0 is difficult to realize. Government organizations are not organized as collectivities but as hierarchical entities with fixed functions and responsibilities. Open learning is needed for innovation but open learning conflicts with the nature of bureaucracy in which formalization and a hierarchical chain of command lines are core principles. The idea of collective leadership certainly conflicts with the traditional idea of government bureaucracies being instruments for their political masters.

4. Challenge 2: Getting Citizens Interested

Governments may develop innovative platforms for communication with citizens, yet, these platforms will only be effective if citizens actually use them. The effectiveness of citizen-government communication has declined in recent years. Bimber (2003) argues that societies have undergone a number of information revolutions whereby changes in information *costs, flows*, and *distributions* have impacted the relationship between governments and citizens. These changes work in two directions: first is

Albert Jacob Meijer et al.

the effectiveness of (mass) communication (campaigns) launched by governments to influence citizens top down and second is the effectiveness of communication and service delivery whereby citizens takes the initiative in starting the communication process: a bottom up process.

Two main explanations exist for the decline in communication effectiveness. First is the changed (infra) structure of our society. Trends as individualization, globalization, increasing complexity of society and the transition from a traditional to a network society, inhibit the government's potential to reach citizens (Van Dijk 2006). In this networked society, the individual is no longer tied to formal structures but creates his own networks, untying himself from governmental institutions. Furthermore, the relationship between governments and citizens has changed. Citizens' trust in government has declined over the years (Chanley, Rudolph, and Rahn 2000). Whereas in earlier days people used to trust governments morally, trust has declined and citizens judge governments directly, based on their performance (Uslaner 2002). This implies that citizens no longer consider all governmental information to be true. Related trend is that Western societies get more driven by risks and uncertainties (Beck 2009). Governments increasingly point citizens to various risks in society (O'Malley 2004), causing citizens to gather information as a natural response. Finally, due to budget shortages, governments have adopted strategies such as privatization and a business like 'customer' approach of citizens (Osborne and Gaebler 1992). This has turned citizens into consumers (Vigoda 2002) who are less likely to be influenced by governments.

The second explanation concerns the changes in our ways of communication and the availability media to choose from. Multidirectional flows via electronic and interpersonal media evolved alongside uni-directional flows via the mass media. First reason for this change is the increase in the number of media such as mobile phones and the Internet. The latter facilitates media such as websites, e-mail, chat, and social (network) media like Facebook. Technologies like Web 2.0 are also moving from the private and business sphere into the public sector. The rapid diffusion of these media has shifted media use from the traditional to interactive media (and self-service) (Estabrook, Witt and Rainie 2007). Nevertheless, these new media are not replacing the old media. Research shows that citizens use more media in parallel for their contacts with governments (Pieterson and Ebbers 2008). Besides, the Internet and especially so called 2.0 or social me-

155

dia have impacted our social networks and facilitate the exchange of information within peoples' networks (Resnick 2002). This hampers governments using merely formal communication channels to control their information flows to citizens and use their top-down flow of information. Since citizens can easily initiate their own platforms for sharing opinions and debating about public issues, the bottom up flow is being emphasized. Digital natives, as the generation who grew up with Internet is often called (Gasser and Palfrey 2008), create user-generated content and share it with others based upon their own initiatives.

Citizens have different incentives to use social media in general. Shao (2008) deduced four factors which are relevant for motivation to use social (user-generated) media: information, entertainment, social interaction and self-expression. Information seeking is driven by people's curious nature and desire to increase knowledge of one's self, others and the world. Entertainment is driven by escapism, emotional release, relaxing, enjoyment, time spending and arousal. Social interaction is driven by the social nature of people to interact with others. Self-expression refers to the expression of one's own identity and individuality and can be a process by which people attempt to control the impressions others have of them. Shao (2008) argues individuals use user-generated media in different ways: consuming, participating and producing. The motives are related to these uses. People consume content for information and entertainment, participate for social interaction and community development and produce their own content for self-expression and self-actualization. Applied to citizen-government communication, one could argue these four motivations are also prevalent for the specific use of social media.

Apart from the satisfaction that is gained from the above factors, people seek instant gratification through behavioral incentives, which can also be derived from underlying behavioral determinants. For example, citizens may be looking for entertainment and prefer Twitter over a website, based on the ease of use of the former channel. These more general incentives to use certain communication channels for government-citizen communication have been studied by Pieterson (2009). He empirically confirmed that four groups of factors determine the use of channels by individuals: channel characteristics, task characteristics, situational factors and personal characteristics. These factors need to be studied separately as well as in relation to each other.

Channel characteristics are divided into two sorts channel characteristics: intrinsic and extrinsic. Intrinsic characteristics are the number and kind of the cues of a channel. For example, you can't play a video on a newspaper. Extrinsic channel characteristics are subjectively constructed and situational influenced perceptions of the channel, like immediacy of feedback, level of certainty, personalization, ease of use, interactivity etcetera. These characteristics differ from person to person, depending on personal experience. Task characteristics are the perceptions of the tasks that have to be fulfilled by the user. The complexity and ambiguity of a task are founded to be the most influential task factors when it comes to channel choice (Ebbers, Pieterson and Noordman 2008). Situational factors are derived from the context of use. Factors as (geographical) distance towards the channel or the available time are situational constraints that play also an important role in channel choice. Last but not least, personal characteristics can be derived from demographic features like age or gender, and psychographic traits, like state of mind, earlier experiences, habits, and trust (Pieterson 2009). Pieterson (2009) concludes that habits appear on of the most important drivers of channel choice, where other theories often neglected habitual decision making concerning channel choice. These focused solely on rational decision making (i.e. Media Richness Theory, Daft and Lengel 1986) and the elaboration between task and channel.

Combined, both frameworks (Shao 2008; Pieterson 2009) can help us understand the incentives citizens have to use Government 2.0. Although empirical evidence of the (combined) frameworks in the Government 2.0 context is still lacking (as well as scientific studies on citizens' use of Government 2.0 in general), the framework offers a promising direction and it shows us that interaction and production of information are key factors in the distinction between Government 1.0 and 2.0, from a citizen perspective. Or, as Mengel, Schweik and Fountain (2009) put it: the information paradigm in government is moving away from the "need to know tradition" and towards a "need to share" culture. However, the bureaucratic structure of government limits this dialogue. Regulations and reporting structures hamper the collaboration, creating and sharing between governments and citizens. Government itself is more focused on one-way (mass media based) communication, given its hierarchical top-down structure (Sternstein 2006; Kraemer and King 2003). This leads to a paradox: citizens who are finally enabled to engage in (interactive) communication with government organizations cannot do so, because the government's bureaucratic structure inhibits this communication.

Input from citizens is only valuable when it can be processed according to formal procedures in governmental agencies. These bureaucratic procedures presume neutral and factual information. It clashes with the citizen's desire to use communication for social interaction and self-expression. Procedures are mostly based on information exchange, not the expression of emotions and one's self. Since "sharing" is one of the most distinctive concepts between the 1.0 and the 2.0 era, the contradiction with the top down information flow of governments grows even more, because social media initiatives grow exponentially. Self-expression and social interaction might be the incentives for citizens to interact online, but if there is a lack of platforms where those incentives can be put into practice, government-citizen communication cannot be established.

As a consequence of the top-down structure, government online communication is mostly designed as basic information platforms. Little attention has been paid to the overall view on user experience in interaction (Mahlke 2008) of governmental online communication. Yet, instrumental, for instance ease-of-use, as well as non-instrumental quality aspects, for instance visual attractiveness, are both included and essential in establishing a "good" user experience and, consequently, acceptance and usage. Or, as Van der Heijden (2006) showed us: enjoyment is of great value in web acceptance. Hence, the entertainment incentives of citizens might not be fulfilled either in online government-citizen communication since the focus is on information exchange in a formal way.

5. Challenge 3: Developing Mutual Trust

Government and citizens may be motivated to meet each other in Government 2.0 environments but the success of these government-citizen relationships depends on their mutual trust (Bannister & Connolly, 2011). Particularly in online interactions, trust can never be taken for granted; it has to be established. Since online interactions involve communications at a distance, literally behind screens, traditional trust-enhancing factors that we rely on in face-to-face interactions may not necessarily apply. It is a truism to state that trust has many meanings (McKnight and Chervany 1996). For the purposes of our paper, we can best focus on the context of virtual relationships, where Haenni *et al.* (2009, p. 40 ff.) define trust as 'the positive opinion of a trustor about a trustee's trustworthiness relative to some trust context'. Trustworthiness is someone's 'compound property of being competent and honest with respect to the actions and statements in some trust context', while a trust context is 'a particular class of actions or statements, which are not further distinguished when judging an agent's trustworthiness.' These definitions highlight that trust is a subjective, context-dependent characteristic of one party in relation to another party. Whether citizens and governments trust each other within the setting of a particular web 2.0 context will depend on several variables. Generally, trust has three primary dimensions: competence (is the trustee competent in performing her task?), benevolence (does the trustee care for the trustor?) and honesty (does the trustee perform her duties truthfully?) (Grimmelikhuijsen 2009). What remains implicit in these dimensions is that the trustee must be available and known, otherwise competence, benevolence and honesty cannot be sufficiently perceived by the trustor. Therefore, Cofta (2007) identifies two additional, we could say preconditional, dimensions: availability (is the trustee available when needed?), and identity (is the identity of the trustee established?).

Closely related to the enablers of trust in the trustee are enablers of confidence in the reliability of the trustee's statements. In governments 2.0 applications, the latter are perhaps even more important: do governments and citizens trust the *content* of their web 2.0 interactions? Content reliability can be gauged from two types of criteria: content criteria, related to the content itself, for example consistency, coherence, and accuracy; and pedigree criteria, related to the information source, for example whether information comes from an authoritative source or from a previously reliable source (Vedder and Wachbroit 2003). In online contexts (as in many offline contexts), people find it hard to apply content criteria and usually rely on pedigree criteria (Vedder and Wachbroit 2003). In other words, trust in the Web 2.0 content often boils down to trust in the content's source, that is, in the counter-party who contributes content. Since many pedigree criteria are connected to the information's source, knowing who the source is becomes important. This underpins the importance of identity as a preconditional dimension of trust: it is a facilitating enabler for the other enablers of trust.

What, then, is identity? Given our focus on online interactions, we use a technical-organizational definition: identity is 'any subset of attribute values of an individual person which sufficiently distinguishes this individual person from all other persons within any set of persons' (Pfitzmann and Hansen 2010, p. 30). An identity thus is a collection of attributes that together uniquely identify an individual within a relevant group in a particular context; this can be 'Mr. Cameron from Downing Street, 10', or 'the tall guy in the brown coat who always takes the same morning train'. One can easily see that many different collections of attributes are possible to identify people within certain groups.

Gary T. Marx (2006) distinguishes five types of identity knowledge that can be placed on a continuum, ranging from identity information very close and specific to the individual (core identification and unique identification) through identity information specific to the type of individual (sensitive information and private information) to any identity information that can be attached to a person (individual information). These five types can be thought of as concentric circles, with core identification as the inner, most limited category, and individual information as the outer, most comprehensive category. It is useful to distinguish between these types of identity information, precisely because identification is such a key element in government-citizen relationships.

A central policy question is how much and what kind of identity information is necessary in various contexts. In particular, whether identification of a unique person is appropriate and, if so, what form it should take (Marx 2006). For government 2.0 applications, one can hypothesize that, based on identity being a key facilitating enabler for trust; trust in applications is proportional to the availability of identity information. In particular, one can hypothesize that trust increases as identity information comes closer to the core of the identity circles.

From a policy perspective, one might therefore conclude that for successful government 2.0 applications, strong identity management is needed to establish participants' identity and to enhance identity knowledge through providing more – and more personal – types of identity information. However, this conclusion is not evident, since strong identity management requires more effort from participants and therefore might raise the threshold for civil servants and citizens to participate. More relevant from the perspective of trust, however, is that there are also at least two downsides to high levels of identity knowledge that risk *diminishing* trust, especially on the citizen side. These downsides are the risks to the self-development and privacy, which are particularly visible in today's context of online interactions.

The first risk is a potentially chilling effect on self-development, which stems from the interrelationship between two forms of identity (Hildebrandt 2008). So far, we have focused on identity in the identity-management sense, which is an outsider's perspective of *idem* identity: are we talking about the *same* person? Another aspect of identity is the insider's perspective of *ipse* identity: who am I? This form of identity is crucial for self-development: individuals have to be able to develop a sense of self, in order to determine who they are or who they want to be. Both forms are inextricably related: the sense of self closely depends on being identified in social practices, and vice versa: identity management often relies on information that is also important for building a personal identity. In online interactions, particularly if profiling technologies are used for identifying or characterizing persons, identification based on *idem* identity characteristics carries the risk that people are identified with certain groups (with whom they may not share all characteristics) and perhaps consequently stigmatized or discriminated. Moreover, people can also start to self-identify (*ipse* identity) with the categories thus stamped on them. Forcing citizens to be identified in web 2.0 applications, particularly if this involves government-created identities or 'imposed personae' (Clarke 1994), may, in the long run, amount to restricting their self-development (Hildebrandt and Koops 2010).

The second risk is the potential of privacy infringement of Web 2.0 participants, stemming from the fact that identity information often (although not always) relates to personal information. The information becomes more sensitive if it comes closer to the center of Marx's circles of identity knowledge. From an informational-privacy perspective, the amount of personal data disclosed and processed should be kept to the minimum of what is necessary for the purpose at hand. A central data-protection principle, enshrined in the Council of Europe Convention 108 and the European Union's 1995 Data Protection Directive, is that personal data should not be excessive in relation to the purposes for which they are collected, stored, or processed. This data minimization or purpose-binding principle points exactly the opposite direction from the hypothetical conclusion above that trust requires establishing as much identity knowledge as possible.

Privacy concerns are compounded in the context of web 2.0, particularly with social media where traditional social contexts blur. Individuals always play roles in social life, e.g., husband, employee, fire brigade volunteer, clarinet player, etc., presenting themselves to their audiences in different ways (Goffman 1959). These contexts are governed by norms and social practices particular to the context, for example related to the questions you are expected or allowed to ask (Nissenbaum 2010). In today's social media, audience segregation is difficult to manage, resulting in 'friends' from various contexts seeing information they would not acquire in offline contexts. This infringement of 'contextual integrity' is one of the crucial current threats to privacy (Nissenbaum 2010).

Although self-development and privacy are traditionally seen as citizen's concerns vis-à-vis the state, Web 2.0 introduces a complicating factor: state officials can take dual roles on the same media, as officials and as citizens. The networks in new media do not contain straightforward distinctions between 'the state' and 'the citizen', making the issue of 'contextual integrity' salient for all parties involved. Guidelines for civil servant participation in social media tend to stress role specification, for example in Britain: 'Wherever possible, disclose your position as a representative of your department or agency' (Cabinet Office 2008). At the same time, most guidelines warn against giving too much (personal) information, because of the Internet's everlasting memory and the potential for abuse of information. Civil servants are allowed or stimulated to participate in web 2.0 as private persons under a separate account, but warned that citizens can find them through search engines using identity information to combine their public-function and private profiles; hence, they should be careful which information they provide, both as civil servant and as citizen. Providing more identity information, then, also poses risks on the government side of web 2.0.

In sum, we can conclude that identity is a major factor in creating trust in online applications, but that it is a double-edged sword. Having more identity knowledge of counter-parties will enhance trust, but having to provide identity knowledge to counter-parties risks diminishing trust in a context where risks to privacy and self-development arise. For the success of government 2.0 applications, this challenge implies that applications must run the gauntlet of stimulating the exchange of identity information without forcing people to disclose more identity information than they feel comfortable in providing in the particular context of the application.

6. Challenges to the Realization of Government 2.0

In this paper, we have discussed three key success factors that emerge from a literature review on government 2.0. First, leadership in government is crucial since governments need to be willing to shift their interaction patterns from formal interactions with representatives of interest groups to informal information exchanges with individuals in networks – a shift that cannot take place without strong leadership. Second, incentives for citizens are a key component since government initiatives that are not used by citizens will have no effect. Citizens need to be willing to participate in these networks. Various activities demand their attention and government initiated networks are in competition with a variety of other networks. And third, trust needs to be established in these government-citizen interactions to make the networks viable and robust. This requires reflection on the trust-enhancing and trust-diminishing factors at play in a networked environment without hierarchical relationships and without face-to-face contacts. Knowledge of identity, on both sides of the interaction, is a crucial trust-related factor but also a two-edged sword. Knowing others' identity is expected to enhance governments' and citizens' trust and willingness to participate, but having to provide identity knowledge of one-self might decrease trust because of the risks of abuse of online identity information.

The literature review provided important insights in the difficulties of realizing Government 2.0 and transforming relations between government and citizens. More specifically, we identified three challenges:

1. Creating new (collective) leadership roles that are fundamentally different from bureaucratic roles.
2. Making serious communication attractive to citizens who are increasingly motivated by game-type interactions and 'fun'.
3. Stimulating the exchange of identity information without forcing people to disclose more identity information than they feel comfortable.

These challenges may explain why it is difficult to realize Government 2.0 and why all the 'great ideas' of gurus such as Eggers (2005) and Tapscott Williams and Herman (2008) have not yet been realized.

Our discussion suggests that there are no easy, one-size-fits-all ways to address the challenges of leadership, citizen incentives, and trust and identity. Each factor in itself is multi-faceted and nuanced, while the possible interaction of the three factors – and possibly others – makes the picture even more complex. Being relatively at the start of a new technology that has the potential to transform governance, it is too early to aim at solving problems and finding the golden rule of successful Government 2.0. To avoid myopia and to acknowledge its character as an institutional transformation, we propose that research into Government 2.0 should take a contextual and historical perspective.

Realizing Government 2.0 means looking beyond the technology and understanding its potential in a specific situation. Agents of change should understand the specific need for leadership and aim to create room within bureaucratic organizations to experiment with new forms of leadership. Government organizations should be willing to investigate whether more playful interactions with citizens can help to engage on serious issues. They should acknowledge the sensitive nature of trust and be careful not to demand too much information from citizens. We would like to emphasize that the realization of Government 2.0 is not so much about general design guidelines and one-size-fits-all approaches but rather about creating innovative and specific niches that help organizations to develop technological practices that fit their context and historical development.

References

Alvarez, J. L. & S. Svejenova. (2005). Sharing Executive Power: Roles and Relationships at the Top. Cambridge: Cambridge University Press.
Bannister, F. & Connolly, R. (2011). Trust and transformational government: A proposed framework for research, Government Information Quarterly, 28(2), 137-147.
Beck, U. (2009). World at Risk. Cambridge: Polity Press.
Bimber, B. (2003). Information and American democracy: Technology in the evolution of political power. New York: Cambridge University Press.
Boase, J., Horrigan, J., Wellman, B. & Rainie, L. (2006). The Strength of Internet Ties. Washington, D.C.: Pew Internet & American Life Project.

Boin, A. & 't Hart, P. (2011). Leiderschap in Publieke Organisaties. In: M. Noorde-graaf, K. Geuijen and A. Meijer (Eds.), Handboek Publiek Management. The Hague: Boom Lemma, pp. 115 – 132.

Borins, S. (2010). Strategic Planning from Robert McNamara to Gov 2.0, Public Administration Review, 70(1), 220-1.

Cabinet Office. (2008). Participation online. Guidance for civil servants. June 2008. Retrieved from: http://www.civilservice.gov.uk/about/resources/participation-online.aspx, 8 March 2011.

Chanley, V.A., Rudolph, T.J. & Rahn, W.M. (2000). The Origins and Consequences of Public Trust in Government: A Time Series Analysis, Public Opinion Quarterly, 64(3), 239-56.

Chesbrough, H.W. (2003). Open Innovation: The new imperative for creating and profiting from technology. Boston: Harvard Business School Press.

Chun, S.W., Shulman, S. Sandoval, R. & Hovy E. (2010). Government 2.0: Making connections between citizens, data and government, Information Polity 15(1-2), 1 -9.

Ciborra, C. (2002). The Labyrinths of Information. Challenging the Wisdom of Systems. Oxford: Oxford University Press.

Clarke, R. (1994). The Digital Persona and its Application to Data Surveillance, The Information Society 10, 2. Retrieved from: http://www.rogerclarke.com/DV/DigPersona.html, 8 March 2011.

Cofta, P. (2007). Confidence, trust and identity, BP Technology Journal, 25(2), 173-8.

Coursey, D. & Norris, D.F. (2008). Models of e-Government: Are They Correct? An Empirical Assessment, Public Administration Review, 68(3), 523–536.

Daft, R. L. & Lengel, R. H. (1986). 'Organizational Information Requirements, Media Richness and Structural Design', Management Science, 32(5), 554-71.

Ebbers, W. E., Pieterson, W. J. & Noordman, H. N. (2008). Electronic Government: Rethinking Channel Management Strategies, in: Government Information Quarterly, 25(2), 181-201.

Eggers, W.D. (2005). Government 2.0: Using Technology to Improve Education, Cut Red Tape, Reduce Gridlock and Enhance Democracy, Plymouth (UK): Rowman & Littlefield Publishers.

Ellison, N. B., Steinfield, C. & Lampe, C. (2007). The Benefits of Facebook "Friends:" Social Capital and College Students' Use of Online Social Network Sites, Journal of Computer – Mediated Communication, 12(4).

Estabrook, L., Witt, E. & Rainie, L. (2007). Information searches that solve problems. How people use the internet, libraries, and government agencies when they need help. Washington, DC: Pew Internet & American Life Project.

Frissen, V., Van Staden, M. , Huijboom, N., Kotterink, B., Huveneers, S., Kuipers, M. & Bodea G. (2008). Naar een 'User Generated State'? De impact van nieuwe media voor overheid en openbaar bestuur, Rapport voor het ministerie van

BZK, Den Haag. Retrieved from: http://www.minbzk.nl/111201/naar-een-user, 15 May 2009.

Gasser, U. & Palfrey, J. (2008). Born Digital: Understanding the First Generation of Digital Natives. New York: Basic Books.

Goffman, E. (1959). The presentation of self in everyday life. Garden City, N.Y.: Doubleday.

Grimmelikhuijsen, S.G. (2008). What Drives Transparency Of Municipal Govern-ments: Push Or Pull?, Paper presented at the EGPA conference of September 3rd – 5th, 2008, Rotterdam.

Grimmelikhuijsen, S.G. (2009). Do transparent government agencies strengthen trust?, Information Polity, 14(3), 173–86.

Haenni, R., Jaquet-Chiffelle, D.-O., Anrig, B. & Benoist, E. (2009). Core Concepts and Definitions, in: D.-O. Jaquet-Chiffelle and H. Buitelaar (Eds.), D17.4: Trust and Identification in the Light of Virtual Persons, FIDIS deliverable p. 38-58. Re-trieved from: http://www.fidis.net, 1 June 2009.

Heinze, N., & Hu, Q. (2005) e-Government Research: A Review via the Lens of Struc-turation Theory. Proceedings of the Ninth Pacific Asia Conference on Informa-tion Systems (PACS2005), Bangkok, july 7-10, 891-904.

Hildebrandt, M. (2008). Where Idem meets Ipse: Conceptual Analysis, in: M. Hildebrandt, B.-J. Koops and K. De Vries (Eds.), D7.14a: Where Idem-Identity meets Ipse-Identity. Conceptual Explorations, FIDIS deliverable, (p. 12-17). Re-trieved from: http://www.fidis.net, 1 December 2008.

Hildebrandt, M. & Koops. B.J. (2010). The Challenges of Ambient Law and Legal Protection in the Profiling Era. Modern Law Review, 73 (3), 428-460.

Jung, D., Chow, C. & Wu, A. (2003). The Role of Transformational Leadership in Enhancing Organizational Innovation: Hypotheses and Some Preliminary Find-ings, The Leadership Quarterly, 14, 525-44.

Katz, E. (1957). The Two-Step Flow of Communication: an Up-To Date Report on a Hypothesis, The Public Opinion Quarterly, 21 (1), 61-78.

Ke, W. & Wei, K.K. (2004). Successful e-Government in Singapore. Communications of the ACM, 47 (6), 95-99.

Kingdon, J. (2003). Agendas, Alternatives, and Public Policies. Second Edition. New York: Longman.

Kraemer, K. & King, J.L. (2003). Information Technology and Administrative Reform: Will the Time After e-Government Be Different? Paper presented at the Heinrich Reinemann Schrift Fest, Post Graduate School of Administration. Re-trieved from: http://www.crito.uci.edu/publications/pdf/e-Government.pdf, 8 March 2011.

Lin, N. (2001). Bulding a Network Theory of Social Capital, in: N. Lin, K. S. Cook and R. S. Burt (eds.), Social capital: theory and research. New Brunswick, NJ: Trans-action Publishers.

Luk, S.C.Y. (2008). The impact of leadership and stakeholders on the success/failure of e-Government service: Using the case study of e-stamping service in Hong Kong, Government Information Quarterly, 26(4), 594-604.

Mahlke, S. (2008). User Experience of Interaction with Technical Systems. Theories, Methods, Empirical Results, and Their Application to the Design of Interactive Systems. Saarbrücken: VDM Verlag.

Marx, G.T. (2006), Varieties of Personal Information as Influences on Attitudes towards Surveillance, in: K.D. Haggerty and R.V. Ericson (Eds.), The New Politics of Surveillance and Visibility, Toronto: University of Toronto Press.

McKnight, D.H. & Chervany, N.L. (1996). The Meanings of Trust. Working Paper 96-04. Retrieved from: http://www.misrc.umn.edu/wpaper/WorkingPapers/9604.pdf, 8 March 2011.

Meijer, A. & Zouridis, Z. (2006), e-Government is an Institutional Innovation. In: V. Bekkers, H. van Duivenboden & M. Thaens (Eds.), Information and Communication technology and Public Innovation. Assessing the ICT-Driven Modernization of Public Administration, (pp. 219-29), Amsterdam: IOS Press.

Meijer, A., Boersma, K. & Wagenaar, P. (eds). (2009). ICTs, Citizens and Governance: After the Hype, Innovation and the Public Sector, Volume 14, Amsterdam: IOS Press.

Mergel, I. A., Schweik, C.M. & Fountain, J.E. (2009). The Transformational Effect of Web 2.0 Technologies on Government. Retrieved from: SSRN: http://ssrn.com/abstract=1412796 1 June 2009.

Millard, J. (2006). e-Government for an inclusive society: flexi-channelling and social intermediaries. Paper presented at the eGOV conference 2006, Krakow, Poland.

Monge, P.R., & Contractor, N.S. (2003). Theories of communication networks. Oxford; New York: Oxford University Press.

Moynihan, D.P. Pandey, S.K. &. Wright, B.E. (2012). Setting the Table: How Transformational Leadership Fosters Performance Information Use, Journal of Public Administration Research and Theory, 22(1): 143-164.

Mumford, M., Scott, G., Gaddis, B. & Strange, J. (2003). Leading Creative People: Orchestrating Expertise and Relationships. In: The Leadership Quarterly, 13, 705-50.

Nissenbaum, H. (2010). Privacy in Context. Technology, Policy, and the Integrity of Social Life, Stanford, CA: Stanford University Press.

Norris, D.F. (2010). e-Government 2020: Plus ça change, plus c'est la même chose. Public Administration Review, 70(1), 180-181.

Noveck, B. (2009). Wiki-Government. How open-source technology can make government decision-making more expert and more democratic. Washington DC: Brookings Institution Press.

O'Malley, P. (2004). Risk, Uncertainty and Government. London: The GlassHouse Press.

Orlikowski, W. J. (1992). The duality of technology: Rethinking the concept of technology in organizations, Organization Science, 3(3), 398–427.

Orlikowski, W.J. (2000). Using Technology and Constituting Structures: A Practice Lens for Studying Technology in Organizations, Organization Science, 11 (4), 404-428.

Orlikowski, W. J., Yates, J., Okamura, K. & Fujimoto, M. (1995). Shaping electronic communication: The metastructuring of technology in the context of use. Organization Science, 6(4), 423–44.

Osborne, D. & Gaebler, T. (1992). Reinventing Government: how the entrepreneurial spirit is transforming the public sector. Readin: Addison-Wesley.

Osimo, D. (2008). Web 2.0 in Government: Why and How. Technical Report. JRC, EUR 23358, EC JRC.

Pfitzmann, A. & Hansen, M. (2010). A terminology for talking about privacy by data minimization: Anonymity, Unlinkability, Undetectability, Unobservability, Pseudonymity, and Identity Management, Version 0.33. Retrieved from: http://dud.inf.tu-dresden.de/Anon_Terminology.shtml, 1 April 2010.

Pieterson, W. (2009). Channel Choice; Citizens' Channel Behavior and Public Service Channel Strategy. Enschede: University of Twente.

Pieterson, W., & Ebbers, W. (2008). The Use of Service Channels by Citizens in the Netherlands; implications for multi-channel management, International Review of Administrative Sciences, 74, 1.

Resnick, P. (2002). Beyond Bowling Together: SocioTechnical Capital. In: Carroll, J.M. (ed.) HCI in the New Millenium. Addison-Wesley, 247-272.

Sabatier, P. (2007). The Need for Better Theories, in: P. Sabatier (ed.) Theories of the Policy Process. Cambridge: Westview Press.

Scharpf, F. (1997). Games Real Actors Play: Actor-Centered Institutionalism in Policy Research. Cambridge: Westview Press.

Selznick, P. (1957). Leadership and Administration. New York: Harper Collins.

Shao, G. (2008). Understanding the appeal of user-generated media: a uses and gratifications perspective, Journal of Internet Research, 19, 7-25.

Sproull, L. & Kiesler, S. (1991). Connections. New ways of working in the networked organization. Cambridge: The MIT Press.

Sternstein, A. (2006). Web 2.0 for feds. Retrieved from: http://www.fcw.com/print/12_43/news/96857-1.html, 8 March 2011.

Tapscott, D., Williams, A.D. & Herman, D. (2008). Government 2.0: Transforming Government and Governance for the Twenty-First Century. New Paradigm, January 2008, 1-25.

Uslaner, E. M. (2002). The moral foundations of trust. Cambridge: Cambridge University Press.

Van der Heijden, H. (2003). Factors influencing the usage of websites: the case of a generic Portal in the Netherlands, Information & Management, 40(6), 541–9.

Van Dijk, J. (2006). The Network Society, Second Edition. London: Sage Publications.

Albert Jacob Meijer et al.

Vedder, A. & Wachbroit, R. (2003). Reliability of Information on the Internet: Some Distinctions, Ethics and Information Technology, 5, 211-5.

Vigoda, E. (2002). From responsiveness to collaboration: Governance, citizens, and the next generation of public administration, Public Administration Review, 62(5), 527-40.

Wright, B.E. & Pandey, S.K. (2010) Transformational Leadership in the Public Sector: Does Structure Matter? Journal of Public Administration Research and Theory, 20 (1): 75-89.

Zinger, J. T., Blanco, H., Zanibbi, L. & Mount, J. (1996). An Empirical Study of the Small Business Support Network; The Entrepreneurs' Perspective, Canadian Journal of Administrative Sciences / Revue Canadienne des Sciences de l'Administration, 13(4), 347-357.

Is e-democracy more than democratic?
An examination of the implementation of socially sustainable values in an e-Democratic processes

Gustav Lidén

Department of Social Sciences, Mid Sweden University, 851 70 Sundsvall, Sweden

gustav.liden@miun.se

Originally published in Electronic Journal of e-Government Volume 10 Issue 1 (2012) http://www.ejeg.com

Editorial Commentary

E-democracy is a pillar of e-Government. It is often claimed that ICT can increase citizens' participation, thus fostering democracy. However, Lidén's chapter argues (on the basis of empirical research) that e-democracy can be effective only where there is already democracy. In other words, the use of ICT alone cannot itself transform the relationship between government and citizens. What is needed to make e-democracy effective, is its integration within a system of values, for instance the values of sustainable development. In fact, by considering three e-democracy projects in several Swedish municipalities, the paper shows that adding a socially sustainable perspective to e-democracy provides adequate opportunities for analysing social development, without losing the qualities desired in a democratic society. Whereas what Lidén's contribution considers a sort of 'evolution' of democracy toward e-democracy,

Litvinenko's chapter discusses the possibility of considering e-democracy as a radical transformation of democracy. Litvinenko discusses the case of the success of the "Pirate Party" in Germany, which she considers as setting a new round of the discussion concerning the reform of representative democracy in accordance with the new age of social media. If e-democracy is considered as an evolution of democracy, then the use of ICT can be considered as a way to improve traditional democracy by making it more participative. If e-democracy is considered as a new form of democracy instead, completely new problems must be addressed concerning the meaning of democracy and representativeness.

Abstract: A growing literature tries to contribute to a more balanced view of the concept of e-democracy. However, one seldom discussed aspect is the concept's inadequate dimension on what a desirable development of society consists of. By adding certain values, today most pronounced in the theory of social sustainability, this article examines the awareness of such in three e-democratic projects in Swedish municipalities. This is carried out through a qualitative inquiry that uses different types of data and that regards social sustainability as an ongoing process that is suitable to be analysed in relation to other structures in society. The empirical part reveals different important topics. First it shows that the consciousness of socially sustainable values varies between the examined cases. Second, this variation can be due to both the varying success of e-democracy and to conditions inside the political organizations. In conclusion, this paper reveals that the consequence of adding a socially sustainable perspective to e-democracy is that it provides adequate opportunities for analysing social development without missing out qualities that are desired in a democratic society.

Keywords: e-democracy, social sustainability, democratic theory, political participation, political equality, Sweden

1. Introduction

A buzz word since the 1990s, e-democracy has been embedded in a great variety of positive values. The use of information and communications technology (ICT) in democratic processes is said to provide the potential to strengthen participation (Clift, 2003) and deliberative processes (Barber, 2003) and even result in a total transformation of the balance of power in favour of a plebiscitary public (Coleman, 2007). Particular examples of e-democratic projects show how citizens can get involved in everything from budgetary processes (Miori and Russo, 2011) to how local communities

work with an integrated strategy of concentrating administrative and business services with participatory features on the web (Komito, 2005). However, a growing literature is critical to the unbalanced view of the effects of
e-democracy (e.g. Hindman, 2009; Kampen and Snijkers, 2003; Ward and
Vedel, 2006), and out of this arises a field that states that the notion of e-
democracy is insufficient for society in many ways. This description is in
line with calls for for e-democracy to be complemented with other values,
founded on a normative idea of what a desirable development is. Building
on this idea of a 'good society' (Dahl, 1989), this article argues that values
other than those found in the theory of e-democracy must be searched for
and emphasized in our understanding of this concept.

Theoretically this study is based on the idea of a required relationship between democratic theory and e-democracy. Although traditionally this
connection is not necessarily assumed in e-democratic theory, it has begun
to be called for in the literature (Macintosh et al., 2009). However, as has
been argued above, more normative claims, neither emphasized in the
general democratic theory nor in the e-democratic theory, also need to be
initiated in an understanding of e-democracy. This is because of their ability to point out a desirable development. Today, such values are most
stressed in the theory of social sustainability and when introduced they
can give a wider understanding of such a development. To examine this,
this article studies how socially sustainable values are reflected on in the
work with e-democracy in three Swedish municipalities. The purpose is
thereby to examine awareness of social sustainability in some examples of
e-democratic projects by answering the following question: Has social sustainability contributed to the development of e-democracy in line with
what can be said to be a desired development towards a 'good society',
and if so how has it done so? Associated with this question is the importance of reflecting upon explanations to the potential variation in the
awareness of social sustainability in such development processes.

There are several reasons for relating e-democracy to the perspective of
social sustainability. In the extensive democratic theory several minimalistic perspectives are presented on democracy: democracy is the method for
arriving at political decisions taken by representatives elected by the people (Schumpeter, 1994); democracy is a political system which supplies
regular constitutional opportunities for changing the governing officials
(Lipset, 1959); and democracy is a political system where groups compete

for power and where power holders are elected by the people (Vanhanen, 1997). These ideas are in accordance with the rather constricted view on democracy that is favoured in the liberal tradition. The essential weakness of such definitions is the exclusive focus on the institutional arrangement for distributing political power and the role of these power holders. Although these are core functions in a democratic society, such types of definitions, electoral ones, miss out crucial dimensions (Diamond, 1999; Tilly, 2007), for example the protection of human rights and the maintenance of civil liberties. The same is true of definitions of e-democracy, which are often just as minimalistic. Deriving from Dahl (1989), and even if the concept of a 'good society' is more than blurred, it seems reasonable to argue that e-democracy also needs to be complemented with additional values. If dimensions deduced from social sustainability are added to e-democracy we seem to get closer to the idea of an ideal society.

2. A theoretical framework

The theoretical framework will be divided into three parts. First, e-democracy is theoretically determined and defined. Second, social sustainability is described and related to democracy. Third, the approach in this article will be specified in relation to the two theories and their common denominator, creating a unified framework for the empirical research.

2.1   e-Democracy

In retrospect, much of the research carried out on e-democracy must be characterized as quite empirical and case-orientated. Explicitly focusing on e-democracy, it should be noticed that the concept can be approached from several different perspectives: different e-democratic processes (van Dijk, 2000; Grönlund, 2009; Vedel, 2006); different variations of an e-democratic political system (van Dijk, 2000; Päivärinta and Sæbø, 2008; Åström, 2001); explanations of a successful e-democracy (Carrizales, 2008; Norris, 2001) and different features in e-democracy (Breindl and Francq, 2008; Oates, 2003). There are, though, some important contributions in particular that add theoretical leverage to the understanding of e-democracy. The point of departure in this article is based on an obvious relationship between a political system and its virtual variants (Macintosh et al., 2009; Norris, 2001) and sets the direction for how e-democracy should be analysed. As argued by Norris (2001: 107) an e-democratic system will mirror the traditional political system. A consequence of this fact is that an e-democracy cannot by itself be totally democratic if the political system in which it is embedded is not democratic either (Lidén, 2011). This idea has, however, been excluded in contemporary research and needs to be considered, resulting in distinct claims about e-democracy that underline the importance of civil and political rights.

Deriving from the aforementioned, an instrumental perspective of e-democracy provides the best possibilities both for a comprehensive theoretical understanding and for analytical purposes (Vedel, 2006). Choosing this approach, which is consistent with much of the earlier research literature, provides several advantages. First, it allows analysis of both the context and the consequences of e-democracy. This is due to the possibility of dividing the phenomenon into different processes as exemplified by Vedel (2006) and others (van Dijk, 2000; Grönlund, 2009). Second, it highlights the fact that besides sustaining democratic principles e-democracy is not about contents, but rather about procedures. Based on this the following definition will be applied in this article: *e-democracy is constituted from the possibility of the usage of ICT in political processes concerning information, discussion and decision-making and in addition includes these being permeated by the political and civil rights that are characterized as democratic.* I now turn to discuss social sustainability.

2.2   Social sustainability

Social sustainability must be understood in accordance with at least two influencing factors. First of all, it must be noticed that social sustainability is one part in the much discussed paradigm of sustainable development. Hence, if we want to understand social sustainability its relations with other aspects of a sustainable development cannot be ignored. Second, social sustainability is a concept that is a vital part in the contemporary discussion of a successful global development. That means a development that meets the needs of the present without compromising the ability of future generations to meet their own needs (WCED, 1987: 8).

Much of the initial conceptualization of sustainable development is related to the UN body *The World Commission on Environment and Development* (WCED), which in 1987 reported their work in the publication *Our Common Future*. The main point in the report was the statement about the interconnection between ecological, economical and social dimensions. This approach was intensified with the following UN conference on Environment and Development in Rio de Janeiro in 1992. An especially important outcome of the Rio summit was the action plan *Agenda 21* which stresses the importance of sustainable development being considered in relation to local actors (Olsson, ed., 2005).

Sustainable development has clearly become an important topic in the global political discussion (Sneddon et al., 2006). Elaborating on a scientific perspective on sustainable development is, however, more problematic. Several scholars (e.g. Lélé, 1991; Tikjoeb, 2004) have emphasized the obstacles that appear when an attempt is made to integrate the concepts into a scientific framework. Léle states that: 'The absence of a clear theoretical and analytical framework, however, makes it difficult to determine whether the new policies will indeed foster an environmentally sound and socially meaningful form of development' (1991: 607).

Turning to focus explicitly on social sustainability, it should be noted that this dimension is often described as the vaguest one of the three. There are several reasons as to why. First, social sustainability demands a different approach to the other two dimensions, mainly because it refers to different analytical levels and reflexivity (Lehtonen, 2004). Further, the sustainable development paradigm has been much ignored by social scientists and has not been fully developed (Becker et al., 1997). However, constructing a sound theoretical framework based on definitions of social sustainability can hopefully compensate for this blurry situation. In Lidén (2011) a typology is created that allows for a separation between different perspectives on social sustainability. Arguing that the concept can be divided both through a distinction between analytical and normative qualities and between a view upon it as a condition or a process, four alternative perspectives emerge:

- **A normative condition** is a perspective of social sustainability that indicates a desirable order for a society. One example of this is suggested by Littig and Grießler (2005) when they state that social sustainability is a quality of societies which satisfies an extended set of human needs and fulfils claims of justice, human dignity and participation.

- **A normative process** has a stronger focus upon the situation of societies as changeable. One significant example is given by Polèse and Stren (ed., 2000) who stress the ability of policies and institutions to integrate different groups and cultural practices in a just and equitable way. Such a normative claim is logically related to a procedural viewpoint, pointing to the possibility for societies to develop.

- **An analytical condition** moves a step away from normative claims of what social sustainability should lead to, to a focus on its relationship with structures in society and related concepts. From Bramley et al.'s (2006) two dimensions regarding social sustainability can be identified. First, the authors recognize both an individual and a collectivistic perspective on equality in the distribution of social justice. This can be related to their notion of a society's ability to be viable and functional. Second, and in a more operative sense, social sustainability is related to ideas about social capital, social cohesion and social exclusion.

- **An analytical process** develops this perspective by adding a progressive feature (Becker and Jahn ed. 1999; McKenzie, 2004), focusing on how development of societies can be socially sustainable. An example of how such a goal is met is given by McKenzie (2004) specified in nine goals. With a similar approach Becker and Jahn (ed., 1999) identify three analytical perspectives of social sustainability. Two of them are relevant here, regarding how social patterns and political dimensions are essential in shaping a sustainable society.

This typology is one way of increasing the clarity of the concept. Having pronounced this framework some clarification is needed. Studying the development of e-democracy in some of the Swedish municipalities, importance will be attached to the perspective of viewing social sustainability as a process, admitting that the scope of social sustainability in a social context can never be static. In addition, the analytical dimension of the concept is preferred, creating a focus on the phenomenon's relationship with structures in society and similar social concepts. As have been seen (Becker and Jahn ed., 1999; Bramley et al., 2006; Littig and Grießler, 2005; McKenzie, 2004; Polèse and Stren ed., 2000) social sustainability has been related to several positive values, e.g. cohesion, equality, justice, human dignity, fulfilment of needs, protection of culture and political participation. Of course, a selection of these sub-entities must be carried out. In the literature equality and participation seem to be two of the most frequently attached values. Based on this the operative definition of social sustainability in this contribution will be the following: *A society which in its development process strengthens the elements of political equality and political participation.*

2.3   Using social sustainability to evaluate e-democracy

To be able to apply social sustainability to e-democracy the democratic relevance of the concept must be extracted. Beginning with official statements found in *Our Common Future* the WCED proclaims the importance of political decision-making based on the idea of the subsidiarity principle, which shapes the possibility of citizens' participation. An institutional landscape is necessary, though, to make sustainable changes possible (WCED, 1987). However, social sustainability and democracy can be related to each other in a more analytical way. One example is given by Sachs (1999: 27), who claims:

> *A strong definition of social sustainability must rest on the basic values of equity and democracy, the latter meant as the effective appropriation of all the human rights – political, civil, economic, social and cultural – by all the people.*

Following Sachs, democracy seems to be necessary for the existence of social sustainability. Other scholars (Littig and Grießler, 2005; McKenzie, 2004) present similar arguments, stating that political participation is closely related to both social sustainability and democracy. More precisely, the qualities that democracy has potential to lead to, e.g. inclusiveness, participation and justice in political and civil rights, are though not described as sufficient for social sustainability. Scholars argue (Magis and Shinn, 2009; Schmitter and Karl, 1991) that not even democracies are societies where needs are always fulfilled, participation widespread and equality reached.

The e-democratic research in this area, with its focus on participation and equality, is nowadays quite vast. A suitable review of this literature starts with the meta-analysis carried out by Boulianne (2009). Deriving from 38 earlier studies, she implies that technology could stimulate political par-

ticipation but at the same times raises questions concerning the mechanisms and magnitude of such effects. Contemporary research is divided
when it comes to socially sustainable values of participation and equality.
Norris (2003) and Dunne (2010) argue that if participation increases
through e-democracy it will merely strengthen inequality through additionally stimulating participation among those who are already interested
in political and societal questions. Others have argued (Barber, 2003) and
empirically illustrated (Christensen & Bengtsson, 2011; Taewoo, 2012) that
the lower barriers to access that ICTs bring can activate social groups of
citizens that have previously been more or less excluded from politics. In
the discourse of equality several other aspects are pronounced. Micro perspectives have shown that some resources, such as income and education,
not only determine traditional political participation but also this type of
engagement using ICT (Best & Krueger, 2005; di Gennaro & Dutton, 2006),
creating an unequal participation. The important distinction between being
able to speak and being heard (Fuchs 2010; Hindman 2010) has, moreover,
been attached to this discussion.

Summing up to create theoretical foundations for the empirical analysis
some concluding points should be made. Contemporary literature clearly
shows that democracy and social sustainability can be related. Since I have
argued previously that democracy and e-democracy are social phenomena
that are theoretically and empirically linked to each other, an analytical
approach relating social sustainability and e-democracy appears to be le-
gitimate. In other words, an e-democratic society that, through its development, strengthens political participation and political equality is more
closely related to the notion of a 'good society' and closer to the ideal of
democracy. Additionally, previous research is inconsistent on the question
of how e-democratic processes are permeated with socially sustainable
values. Since it is hard to make any assumptions based on this, a more inductive approach will be used where the empirical results will take the
lead.

3. Method
By examining the Swedish case, this article tries to address the weaknesses
of previous research. Sweden is interesting since it is in the lead when it
comes to characteristics related to information societies (Webster, 2006)
and its local authorities have a mandate to work out their own local public

e-democratic processes. Of the 290 Swedish municipalities, Ockelbo, Älvkarleby and Ovanåker have been chosen. Two principles have guided the selection of cases. First of all they reflect different levels of e-democracy as it has been measured in Lidén (2011). Deriving from this study, e-democracy was measured in accordance with the given definition from the 'supply-side', i.e. the occurrence of functions concerning political information and discussion on municipalities' websites that made it possible to order municipalities according to their level of e-democracy. Ockelbo reflects a low level of e-democracy, Älvkarleby an intermediate level and Ovanåker a high level. As argued by Gerring (2007: 100), the variation in this aspect gives some advantages and for this study it will be crucial when it comes to analysing the awareness of values related to social sustainability. Second, in all other aspects the municipalities are selected on the precondition of having maximal similarities, resembling Mill's method on agreement (Mill, 2004). For example, the three municipalities all have a small number of inhabitants, are located in the same regional context and have a comparable history as industrial communities.

This study employs a qualitative methodology, specified through semi-structured interviews and analysis of official documents. Regarding the interviews, the local councillors have been interviewed to provide data that reflect the political will. Further, civil servants that are responsible for or associated with e-democratic work have also been interviewed, reflecting the local administration. During the ten interviews the relation between e-democracy and social sustainability has been addressed through several thematically ordered questions. In line with the definition of social sustainability, the guiding question has been: *have you consciously worked to ensure that the e-democratic functions of the municipality stimulate political participation* and/or *are characterized by political equality.* Each interview lasted between 35 and 60 minutes and was recorded and transcribed. Official documents have complemented the interviews, creating the possibility of triangulating both data and different perspectives, since interviews represent different positions in the organization (Yin, 2003).

The strategy for transferring the used theoretical framework into methods for analysis can be summarized in several steps that are outlined for answering the research question. As given by the presented concept of social sustainability, this article will define it as processes that strengthen political equality and political participation. The theoretical framework for this

analysis will be based on a perspective where the work with social sustainability is an enduring matter and not static (Becker and Jahn ed., 1999;
McKenzie, 2004). This needs a temporal variation where the chain of
events can be reconstructed chronologically (Gerring 2007). Therefore the
collection of data in the selected cases represents information collected
over several years the analysis of it compounds different material. Moreover, social sustainability will be analysed in relation to other structures in
society claiming that this work has to relate to established cultures and
social hierarchies (Bramley et al. 2006; Becker and Jahn ed., 1999). Meth-
odologically this will be assured by allowing a collection of a rich and thick
empirical material through interviews and documents, but also by establishing a strong connection between theory and method. The latter has to
do with the argumentation above, where democracy and social sustainability are presented as concepts that it is possible to relate to each other. All
in all this not only provides triangulation of data but also create a cohesive
model for analysis that includes different important perspectives.

4. Findings: three Swedish municipalities

A few earlier examples of in-depth studies exists concerning how Swedish
municipalities use e-democratic processes in their relation with citizens
(e.g. Grönlund, 2003; Ranerup, 1999; Öhrvall, 2002). Likewise a few studies
examine the socially sustainable aspects of e-democratic projects (e.g. Bailey, 2009; Lombardi and Cooper, 2009; Maier-Rabler and Huber, 2010). The
empirical part of this paper will try to contribute to this research by exploring how social sustainability has contributed to a desired development.

Some relevant variables for the three cases are presented in table 1. As
argued above, the three municipalities reflect the whole range of the level
of e-democracy, from the most undeveloped to the most successful. In
accordance with the criteria for selection they are, though, similar when it
comes to potential influencing variables. Their population size is in all three
cases small, way below the national average of more than 30 000 inhabitants. Consistent with significant research in political science (Diamond and
Morlino ed., 2005; Putnam 1992), political participation, in this example
quantified through the measurement of voter turnout, could reflect the
quality of both democracy and the local political culture. The national average for the latest parliamentary elections was 84.6 per cent, and it is
shown that two of the municipalities are below this value. However, a cau-

tious assumption could be made of this determinant influence for Ovanåker's level of e-democracy. The level of the average income is presented in the last column. All three municipalities are below the national average of 264.7 thousand Swedish crowns annually per adult citizen. I will now discuss the findings from the three cases in turn.

Table 1: Descriptive statistics of selected cases

Case	Level of e-democracy	Population size (2011)	Voter turnout (2010)	Average income (2010)
Ockelbo	Low	5907	81.7	243.5
Älvkarleby	Intermediate	9089	80.9	256.0
Ovanåker	High	11 404	84.8	239.6

Source: Statistics Sweden (2012); Swedish Elections Authority (2012).

4.1   Ockelbo: low level of e-democracy

The small community of Ockelbo is situated in the middle of Sweden within a commutable distance north from the regional centre Gävle. Ockelbo has one of the lowest values of e-democracy found in Sweden. (It should be added that this website was changed in January 2010. This strengthens the municipality's level of e-democracy somewhat. This study is however based on the earlier version). The official website has few functions that provide citizens with relevant political information. The exceptions were that the budget and the calendar for the municipal council's meetings could be found on the website. No functions that involved citizens in discussion or decisions processes as described by Vedel (2006) were to be found on the website.

On the subject of social sustainability, Ockelbo has, in an explicit way, worked with these types of questions in the local development project 'Ett hållbart Ockelbo' (a, b) for several years. The social dimension has been important throughout this project and has been expressed partly by a focus on citizens' participation and a bottom-up perspective by involving citizens in the local development of the municipality. This is analogous with the relation between democracy and social sustainability that Sachs (1999) and Magis and Shinn (2009) have emphasized, though it seems quite unclear to what extent this has actually influenced the development process of the internal work with e-democracy. The local councillor even states that stimulating citizens' involvement in political matters so far has not been a priority area. The employers of the administration do, however, emphasize that the importance of a participatory perspective has been omnipresent during recent years when working with e-democracy. But more pragmatically the functions directly stimulating participation are more advanced and a phase further on (personal interview, 9 September 2010). However, it is quite obvious from interviewing the administration staff that a desirable e-democracy demands vital communication channels between the municipality and the citizens.

Turning to political equality, the local council does not distinguish between what is done online and the regular democratic work in the municipality. At the same time it argues that political information and participation online should only be considered as a complement to the official website. In the words of the head of the municipalities' administration: 'publishing things on the website is not the same as then assuming that everyone is then aware of that information' (personal interview, 9 September 2010). The question of how inclusive this e-democracy is cannot be described as current in the local dialogue. A plausible reason for this is that Ockelbo, according to several of the respondents, is described as a municipality where the space between the ordinary citizen and the political leadership is small (personal interview, 9 September 2010). Although this says nothing much about the distance created by or the inclusiveness of the online channels, interpreting this as a situation where an awareness of political equality is salient seems distant.

Summing up, social sustainability has been a discussed topic over the years in Ockelbo. As reported, this perspective has been important in developing a plan for local development but has not evidently embedded the e-democratic development process in the same way. Undoubtedly, traces can be identified from the idea of social sustainability, mostly through a low level of awareness, but these cannot be described as dominating ideas. Most significant are the values of social sustainability found at the imple-menting level in the administration.

4.2   Älvkarleby: intermediate level of e-democracy

Älvkarleby is located in the middle of Sweden, about 20 kilometers south from the regional centre Gävle. The overall level of e-democracy in the municipality has been described as intermediate. More exactly, several functions regarding political information are shown on the website. Among others, protocols from the city councils and general information about the political situation can be found. Citizens can interact with decision-makers via the website by accessing the contact information of some leading politicians, and there is a function enabling citizens to submit complaints and opinions. In other words, the website both provides information and facilitates discussion processes (Vedel, 2006).

Turning to the possible awareness of social sustainability when it comes to e-democracy, the interviews create solid material. Both representatives of the political leadership and the administration show awareness of how the website can contribute to a growing political participation. During the last few years effort has mainly been put into providing relevant and current information, with the aspiration that it will create a foundation for participation. One of the employers at the local administration has formulated this ambition as follows: 'Some information also encourages participation in a second stage' (personal interview, 9 June 2010). Concerning the quality and type of information, the person in charge of presenting political information has a clear viewpoint. The cost of publishing pre-existing written documents, e.g. protocols, on the website is negligible and therefore it is an inexpensive method that possibly strengthens participation. However, more explicit functions for increasing interactivity are often more expensive and time-consuming and can result in the need for legal considerations (personal interview, 24 May 2010), for example in web streaming of council meetings and in web based diaries. One can, though, reflect upon the need for specific efforts to strengthen participation that are both indirect, through information, and direct, through a participatory function and inexpensive solutions.

Regarding political equality as a way to achieve social sustainability, it must be interpreted that the municipality has a clear understanding of the importance of continuously reflecting upon these questions, as has been discussed in the literature (Becker and Jahn, 1999; McKenzie, 2004; Polèse and Stren, 2000). The local councillor and the people in the administration that are responsible for the practical questions about e-democracy show a clear consciousness of inequality of access to e-democratic functions but also a bias in the actual willingness to take part in the local political development (cf. Norris, 2003; Dunne, 2010). Linking the uneven distribution (based on age) in the local council to a similarly uneven distribution concerning usage of e-democratic functions, the secretary of the municipality emphasizes the importance of complementing online information with physical information (personal interview, 24 May 2010). This awareness represents an understanding of a general structural problem, but the reference to this as merely a generation gap is simplified (van Dijk, 2005). However, it is obvious that the question of political equality is on the agenda, acknowledged both by the political leadership and the administration, and access to the information society, not just alternatives to it, is facilitated by the municipality.

In conclusion, socially sustainable values have been reflected upon in the work on the e-democratic process in Älvkarleby. The interviews must be interpreted as political participation, and equality is a dimension that has been considered in this work. This is partly to do with the respondents' natural way of discussing social sustainability and similar concepts.

4.3   Ovanåker: high level of e-democracy

The municipality of Ovanåker is located in the interior part of the middle of Sweden. In relation to Ockelbo, Ovanåker is situated about 50 kilometers further north. The overall level of e-democracy in Ovanåker is high. Of the examined functions, a majority can be found on the official website. Functions that are lacking concerning access to the municipality's diary through the website and information about incoming complaints and opinions.

In relation to the other two municipalities, in one way, Ovanåker has a more elaborated perspective on political participation. The local councillor claims that participation is essential; however, without the relevant information participation will not be stimulated (personal interview, 15 April 2010). The representatives of the administration develop this argumentation, referring to the fact that democratic functions and more administrative tasks can be coped with more efficiently online. Regarding this ambition to date, the head of the administration states the objective is: '... to make this communication into the municipality more effective and to make routines more effective so that we will have more time to meet the local citizens' (personal interview, 15 April 2010). In other words, the goal of e-democracy is not only to stimulate participation through online channels but also to create resources to be used in the ordinary way of maintaining a dialogue with the inhabitants. This view of e-democracy as a way of

achieving efficiency has not been found elsewhere. According to the literature (Becker and Jahn ed., 1999; McKenzie, 2004), a more genuine wish for
participation should be interpreted as more socially sustainable.

The reflection about political equality is somewhat blurred in the case of
Ovanåker. The interviews give different descriptions of the awareness of
political equality in the process of e-democracy. One of the respondents
representing the administrations says, however, that this question has
been up for discussion. The topic discussed was that participation in the
information society can reinforce a class barrier and can exclude significant
sections of the citizenships (personal interview, 15 April 2010). This understanding results in a view of e-democracy as a complement to the traditional opportunities for citizens to take part in the political process and it
can also be associated with the analytical dimension of social sustainability
that includes the importance of social hierarchies (Becker and Jahn, 1999).
Moreover, this should not be regarded as the same as coping with the digital divide, but merely a way to create an alternative to the information
society. An empirical investigation that verifies the importance of this
working method is the result of an online survey that Ovanåker carried out
in 2009 aimed at its youth. Concerning political equality this survey shows
that a majority of the respondents feel that they have few or no possibilities to influence the decision-makers. Further, few of the respondents use
the municipality's website as a channel to present their opinions
(Ovanåkers kommun, 11 June 2009). In other words, Ovanåker has examined the topic of political equality in the municipality. Even if the results
among the youth are discouraging the problem has at least partly been
identified.

To sum up, in many ways, over time Ovanåker presents a pragmatic view
on social sustainability. The use of e-democracy is not only based on its
one intrinsic value but also in accordance with the practical effects it can
have on the administration. The ideas of strengthening political participation and equality are also to be found in the discussion regarding the e-
democratic processes in Ovanåker.

4.4   Discussion: three cases of e-democracy
The three examined cases highlight important similarities but also crucial
differences in the awareness of social sustainability in relation to e-

Gustav Lidén

democracy. Answering the research question will be facilitated if there is a discussion first about those aspects that in some way indicate similar patterns among the cases. The ambition of supplying citizens with adequate political information seems to be evident in all three cases. In Ockelbo, this has been described as the initiating stage, and representatives from the other two municipalities, even if they have a more developed e-democracy, also stress this dimension. This stage of development is verified by the applied theoretical foundation (Vedel, 2006) where more explicit forms of participation, i.e. discussion and decision-making, follow. In accordance with their higher value of e-democracy, Älvkarleby and Ovanåker have some functions of strengthening participation. The interviews do, however, show that to a certain degree these are strongly related to economic costs, where the implementation of such functions often has expensive consequences (Andersen, Henriksen and Secher, 2007; Carrizales, 2008). In short, not just democracy but also a socially sustainable e-democracy is costly. The lack of interest in these questions that has been identified in research from a British context can, however, not be verified (Kolsaker and Lee-Kelley, 2009). Rather, civil servants give an enthusiastic impression and have contributed to the work of strengthening participation and thereby letting e-democracy be influenced by socially sustainable values. Also when it comes to the issue of political equality similar tendencies can be found. All the municipalities have representatives that are quite clear about the fact that online information needs to be complemented with physical alternatives. In addition, the three examined municipalities provide the view that questions of equality need to be addressed in the whole political system and that the understanding of it in an e-democratic context is constituted of a spillover from the democratic system, as argued earlier by Sachs (1999).

Turning to aspects where apparent differences can be found, some points can be listed. Ockelbo has evidently worked with socially sustainable questions in other areas. The fact that its e-democracy is not especially characterized by such values can, however, most reasonably be related to its development of e-democracy. In other words, it seems irrational to attach socially sustainable values to something that almost does not exist. However, just an awareness of social sustainability is a strong advantage since the emphasis of continuous implementation of such values is exactly what the theory stipulates (Becker and Jahn, 1999; McKenzie, 2004). In both Älvkarleby and Ovanåker, socially sustainable values have contributed to the development of e-democracy. On the topic of political equality they, analysed together, display a desirable development. Representatives of the administration of Älvkarleby mainly address this as a question of willingness and age, saying that access to the internet and participation in the information society are strongly related to these variables. This contradicts the positive statement proposed by Barber (2003) that expects a positive outcome from new technology. One of the respondent employed at the municipality of Ovanåker discusses this in relation to a more traditional explanation of political exclusion, namely social position. Integrating these perspectives would have given the best possibility of addressing political equality. Differences between age groups clearly exist but they are complemented with influences from social indicators such as education, income and occupation (van Dijk, 2005; Norris, 2001, 2003). The actual status of the willingness to participate is more complex and can be understood both as influenced by other explanations and as an important factor influencing them. The relationship is probably reciprocal. To sum up, Älvkarleby and Ovanåker have some analytical dimensions in the understanding of political equality in e-democracy, but seem to lack important ones.

5. Concluding remarks

This article has clarifiedthat the awareness of social sustainability varies between e-democratic projects. The research question can thereby be answered. However, the potential explanations of the variation in the awareness of social sustainability should also be discussed.

First of all we can see a variation between the three municipalities where Ockelbo has let socially sustainable values have an impact of the development on e-democracy to a lesser extent than the other two cases. As argued above, the municipalities of Älvkarleby and Ovanåker have articulated an awareness that can clearly be traced. The empirical examination shows that the level of e-democracy is not a necessary condition for considerations of social sustainability, since the emphasis on political participation and equality in democratic processes through ICT are at least as high in Älvkarleby as in Ovanåker. One must therefore search for other explanatory variables. Earlier research has implied that socioeconomic variables (Medaglia, 2007), population size (Lidén, 2011) and civic engagement (Norris, 2001) can have a positive relationship with e-democracy, and contemporary theorizing (Maier-Rabler and Huber, 2010) argues that a sustainable e-democracy requires educated and skilled citizens that can be a part of such a society. With a focus on political organization, research has shown the importance of economic resources (Andersen, Henriksen and Secher, 2007; Carrizales, 2008) and commitment (Kolsaker and Lee-Kelley, 2009) for e-democracy. Several structural factors could be of importance. With citizens that are well educated and interested in politics, they are likely to participate more and so there is an increasing in the chances of them influencing the e-democratic processes and simultaneously social sustainability in regard to participation. When it comes to equality in such processes, the answer is harder to find since none of the discussed determinants takes into account the distribution of resources. Awareness and a strategy for neutralization of political inequality, as found among some of the municipalities, must be regarded as crucial. To conclude, the consequence of adding a socially sustainable perspective to e-democracy it that it provides better opportunities to evaluate social development without the risk of ignoring qualities that are essential for a desirable direction when it comes to the use of ICT in democratic processes.

Acknowledgement

I would like to thank Katarina L Gidlund, Anders Larsson, and Katarina Giritli-Nygren for valuable comments on earlier drafts of this manuscript.

References

Andersen, K. V., Henriksen, H. Z. and Secher, C. (2007) 'Cost of e-participation: the management challenges', *Transforming Government: People, Process and Policy*, vol. 1,no. 1, pp. 29-43.

Bailey, A. (2009) 'Issues affecting the social sustainability of telecentres in developing contexts: A field study of sixteen telecentres in Jamaica', *The Electronic Journal on Information Systems in Developing Countries*, vol. 36, no. 4, pp. 1-18.

Barber, B. R. (2003) *Strong Democracy: Participatory Politics for a New Age*, Berkeley: University of California Press.

Becker, E. and Jahn, T. (ed.) (1999) Sustainability and the Social Sciences: A Cross-Disciplinary Approach to Integrating Environmental Considerations into Theoretical Reorientation, London: Zed Books.

Becker, E., Jahn, T., Stiess, I. and Wehlin, P. (1997) *Sustainability: A Cross-Disciplinary Concept for Social Transformations*, MOST Policy Papers 6, United Nations Educational, Scientific and Cultural Organization, Paris.

Best, S. J. and Krueger, B. S (2005) 'Analyzing the representativeness of internet political participation', *Political Behavior*, vol. 27, no. 2, pp. 183-216.

Boulianne, S. (2009) 'Does internet use affect engagement? A meta-analysis of research', *Political Communication*, vol. 26, no. 2, pp. 193–211.

Bramley, G., Dempsey, N., Power, S. and Brown C. (2006) 'What is "social sustainability", and how do our existing urban forms perform nurturing it?', the Planning Research Conference, London, April 2006.

Breindl, Y. and Francq, P. (2008) 'Can Web 2.0 applications save e-democracy? A study of how new internet applications may enhance citizen participation in the political process online', *International Journal of Electronic Democracy*, vol. 1, no. 1, pp. 14-31.

Carrizales, T. (2008) 'Critical factors in an electronic democracy: A study of municipal managers', *Electronic Journal of e-Government*, vol. 6, no. 1, pp. 23-30.

Christensen, H. S., and Bengtsson, A. (2011) 'The political competence of internet participants', *Information, Communication & Society*, vol. 14, no. 6, pp. 896–916.

Clift, S. (2003) E-Democracy, E-Governance and Public Net-Work.

Coleman, S. (2007) 'E-democracy: The history and future of an idea', in: Mansell, R., Avgerou, C., Quah, D. and Silverstone, R. (ed.) *The Oxford Handbook of Information and Communication Technologies*, Oxford: Oxford University Press.

Dahl, R. A. (1971) *Polyarchy: Participation and Opposition*, New Haven: Yale University Press.

Dahl, R. A. (1989) *Democracy and Its Critics*, New Haven: Yale University Press.

Diamond, L. (1999) *Developing Democracy: Toward Consolidation*, Baltimore: John Hopkins University Press.

Diamond, L. and Morlino, L. (ed.) (2005) *Assessing the Quality of Democracy*, Baltimore: John Hopkins University Press.

van Dijk, J. (2000) 'Models of Democracy and Concepts of Communication', in: Hacker, K. L. and van Dijk, J. (ed.) *Digital Democracy: Issues of Theory & Practice,* London: Sage.

van Dijk, J. A. G. M. (2005) The Deepening Divide: Inequality in the Information Society, Thousand Oaks: Sage.

Dunne, K. (2010) 'Can online forums address political disengagement for local government?', *Journal of Information Technology & Politics*, vol. 7, no. 4, pp.300-317.

Ett Hållbart Ockelbo – projektbeskrivning, (a).

Ett Hållbart Ockelbo: Slutrapport av projektet till Länsstyrelsen Gävleborg, (b).

Fuchs, C. (2010) 'Class, knowledge and new media', *Media Culture and Society*, vol. 32, no.1, pp. 141–150.

di Gennaro, C. and Dutton, W. (2006) 'The internet and the public: Online and offline political participation in the United Kingdom', *Parliamentary Affairs*, vol. 59, no. 2, pp. 299-313.

Gerring, J. (2007) *Case Study Research: Principles and Practices*, Cambridge: Cambridge University Press.

Gustav Lidén

Grönlund, Å. (2003) 'Emerging electronic infrastructures: Exploring democratic components', *Social Science Computer Review*, vol. 21, no. 1, pp. 55-72.

Grönlund, Å. (2009) 'ICT is not participation is not democracy – eParticipation development models revisited' in: Macintosh, A. and Tambouris, E. (ed.) *Electronic participation: First International Conference, ePart 2009 Linz, Austria, September 2009 Proceedings*, Berlin: Springer.

Hindman, M. (2009) *The Myth of Digital Democracy*, Princeton: Princeton University Press.

Kampen, J. K. and Sninjkers, K. (2003) 'E-democracy: A critical evaluation of the ultimate e-dream', *Social Science Computer Review*, vol. 21, no. 4, pp. 491-496.

Kolsaker, A. and Lee-Kelley L. (2009) 'Singing from the same hymnsheet? The impact of internal stakeholders in the development of e-democracy', *Electronic Journal of e-Government*, vol. 7, no. 2, pp. 155-162.

Komito, L. (2005) 'e-Participation and governance: Widening the net', *Electronic Journal of e-Government*, vol. 3, no. 1, pp. 39-48.

Lehtonen, M. (2004) 'The environmental – social interface of sustainable development: capabilities, social capital, institutions', *Ecological Economics*, vol. 49, no. 2, pp. 199-214.

Léle, S. M. (1991) 'Sustainable development: A critical review', *World Development*, vol. 19, no. 6, pp. 607-621.

Lidén, G. (2011). *Från demokrati till e-demokrati: En jämförande studie av demokratiutveckling i det moderna samhället* [From democracy to e-democracy – A comparative study of the development of democracy in the modern society] Dissertation: Mid Sweden University, Sundsvall.

Lipset, S. M. (1959) 'Some social requisites of democracy', *American Political Science Review*, vol. 53, no. 1, pp. 69-105.

Littig, B. and Grießlers, E. (2005) 'Social sustainability: A catchword between political pragmatism and social theory', *International Journal of Sustainable Development*, vol. 8, no. 1-2, pp. 65-79.

Lombardi, P. and Cooper, I. (2009) 'The challenge of the e-Agora metrics: the social construction of meaningful measurements', *International Journal of Sustainable Development*, vol. 12, no. 2/3/4, pp. 210-222.

Macintosh, A., Coleman, S. and Scheeberger, A. (2009). 'eParticipation: The research gaps', in Macintosh, A. and Tambouris, E. (ed.), *Electronic Participation*, Berlin: Springer.

Maier-Rabler, U. and Huber, S. (2010) 'Sustainable e-participation through participatory experiences in education', *eJournal of eDemocracy and Open Government*, vol. 2, no. 2, pp. 131-144.

Magis, K. and Shinn C. (2009) 'Emergent principles of social sustainability', in Dillard, J., Dujon, V. and Kling, M. C. (ed.), *Understanding the Social Dimension of Sustainability*, New York: Routledge.

McKenzie, S. (2004) 'Social sustainability: Towards some definitions', *Hawke Research Institute Working Paper,* Series no. 27, University of South Australia.

Leading issues in e-Government Volume 2

Medaglia, R. (2007) 'Measuring the diffusion of eParticipation: A survey on Italian local government', *Information Polity*, vol. 12, no. 4, pp. 265-280.

Mill, J. S. (2004). System of Logic: Ratiocinative and Inductive Being a Connected View of the Principles of Evidence and the Methods of Scientific Investigation, Whitefish: Kessinger.

Miori, V. and Russo, D. (2011) 'Integrating online and traditional involvement in participatory budgeting', *Electronic Journal of e-Government*, vol. 9, no. 1, pp. 41-57.

Norris, P. (2001) Digital Divide: Civic Engagement, Information Poverty, and the Internet Worldwide, New York: Cambridge University Press.

Oates, B. J. (2003) 'The potential contribution of ICTs to the political processes', *Electronic Journal of e-Government*, vol. 1, no. 1, pp. 31-39.

Olsson, J. (ed.) (2005) *Hållbar utveckling underifrån*, Nora: Nya Doxa.

Ovanåkers kommun, *Ungdomsdialog: Enkätresultat,* 11 June 2009.

Personal interviews, conducted 9 September 2010 in Ockelbo, 15 April 2010 in Ovanåker and 24 May 2010 and (on the telephone) 9 June 2010 in Älvkarleby.

Polèse, M. and Stren, R. (ed.) (2000) *The Social Sustainability of Cities: Diversity and the Management of Change*, Toronto: University of Toronto Press.

Putnam, R D. (1992) *Making Democracy Work: Civic Traditions in Modern Italy*, Princeton: Princeton University Press.

Päivärinta, T. and Sæbø, Ø. (2008) 'The genre system lens on e-democracy', *Scandinavian Journal of Information Systems*, vol. 20, no. 2, pp. 51-82.

Ragnerup, A. (1999) 'Elektronisk debatt i kommunal politik', in: *IT i demokratins tjänst*, Statens Offentliga Utredningar 1999:117.

Sachs, I. (1999) 'Social sustainability and whole development: Exploring the dimensions of sustainable developmet', in Becker, E. and Jahn, T. (ed.) (1999) *Sustainability and the Social Sciences: A Cross-Disciplinary Approach to Integrating Environmental Considerations into Theoretical Reorientation*, London: Zed Books.

Schmitter, P. C. and Karl, T. L. (1991) 'What democracy I... and is not', *Journal of Democracy*, vol. 2, pp. 67-73.

Schumpeter, J. A. (1994) *Capitalism, Socialism & Democracy*, London: Routledge.

Sneddon, C., Howarth, R. B. and Norgaard, R. B. (2006) 'Sustainable development in a post-Brundtland world', *Ecological Economics*, vol. 57, no. 2, pp. 253-268.

Statistics Sweden (2012), *Demographic data,* [Online], Available: www.scb.se [20 April 2012].

Swedish Elections Authority (2012), *Election Results,* [Online], Available: www.val.se [20 April 2012].

Taewoo, N. (2012) 'Dual effects of the internet on political activism: Reinforcing and mobilizing', *Government Information Quarterly*, vol. 29, pp. 90–97.

Tikojeb, S. A. (2004) 'Mainstreaming religion in sustainable development: A causal layered analysis', *Journal of Future Studies*, vol. 8, no. 4, pp. 47-60.

Tilly, C. (2007) *Democracy*, Cambridge: Cambridge University Press.

Vanhanen, T. (1997) Prospects of Democracy – A study of 172 countries, London: Routledge.

Vedel, T. (2006) 'The idea of electronic democracy: Origins, visions and questions', *Parliamentary Affairs*, vol. 59, no. 2, pp. 226-235.

Ward, S. and Vedel, T. (2006) 'Introduction: The potential of the internet revisited', *Parliamentary Affairs*, vol. 59, no. 2, pp. 210-225.

WCED (1987) *Our Common Future*, Oxford: Oxford University Press.

Webster, F. (2006) *Theories of the Information Society*, Oxon: Routledge.

Yin, R. K. (2003) *Case Study Research: Design and Methods*, Thousand Oaks: Sage.

Åström, J. (2001) 'Should democracy online be quick, strong or thin?', *Communications of the ACM*, vol. 44, no. 1, pp. 49-51.

Öhrvall, R. (2002) *Det digital torget – en studie av kommunala debattforum på internet*, Demokratins mekanismer, Rapport nr. 1, Uppsala Universitet.

Social Media Applications in e-Government: A Risk Assessment Approach

Seyed Amin Mousavi[1] and Elias Pimenidis[2]

[1]University of East London, London, UK

[2]Department of Computer Science & Creative Technologies, Faculty of Environment & Technology, University of the West of England, Bristol, UK

s.a.mousavi@uel.ac.uk
Elias.Pimenidis@uwe.ac.uk

Originally published in The Proceedings of the European Conference on e-Government (2014) Ed. Elexandru Ionas, ACPIL, pp180-188.

Editorial Commentary

Mousavi's and Pimenidis's research looks at social media in e-Government. The increased acceptance and usage of social media applications warrant that governments use these applications to communicate with citizens. However, the use of these applications needs to be carefully considered, therefore the authors highlight some of the risks and benefits of social media in e-Government. This is important because early risk detection could result in opportunities for government to improve service delivery.

Abstract: Social media is increasingly being used in electronic government. Furthermore, recent research has shown that social media can facilitate transparency and democratization of government processes. Stakeholder and citizen participation is one of the major requirements for successful implementation of electronic governments. Social media applications can support governments in encouraging

195

and empowering their citizens and stakeholders in successful e-Government delivery. Social media such as social networking services, blogs, microblogs and wikis, have proven their capability in attracting and serving a wide range of users. Many researchers have studied how social media applications can be used to serve different positive purposes, such as offering business opportunities or providing e-services. On the other hand, many researchers have studied the negative impacts of social media usage in organisations, such as their impact on productivity and cross-cultural communication, and the fact that they giving rise to new types of security, trust and privacy issues. However, governments are expanding their adoption of social media applications to fulfil various promises, such as user participation and user convenience, efficiency, transparency and improved trust. Therefore, identifying new benefits and addressing the current and emerging risks in using social media applications should be a prime concern of practitioners and researchers in the electronic government field. This paper discusses the goals of electronic governments that can be served by social media; it also explores how such media can transform governance systems. Furthermore, this work highlights the potential risks and benefits derived from using social media to reach different stakeholders and communicate with users of electronic government services. To this effect, the authors propose a risk assessment approach that would maximize the benefits of utilizing social media in e-Government delivery.

Keywords: e-Government, social media, risk assessment

1. Introduction

Currently, social media sites account for a high share of internet traffic, and internet users are spending more and more time on such sites. Moreover, these types of activities on a network of networks are considered convenient and fashionable, and provide a universal form of communication. This paper proposes a risk assessment approach for using social media applications in electronic government. Analysing the capability of social media in its various forms is an essential step in using the power of social media to achieve electronic government goals. Social media's functionality and the specific strength of its different forms support the management of existing opportunities and threats in adopting them in the public sector.

This paper has five sections: after this introduction section, the second section reviews the objectives of electronic governments that may be served by using social media; the third explores the latest statistics on the purposes, uses and capabilities of social media websites; the fourth section concerns the risks and benefits of social media in electronic governments;

in the penultimate section we review the three main concerns and look into the capabilities of social media sites and the possible threats to them; finally, the conclusion discusses a risk assessment approach.

2.   Electronic Government goals and objectives

As governments seek to achieve their goals and objectives by adopting existing ICT facilities, the current diffusion of social media has shown its capability in providing a number of tools and approaches to support making electronic government goals a reality. E-Government objectives cover a range of activities, such as providing greater access to government information, providing digital services, promoting civic engagement and offering development opportunities. Successful utilization of electronic governance requires effective use of information and communication technologies by citizens, businesses, and government officials which can improve and streamline any activity requiring government involvement.

Any governmental use of ICT facilities is based on defined relationships between stakeholders of electronic governments. Although there are different ways of categorising two-way relationships between e-Government stakeholders, as shown in Figure 1, most researchers have classified these relationships into three basic groups: G2G, G2B and G2C.

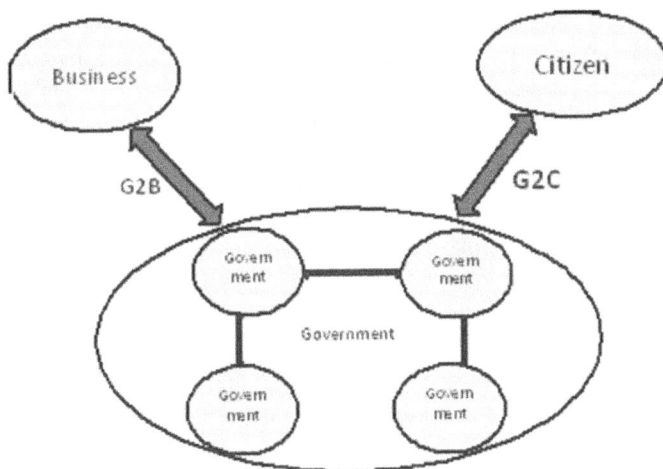

Figure 1: Basic relationships between electronic governance stakeholders

However, social media is mostly used to facilitate B2B, B2C and C2C communication; investigating the common factors between these two relationship groups can lead to the identification of tools and applications that can support the enhancement of e-Government relationships.

3. Social media sites (SMS)

Social media's primary aim is to enable social interaction amongst its users. Social media as internet-based applications facilitate, generate and share content, and exchange information, knowledge and ideas, between participants in a social network. In terms of creating and exchanging user generated content, social media utilises some of the technologies and concepts of Web 2.0, as described by O'Reilly (2007). This platform consists of a set of technologies such as microblogs, blogs, Really Simple Syndication (RSS) and Social Networking Sites (SNS). (Kaplan & Haenlein, 2010).

In terms of user generated content and social networking, the most popular social media sites are Facebook, LinkedIn, YouTube and Twitter. (Kuzma, 2010). Based on the findings of the Pew Research Centre, 73% of internet users are using some kind of social networking site. Currently, the social networking platform with the highest number of users is Facebook (Duggan and Smith, 2013). In regards to evaluating the types of users of a social network, and the purposes of their usage, LinkedIn is very successful and thus it achieves its users' trust; this could be due to the level of confidence their users' have in the information provided. Researchers consider the major benefits achieved by LinkedIn to be: information integrity (Barriger 2009), reliable referral (due to the professionally structured orientation of the site), track companies (used by users), employer search optimization and quality connections (Kaplan 2010). On the other hand, this SNS has some risks, namely identity theft, which could occur after a breach in security settings, and use of API, which allows users to synchronize LinkedIn post content with other SNS. In order to mitigate this risk, some research (Anderson 2012) suggests the implementation of strict privacy measures to help distinguish the professional and personal lives of the users. Another risk factor is the collation of large quantities of information about users; this can be misused by cyber criminals or by people with other malicious intentions who wish to attack users or their connections.

Kaplan and Heinlein (2010) conducted a survey on six hundred professionals, and their findings show that, while Facebook is more effective for business to customer (B2C) networking, LinkedIn is the best social media for networking between businesses (B2B). Concurrently, according to Duggan and Smith (2013), the social media website most used by online adults is Facebook (71%) and the second is LinkedIn (22%).

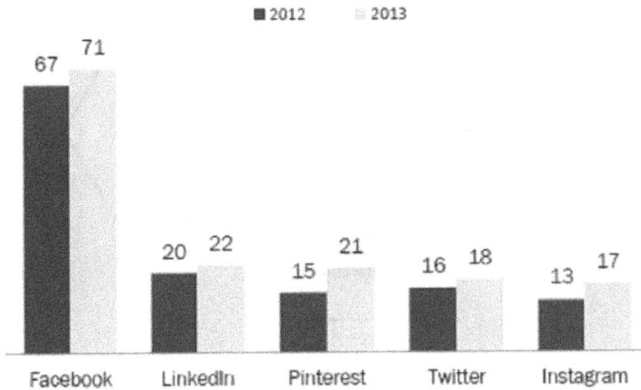

Figure 2: Bar chart showing the percentage of online adults who use certain social media websites in 2012/13 - by Duggan and Smith (2013)

Kietzmann et al. (2011) looked at some popular social media sites, including Facebook, LinkedIn and YouTube, and tried to classify the main social media 'building blocks'. They classified social media functionality into seven blocks; as demonstrated in Figure 3, these blocks are identity, conversations, sharing, presence, relationships, reputation and groups.

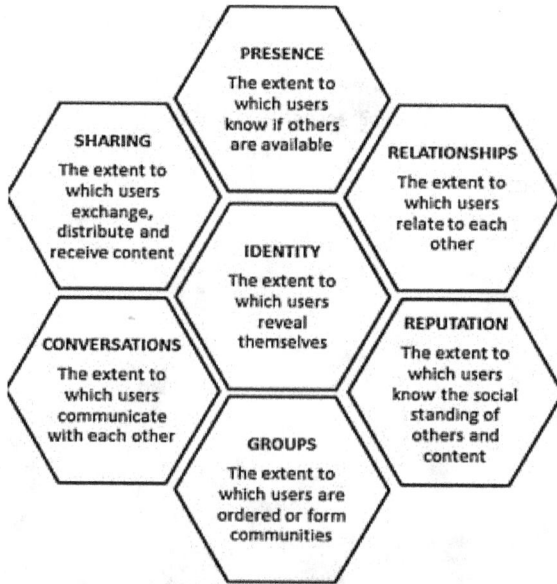

Figure 3: The honeycomb of social media - by Kietzmann et al. (2011)

This honeycomb-like diagram can be used as a key to help understand and utilize different social media sites' functionality and capabilities for serving specific electronic governance requirements. Kietzmann et al. (2011) reveal the argument that, although the studied social media sites cover these seven blocks, different sites focus on different blocks more than others. For example, while Facebook is more focused on managing the structures and individuals within a network of relationships, LinkedIn is more focused on the 'identity block' which is more concerned with data privacy controls and provision of tools for user self-promotion.

4. Risks and benefits of social media in electronic government

Social media in e-Governments is defined as a group of tools, technologies and applications that allow government agencies to improve and enhance their engagement with citizens, businesses and other government agencies, using Web 2.0 concepts. This approach towards social media in e-Government draws attention to the social dimension of Web 2.0 technologies, which emphasize active individual participation on a network by creating, commenting, editing, sharing and rating web content (Chun et al., 2010). These methods of interaction generate a numerous amount of data resources that can by used by the public sector to achieve some of the main goals of electronic government, such as transparency, stakeholders' participation and collaboration. Furthermore, the studies of Mergel (2012) highlight the capability of social media in the public sector to feed dialogues on political issues, enhance democratic and political engagements, and consequently identify existing political and social problems and crowdsource solutions accordingly.

Social media applications in e-Government can be used effectively in the design, delivery and improvement of public electronic services. In order to improve the quality of public electronic services by using social media, the main factors need to be identified and considered; no difference between private and public sector should be ignored in this process. Buckley (2003) argues that, excluding profit orientation, there is no major difference between public and private sectors when it comes to the provision of electronic services. The four main measures of electronic service quality are user satisfaction, reliability, efficiency and privacy. As an example, Buckley (2003) considers click-stream (the determining of how users are drawn to specific electronic services and at what point they exit by tracking access and entry points of the website), return rate of users and total cost per user as measurable criteria. These measures are helpful in the testing phase and help developers identify the shortcomings of provided electronic services. Observing and taking into account the high amount of produced data, and monitoring the manners of interactions between participants may lead to co-production of services and public policies, which can refine public policies and improve the quality of electronic services.

Governments can utilize social media to publish and share government information, targeting citizens, businesses, government employees and other government agencies (Chang & Kanan, 2008), or they can use it to conduct required recruiting activities (Dorris, 2008).

Social media can also be adopted to inform citizens of what governments are doing; this helps breed accountability and transparency (Bertot, Jaeger & Grimes, 2010), which are some of the initial aims of electronic government development. This adoption can serve e-democracy as well, enhancing citizen participation and voting.

Social media can be used by governments for a number of purposes: disseminating information for the audience; sharing information between different governmental bodies; and reaching out to citizens and other users for the purpose of recruiting. Compared to the conventional aim of electronic governments to achieve transparency, trust and efficient business conduction, adopting social media can enhance the participation of communities in the process of decision making (Chun et al., 2010). Therefore, the adopting of social media by governments does not only serve existing goals of electronic government but opens new windows, like enhancing the participation of non-governmental organizations and social communities in the different processes.

As discussed earlier, businesses and citizens are also stakeholders of electronic government; these advantages shouldn't be ignored when adopting social media for electronic government. On the other hand, these promises increase stakeholders' expectations and raise a new risk; while citizens have broader access to information and more tools to participate with, for successful communication there need to be someone on the other side to respond and serve. This means that some additional resources and expertise are required for successful electronic government practice.

Failing to supply these requirements can lead to the citizens' inconvenience and dissatisfaction, which will affect their involvement and participation in required processes. Furthermore, this shortcoming has a negative impact on government accountability, stakeholders' trust and democracy.

Some researchers (Kuzma 2010; Landsbergen 2010; Lacigova et al. 2012) have compared two methods of governments using social media: using popular existing social media sites or creating social government sites. Lacigova et al. (2012) have conducted two European projects on e-participation, and their findings show that utilizing citizens' already preferred media channels has a higher chance of succeeding in engaging people. Moreover, Landsbergen (2010) suggests that the using of existing social media applications by governments is more efficient, both fiscally and in communicating with citizens, than creating a government social networking site. The creating of such aforesaid sites does provide the government with more control over the content and structure, and might reduce concerns about privacy and trust; however, current studies show that creating dedicated websites for this purpose has less chance of succeeding in engaging people.

Kolsaker and Lee-Kelley (2008) found that for successful implementation of electronic government, citizens must be considered at all stages, and failing to engage citizens in this process can lead to isolation and social exclusion of vulnerable members of society. Inadequate approaches of citizen-centric developments may lead to user vulnerability, thus reducing public trust. Carter and Belanger (2004) suggest that trustworthiness is a factor influencing citizen participation in e-Government. Another requirement for successful e-governance is the education and training of users such as government employees and citizens. Addressing these issues is essential for successful citizen participation in electronic government.

The following sections look at these three major areas in more detail. Each section will review the latest research in the corresponding area, and highlight the main potential benefits and risks of social media applications in e-Government.

4.1 Social media contribution to trust

According to Becerra and Gupta (1999) trust in the government refers to the individual's perceptions relating to the ability and integrity of the agency to offer the services. Gefen et al. (2005) recommend that technology adoption is strongly affected by trust in an agency which provides services. In order to develop electronic government, it is essential to build trust between different stakeholders (government agencies, businesses and citizens). Eastlick et al. (2006) argues that trust and commitment are central mediating agents of any online relationship between different entities and Tan and Theon (2001) note that an integral part of adopting electronic government is trust. Thus, the need for building trust between governments and other stakeholders of e-Government is considered a fundamental principle of designing, developing and using e-Government systems.

The emerging global use of social media can cultivate trust, as well as increasing the vulnerabilities of its users. As discussed in section 4, there are more dimensions to the users' vulnerability, such as the observing and monitoring of their behaviour. However, looking into the comparatively successful practice of social media such as LinkedIn (section 3) highlights the key points in achieving the users trust.

Failure to build trust may lead to failure in obtaining citizen participation. Jahankhani and Varghese (2004) discuss three types of trust: process-based trust, characteristic-based trust and institutional-based trust. These three types of trust need to be addressed: in process-based trust, citizens draw from at their past experiences with particular government agencies; in institutional-based trust, citizens look at the accountability of the particular government agencies; and in characteristic-based trust, citizens judge the quality of service that they can get online.

Social media sites such as Twitter can be used very effectively to gain the trust of participants. Twitter can be used primarily to understand the core needs of electronic government stakeholders. Furthermore, public service providers can use the 'tweet' and 'retweet' actions which encourage their citizens' e-participation and highly affect their trust.

Zucker (1986) regards institutional-based trust as a predictor of electronic service adoption; this form of trust refers to the individual view of the institution, and includes regulations and structures which make an environment feel safe.

Teo and Liu (2007) argue that the concept of trust is crucial because it affects a number of factors which are essential for online transactions. They concluded that trustworthy relationships must be developed between different associated parties. There are other associated concepts regarding trust, such as security and privacy. Privacy in the context of e-Government can be considered as protecting personal information that is collected by the government and its agencies. Consumers having privacy concerns, i.e. losing control over their personal information, will weaken their relationships with businesses and has a definitive effect on whether they go online to conduct any relations or not (Parasuraman and Zinkhan, 2002). Dutton (2005) argues that exchanging citizen information for services provided by electronic governments is the cause of the debate about trust. Dutton (2005) also found that collecting data about citizens can raise concerns over the misuse of data, and therefore has a negative effect on trust. On the other hand, absence of the required data will affect accountability and therefore also has a negative effect on trust.

Social media enables government agencies to obtain information on citizens directly but there is a possibility of obtaining information about consumers indirectly by tracking their online activities. This type of information is highly valuable, it can be used for improving government services or it can be sold third parties for commercial purposes. If citizens or businesses don't have confidence in the way that their information will be treated, they will not go online to interact or communicate with government agencies, i.e. they will not trust the new system and therefore the chance of engaging in electronic government transactions will significantly reduce.

Dutton (2005), also suggests that trust in electronic government is significantly affected by the security and privacy of information on citizens, and therefore technological measures such as providing firewalls and authentication systems will contribute to public trust. Adopting social media in e government merges a number of security concerns. As social media includes communication between two parties on a third party platform (SMS), the risk of cloning profiles, inserting malware into government portals and database attack increase (Bertot et al., 2012, Danchev, 2013). Moreover, the advancements in social engineering have been advantageous to social media by instating it as a global and popular communication platform. Therefore, additional measures need to be in place to protect participants and electronic government infrastructures.

Another factor which plays a considerable role in participants' trust is the type of services that they might apply for; findings of a study conducted by Brooks et al (2008) in two local authorities in the UK show that regardless of their concerns over privacy and security, citizens are more willing to vote online as compared to any other electronic services which requires an exchange of data. On the other hand, even when authentication measures, and security and privacy laws are in place, groups of people are not willing to pay their council tax online. Ensuring security and privacy of citizens' data, and providing authentication measures enhances the level of trust in electronic government. This indicates that users of electronic government systems in the chosen sample are more concerned about the security of their financial transactions than of their participation the e-voting system.

As discussed above, social media cannot satisfy all the required dimensions of trust but it serves various types of trust, and can be used as a good platform to facilitate users' involvement in electronic government. This enhances acceptance and utilization of provided electronic public services.

4.2   Education and training

As discussed in section 3, one of the requirements for successful e-governance practice is the educating and training of users of the system; consequently, social media websites can be used as a platform for e-learning.

Nichols (2008) has defined e-learning as "pedagogy empowered by digital technology"; Electronic learning involved the online delivery of information for the purpose of training or education. E-learning can provide access to learning in various formats, times, and places, almost completely on the web as a learning environment (Trajkovic et al. 2000).

Online learning centres can be used in government as an infrastructure for online training and education. Boxer and Johnson (2002) suggest that the centre for learning and training must serve as the central point for all government learning activities. On the other hand, government agencies are suffering from a lack of resources and expertise to design, develop and implement relevant courses. Also, different agencies might produce similar courses which can be considered a waste of resources due to the associated labour and licensing costs. Another problem is brought into consideration by Bose (2004), as many agencies are struggling to convene agency mandated and legislative training needs. Therefore, one of the key factors in successful development of e-Government is using an appropriate learning environment and platform, and having an appropriate level of investment in identifying and designing required courses, which enable a wide range of stakeholders with different needs and levels of expertise. Talug (2012) verifies that social networks provide a platform for new prospects and creative learning styles that enable new life-long experiences, collaborations and interactions.

Talug (2012) highlights the potential of social media websites to motive active learning with a high degree of flexibility in time and location for end users. In addition to social media sites like YouTube providing facilities that enable learners to repeat learning, Facebook can be used for wider discussions and interactions on chosen issues. This approach forces governments to concentrate more on designing educational content than defining the structure of the learning environments.

Social media websites can be used as learning platforms which serve all government organisations; citizens can address issues and enable government agencies, as well as other citizens, to benefit from the potential of electronic government.

Furthermore, user registration and training information can be tracked and can be used in addition to users' feedback in planning and managing professional development and training. This information is also helpful for further development and improvement of existing courses. The social media websites can be used to discuss: e-articles and e-books, coaching tips for managers and mentors, streaming videos, internet learning conferences, electronic audio and video, and, information on the government agency values, strategy and duties. This method enables users to find information and courses they need by provided search engines. In order to enhance training and education in electronic government, technology can be utilised in many ways, but the key is to find a balance between the benefits and costs; social media sites have shown their capability in streaming required information in a cost-effective and flexible manner.

4.3   Bridging digital divide

The digital divide has been termed as limited or lack of access to the internet and electronic services. As access improves with infrastructure development, reductions in connectivity costs and increases in bandwidth available, a new notion of the digital divide emerges through the lack of availability of suitable, easy-to-use and useful e-services for the wider public. The advent of new technologies embraced by tech-savvy generations leads to marginalization of those who do not have access, or have access but do not have the means or incentives to utilize it. Mobile systems appear to make the breakthrough in terms of accessibility but the infrastructure has to be provided, and services need to be developed in the context of meeting the users' or citizens' objectives (Pimenidis et al 2011, Buys et al 2008). This amply applies to social media, where usage is mostly facilitated through mobile devices, but their content and services usually suit certain age groups, professions or social communities.

Can social media bridge the digital divide in terms of offering enriched content combined with ease of access? Is the attraction so strong that it can lead to someone that does not use the internet to do so for the single reason of using social media? Zickuhr and Smith (2011) appear to think so, based on their discussion of the data included in "the Pew Internet Project studies" report. By late 2011 social networking sites were used by 65% of all internet users in the USA, including half of all American adults. There was a strong correlation between usage and age, as some 87% of internet users under 30 use these sites, compared with less than a third (29%) of those 65 and older. However, though their overall numbers are still relatively low, older adults have represented one of the fastest-growing segments of the social networking site-using population. This growth, the authors of the report argue, may be driven by several factors including the ability to reconnect with people from the past, find supporting communities to deal with a chronic disease, and connect with the younger generations.

The digital divide is often discussed under a variety of categorizations; these include north-south, developed-developing world, urban-rural, rich-poor and so on. The contemporary divide can take some unusual forms. For example, there exists a divide between those who use the internet and those who could use it but choose not to do so. Another form of divide is between those who are highly sensitive to and those who are indifferent to issues of personal privacy. These two divisions are manifestations of more fundamental factors than a shortage of time, deficiency in technological skills or lack of adequate access to the Internet. Thus, the effectiveness of the use of social media could be affected by the perceived risks inherent in their use.

When a citizen has to deal with the state, transactions have two distinct and important characteristics: firstly, such transactions are often mandatory and secondly, the state is the monopoly provider of the service s/he needs or is obliged to use. In principle, in such circumstances, key public sector values, including equality and fairness, decree that the government cannot force a citizen to use an online service without access to technology, the ability to use it and, perhaps as noted above, support in using it. It may be possible for businesses to offer products and services solely online (and this is increasingly common) but to offer a mandatory government service purely in online form is to discriminate against certain classes of citizens. In practice therefore, even where there is a high quality online service available, as long as there continues to be a digital divide, governments will continue to be obliged to maintain at least one, and possibly several, alternative channels for service delivery. Beneficially though, this might be in terms of bridging the digital divide; the maintenance of services across multiple channels might have considerable impact on cost, coordination and consistency (Ebbers et al, 2008; Janssen et al, 2003; Pimenidis et al 2011). Thus, when considering the various risks that could adversely affect the use and effectiveness of using social media to promote e-Government, one has to consider both voluntary marginalisation or, on the other end of the spectrum, increased costs and degraded performance.

5. In conclusion – a proposed risk assessment approach

From the above sections there appears to be a clear concern that, despite the various benefits that social media can offer, when considering their usage in promoting e-Government services, a thorough risk assessment needs to be performed. This should highlight the potential risks and their impact, and could possibly lead to new government initiatives that could turn the threat into an opportunity and open new avenues into enhance services. To do so, the authors propose that a comprehensive approach to risk management should be adopted. This is standard practice in the management of any project and any e-Government initiative should be considered as a long-term project. The risk management approach should comprise the following simple steps:

- Identify risks in terms of their impact and likelihood of occurrence
- Evaluate risks as to how they could affect the efficiency of services or the marginalization of certain user groups
- Explore the option of creating an opportunity out of the threat by developing strategies to engage (mobile networks, free access points for social media)

- Establish review points and mechanisms that would allow the monitoring of risks and to explore the emergence of new risks – e.g. increase in DD due to isolation

References

Anderson, J., and Stajano, F. (2012). Not that kind of friend: Misleading divergence between online social networks and real-world social protocols.university of Cambridge Computer laboratory, 1(1), 1-6.

Becerra, M. & Gupta, A. K. (1999). Trust within the Organization: Integrating the Trust Literature with Agency Theory and Transaction Costs Economics. Public Administration Quarterly, 23(1), 177-203.

Bertot, J. C., Jaeger, P. T., & Grimes, J. M. (2010). Using ICTs to create a culture of transparency: E-Government and social media as openness and anti-corruption tools for societies. Government Information Quarterly, 27(3), 264-271.

Bertot, J. C., Jaeger, P. T., & Hansen, D. (2012). The impact of polices on government social media usage: Issues, challenges, and recommendations. Government Information Quarterly, 29(1), 30-40.

Bose, R. (2004) Information Technologies for Education & Training in E-Government. Proceedings of the International Conference on Information Technology: Coding and Computing, Anderson School of Management, New Mexico.

Boxer, K. M. & Johnson, B. (2002) How to build an Online center. Training and Development, 56, 36-43.

Brooks, L., Weerakody, V. and Agyekum-Ofosu, C. (2008). 'The Role of Trust in E-Government Adoption in the UK', in Proceedings of eGovernment Workshop '08 (eGOV08), Brunel University, London, UK

Buckley, J. (2003). E-service Quality and the Public sector. Managing Service Quality, 13, 453-462.

Carter, L and Belanger, F '(2004) Citizen Adoption of Electronic Government Initiatives, Proceedings of the 37th Hawaii International Conference on System Sciences.USA.

Buys, P., Dasgupta, S., Thomas, T. and Wheeler, D. (2008) Determinants of a Digital Divide in Sub-Saharan Africa: A Spatial Econometric Analysis of Cell Phone Coverage, The World Bank Development Research Group, Sustainable Rural and Urban Development Team, Washington DC, USA.

Chang, A.M., & Kanan, P., K.(2008). Leveraging Web 2.0 in Government, E-Government/Technology Series, IBM Center for the Business of Government, available at http://www.businessofgovernment.org/sites/default/files/LeveragingWeb.pdf Last accessed 5th January 2014.

Chun, S. A., Shulman, S., Sandoval, R., & Hovy, E. (2010). Government 2.0. Making connections between citizens, data and government. Information Polity: The

International Journal of Government & Democracy in the Information Age, 15, 1-9.

Criado, J., Sandoval-Almazan, R., & Gil-Garcia, J. (2013). Government innovation through social media. Government Information Quarterly, 30(4), 319-326.

Danchev, D.(2013). Twitter hacked, 250,000 users affected, ZDNet Newsletters, available at http://www.zdnet.com/twitter-hacked-250000-users-affected-7000010712/

Dorris, M. (2008). Service transformation in government. The Public Manager, 25-28. available at http://www.thepublicmanager.org/journal/docs/tpm_spring2008_special_issu e.pdf

Duggan, M. and Smith, R. (2013), Social Media update 2013 Users, available at http://pewinternet.org/Reports/2013/Social-Media-Update/Main-Findings.aspx Last accessed 3rd January 2014.

Dutton, W., Guerra, G. A., Zizzo, D.J., Peltu, M. (2005). The cyber trust tension in E-Government: Balancing identity, privacy, security. Information Polity, 10(2), 13-23.

Eastlick, M. A., Lots, L. S. & Warrington, P. (2006), Understanding online B-to-C relationships: an integrated model of privacy concerns, trust, and commitment. Journal of Business Research, 59(8), 877-886.

Ebbers W., Pieterson W. and Noordman H. (2009). Electronic government: Rethinking channel management strategies, Government Information Quarterly, 25, 181–201.

Gefen, D., Gregory, M. R., Warkentin, M., and Pavlou, P. A. (2005). Cultural Diversity and Trust in IT Adoption: A Comparison of USA and South African e-Voters. Journal of Global Information Management, 13(1), 54-78.

Jahankhani, H. & Varghese, M. K. (2004). The role of consumer trust in relation to electronic commerce . Paper presented in the Proceedings of the 4th Annual Hawaii International conference on Business. USA.

Janssen M. Wagenaar R. and Beerens J. (2003) Towards a Flexible ICT-Architecture for Multi-Channel EGovernment Service Provisioning, In R. Sprague (ed.), Proceedings of the 36th Annual Hawaii International Conference on System Sciences, Track 5, 148-157.

Kaplan, A., & Haenlein, M. (2010). Users of the world, unite! The challenges and opportunities of Social Media, Business Horizons, 53(1), 59-68.

Kietzmann, J., H., Hermkens, K., McCarthy, I., P., Silvestre, B., S. (2011). Social media? Get serious! Understanding the functional building blocks of social media, Business Horizons , 54(3), 241-251.

Kolsaker, A. and Lee-Kelley, L.(2008), Citizens' attitudes towards e-Government and e-governance: a UK study, International Journal of Public Sector Management, 21(7), 723-738.

Kuzma, J. (2010). Asian government usage of Web 2.0 social media. European Journal ePractice, 9(1), 1-13.

Lacigova, O., Maizite, A., Cave, B.(2012), eParticipation and Social Media: a Symbiotic Relationship?, European Journal of ePractice ·16, ISSN: 1988-625X

Landsbergen, D. (2010). Government as part of the revolution: Using social media to achieve public goals. Electronic Journal of e-Government, 8(2), 135-147.

Mergel, I. (2012). The socialmedia innovation challenge in the public sector. Information Polity, 17, 281-292.

Nichos, M. (2008) E-Learning in context. E-Primer Series [online]. Available at: http://akoaotearoa.ac.nz/sites/default/files/ng/group-661/n877-1---e-learning-in-context.pdf

Oliveira, G., H., M., Welch, E.,W. (2013). Social media use in local government: Linkage of technology, task, and organizational context. Government Information Quarterly 30 (4) 397-405

O'Reilly, T. (2007). What is Web 2.0: Design patterns and business models for the nextgeneration of software. Communications & Strategies, 65, 17-37 (1st Quarter).

Parasuraman, A. & Zinkhan, G. M. (2002) Marketing to and serving customers through the internet: an overview and research agenda. Journal of the Academy of Marketing Science, 30, 286–295.

Pimenidis, E., Iliadis L.S. and Georgiadis C.K. (2011) Can e-Government Systems Bridge the Digital Divide?, In Proceedings of the 5th European Conference on Information Management and Evaluation (ECIME 2011), Dipartimento di Informatica e Comunicazione, Università dell'Insubria, Como, Italy, 8-9 September 2011, pp. 403 – 411

Picazo-Vela, S., Gutiérrez-Martínez, I. , Luna-Reyes, L., F.(2012). Understanding risks, benefits, and strategic alternatives of social media applications in the public sector. Government Information Quarterly 29 (4) 504-511.

Talug D., Y. (2012), Lifelong learning through out today's occasions namely social media and online games, Social and Behavioural Sciences 46 (1) 4431-4435

Tan, Y. & Theon, W. (2001) 'Toward a generic model of trust for electronic commerce. International Journal of Electronic Commerce, 5(2), 61-74.

Teo, T. S. H. & Liu, J. (2007) Consumer trust in e-commerce in the United States, Singapore and China. Int. J. Management Science, Omega, 35, 22–38.

Trajkovic, V., Davcev, D., Kimovski, G. & Petanceska, Z. (2000) Web-based Virtual Classroom. Proceedings of the 34th International Conference on Technology of Object-oriented Languages and Systems,137-146.

Web-based Virtual Classroom," Technology of Object-Oriented Languages and Systems, 2000. TOOLS 34. Proceedings. 34th International Conference on , vol., no., pp.137,146,

Zucker, L. G. (1986) 'Production of trust: Institutional sources of economic structure,1840-1920. Research in Organizational Behaviour, 8, 53-111.

Social Media and Perspectives of Liquid Democracy: The Example of Political Communication in the Pirate Party in Germany

Anna Litvinenko

Free University of Berlin, Germany,

litvinanna@hotmail.com

Originally published in the Proceedings of the European Conference on e-Government (2012)Ed. Mila Gascó, ACPIL. Pp403-407.

Editorial Commentary

This is the case of the 'liquid' democracy advocated by the Pirates in Germany. However, by examining how the concept of liquid democracy works within the Pirate Party, Litvinenko concludes that it is hardly possible to use the 'network' as an instrument of decision making in politics, whereas it could be an effective tool for civil society to set the political agenda and influence the framing of political discourse.

Abstract: The recent success of the Pirate Party in the local elections in Berlin (8,9 percent) as well as their popularity in Germany on the national level (10 percent according to Forsa-palls in October) started a new round of discussion concerning the reforming of representative democracy in accordance with the new age of social media. This paper examines the reasons for the success of the Pirates, in particular their strategies of political communication, and makes conclusions concerning the challenges and prospects of the idea of a liquid democracy. Although among the Pirate-voters protest voting is widely spread, that does not explain the phenomenon of the marginal "Internet-party" gaining a nationwide popularity. Based on both theoretical and empirical research the author claims that it is the new approach to political communication in democracy that makes the party so attractive. The research has addressed social milieus which do not match with the traditional target groups division by age, profession etc. such as "modern performers" and "post-materialists" (Zolleis, Prokopf, Strauch 2010) as well as to meet the expectations of Internet-users, who are used to and who are willing to participate in politics. In their political communication 'pirates' use social media tools which have been already explored and used in political campaigns all other the world, but unlike other parties they do it consequently and authentically (e.g. they manage their own social media presence, which leads to an even greater overlap of the private and public spheres of communication with voters and politicians). This paper examines how the concept of liquid democracy works within the party, showing that the structure of the party itself resembles more of a network then a political institution, which obviously correlates with the trends of the 'network society' (Castells), but at the same time represents the main weakness of the liquid democracy concept: it is hardly possible to control the content of the network and therefore to use it as an ultimate instrument of decision making in politics. It could still be an effective tool for the civil society to set the political agenda and influence the framing of political discourse.

Keywords: social media, Germany, eParticipation, liquid democracy, pirate party, political communication

1. Introduction

The increasing role of the Internet in the political communication in the 2000s gave hope that the democratic potential of the web that Al Gore praised as early as 1994 would develop very rapidly. Indeed, social media tools do make the creation of the deliberative public sphere (Habermas 1989) more realistic than ever. This model presupposes communication in all directions: "one-to-many," "many-to-one," "many-to-many" and "one-to-one." However, in practice it turns out that political elites are in most cases not ready to use this opportunity for the democratization of political communication. For instance, research conducted at the Technical University of Ilmenau (Heimrich 2011) shows that German politicians rarely have dialogue with citizens via the Internet. Only 22% of them respond to online-messages from citizens on social media. Heimrich makes the conclusion that:

> *"unlike in the U.S., where social networks like Facebook are already*
> *established as an integral part of the communication strategy of*

many politicians, in Germany the use of Facebook in politics is still at the stage of beginning. Parliamentarians still very rarely use the key features of the social web (...)" (Heimrich 2011)

2. Social milieus of 'modern performers' and 'post-materialists' ready for fundamental changes in representative democracy

Meanwhile there already exists a considerable group of internet-oriented citizens who are used to online-tools and want to use them to participate in decision-making. This refers to a great extent to the so-called "Generation of Digital Natives" – young people who were born into the digital world (Hawkins, Schmidt 2008). The gap between the ossified political structures, still oriented to the traditional communication and decision-making patterns, and the new needs of the "network society" (Castells 2007, 2010) leads inevitably to social tensions, which we can observe now in different countries, for example in form of the "occupy" phenomenon. Since the early 2000s a declining trust in political elites has been the global trend which, according to Castells (2007), leads to the "processes of counter-power linked to social movements and social mobilization".

The crisis of representative democracy challenges society to search for new forms of political participation and organization. One of the possible answers to this challenge is the concept of "liquid democracy" represented by Pirate Parties in Europe. In this paper we examine the political communication of 'pirates' with the example of German Pirate Party, which is, according to the results of the local elections as well as to the polls of the German Forsa-Institute, the most successful of existing Pirate Parties.

At the Federal elections in Germany in 2009, the Pirate party, founded four years earlier, won 2% of the vote, and in September 2011 they unexpectedly gained 8.9% of the vote in the local legislative elections in Berlin. In March 2012 'pirates' managed to enter the local parliament of Saarland with 7,4% of votes, leaving behind two established parties such as "Alliance '90/The Greens" (5%) and the Free Democratic Party (1,2%). In October 2011, according to the poll of the Institute for Social Research "Forsa" 10% of Germans said they would vote for the 'pirates' if parliamentary elections took place on the respective Sunday. According to a survey conducted by ARD-TV after the local legislative elections in Berlin, the portrait of the typical voter of the Pirate party is rather contradictory ('Piratenpartei klettert auf zehn Prozent', 2011). Quite unexpectedly it was not only the twenty-year-old Facebook-hipsters who voted for the 'pirates', as the survey showed a scale of all age groups. Thus, in the age group from 35 to 44, 10% of Berliners voted for the 'pirates', in the group from 45 to 59 year old - 8%, from 18 to 35 - 16%. The only group, where 'pirates' were not so successful, was that of the people older than 60 years (3%).

This success can, of course, partly be explained by protest voting. According to the head of the "Forsa"-Institute, Manfred Güllner, 'pirates' took over votes from the other parties, because citizens are dissatisfied with the current policy ('Piratenpartei klettert auf zehn Prozent', 2011). According to Güllner, the majority of these protest voters come from the center-left of the political spectrum, but there are also people who traditionally support the libertarian Free Democrats and the conservative Christian Democratic Union. However, the nationwide popularity of this party and the growth of its membership by 40 percent in 2011 cannot be explained only with the protest voting. It is also the new approach to politics aimed at its democratization that attracts people.

> *'It is true, that many voters and supporters of the Pirate Party spend a lot of their time online, communicating via social networks (...) and that there are interested in issues of Internet policy. But their discontent with the contemporary politics roots primarily in the feeling that the traditional parties are too far from their world. They require a new political culture. More participation, more democracy.'*
> *(Gathmann, 2011)*

Research carried out on the request of the Hans-Seidel-Foundation shows that pirates appeal to the new target group that has been formed rather recently and can be considered as a product of the developed information society (Zolleis, Prokopf, Strauch, 2010). These are the so-called social milieus of 'modern performers' and 'post-materialists' according to classification of Sinus-Institute in Germany.('Sinus milieus', 2011) The first group is well-educated people, internet-oriented, under 30, with a large number of students and self-employed entrepreneurs among them, who understand themselves as "non-conventional, technological and the cultural elite". The second group, "post-materialists", represents creative industry; they are intellectuals, for whom freedom is more important than security and who fight against ossified bureaucratic structures. These people, Internet-oriented and therefore rather influential in the digital public sphere did not, until now feel themselves represented by any political party. This fact inter alia explains on one hand their low participation in traditional democratic procedures such as elections and on the other hand their claims for more direct democracy and their engagement in the anti-elite movements such as "Occupy".

3. A New type of political party challenges the traditional political spectrum

Since the foundation of the Pirate party in 2006 experts have been trying in vain to determine its position on the political spectrum: this party does not seem to fit into the traditional 'left-right' framework (Hofmann, 2011). The analysis of the profiles of the party leaders shows that they have strikingly different backgrounds. For instance, the chairman of the party, Sebastian Nerz, was formerly a member of the conservative Christian Democratic Party; a deputy of the Berlin Parliament changed to the 'Pirates' from the Green Party; some of the leaders are ordinary IT-specialists, others successful entrepreneurs.

As for the political program of the party, it represents traditionally left ideas such as introduction of a basic income for all citizens or free education, as well as typically libertarian ones when it comes to the questions of individual rights (especially freedom of information on the Internet, up to abolishing of the copyright law). One member of the Pirate party, Marcel-Andre Merkle, in his article "We are researchers, not ideologists,"(Merkle, 2011) writes about the necessity to re-think the patterns of political ideologies, "which had been knocked into our heads like Pavlov's reflexes". He argues that economic growth does not necessarily lead to reducing the social sector, freedom does not mean increasing the criminality etc. and points out that the 'pirates' are moving away from traditional ideology, that is also depicted in the title of his article "We are researchers, not ideologists."

Cooperation, knowledge, and communication. Free life. Because the network is based on the main principle (...) [of] network neutrality. "
(Merkle 2011)

Apparently we can observe from the example of the Pirate party the forming of this new type of ideology (it is may be more appropriate to describe it rather as a 'framework for ideas') of the post-Cold-war period, which responds to the crises of traditional political spectrum as described by Schwarzmantel (2011).

The 'pirates' haven't yet determined their position in all the political fields, focusing only on a few domains such as copyright (open access to all sources of information), protection of personal data, reform of the representative democracy (in accordance with the principles of transparency and citizen participation), infrastructure and education. They often emphasize that for them the most important question is not *what* but *how*, meaning that their core aim is to change the whole approach to politics. The party leaders speak less about solutions to the problems, and more about *how* to find solutions within the paradigm of freedom, which is the key concept of the 'pirates' (Merkle 2011).

This 'ideological' vacuum is often criticized by political opponents of the party and is seen as a threat to the political party system in Germany (Spitz 2011). But on the other hand, this approach to the political spectrum seems to be a viable alternative to the conventional one and meets the needs of the new social milieus described above; internet-oriented individualists who want to customize their political views. This means, as Jakob Augstein, the editor-in-chief of the magazine "Freitag" puts it, that they want to make decisions depending on the political field and on depending on each specific case whether they are 'left' or 'right', or they could be 'green' for issues on education or 'conservative' when it comes to road building. It is the 'collective mind' of the key members of the party that according to this concept can find the optimal solutions in each specific case. The instability of such a system is being criticized by its opponents, but this seems to be ay the same time its strength. As Prof. Peter Kruse of the University of Bremen says, creativity relevant to the modern complex society can only expand in an unstable and uncertain environment of a network that permanently provokes its participants to create new ideas. (Kruse über Kreativität, 2007).

4. Political communication of the Pirate Party

The communication policy of the Pirate Party, both internal and external, is based on the maxim "more participation, more democracy." For communication with citizens they use more or less the same tools and platforms as the conventional parties, e.g. Facebook, Twitter, blogs, sites. In addition they have a "piratewiki" project, which is an open platform, where everybody can contribute to the political deliberative process, as well the whole scope of "pirate-media", such as online-magazine "Flaschenpost" or the Internet-radio.

As for the strategies of online political communication they follow the core rules which were refined during the leading-the-way campaign of Barack Obama in 2008, i.e a presence on all popular social networking sites and in the blogosphere, combining online and offline activities, merging of private and public spheres, making content that goes viral, creating a strong horizontal network of supporters, who would attract the new ones among their friends.

According to several recent studies (Heimrich 2011; Knaut 2010), the majority of the German parties use interactive tools in their online-communication rather ineffectively, they still perceive political communication mostly through the model "one-to-many". Thus, only about a quarter of the Bundestag deputies (23%) have an official profile on Facebook, and only one-third (36%) of them use this profile to talk to the citizens regularly (several times a week). Only 22% of politicians respond to the posts of the citizens on Facebook (Heimrich 2011).

The main reason for the underdevelopment of online-communication of political parties in Germany in comparison to the political online-communication in the USA is in our opinion the difference in political systems: in Germany the political parties do not depend on donations from citizens as they do in the US. As a consequence, the German parties do not seem to have enough motivation to use all the possibilities of social media tools.

Unlike other German parties, the 'pirates' do take advantage of all the interactive possibilities of the Web. Based on the analysis of the communication of the Pirate party on Facebook conducted in the period from October to November 2011, the following conclusions can be made:

1. The official page of the 'pirates' on Facebook is more popular than that of the major parties: it has about 38 000 subscribers (whereas the ruling CDU has 16 000 subscribers, the second largest party in the country SPD - about 24, 000);
2. The activity of the party in social networks is much higher than that of conventional parties (thus, on the official Facebook-page 3-4 postings a day can be listed, with the amount increasing on special events such as party reunion in early December 2011, when the overage amount was 8 postings a day);
3. Official Facebook accounts of the 'pirates' are highly interactive, with citizens writing dozens of comments and posting their own content on the wall of 'pirates' on Facebook;
4. The political communication of 'pirates' in social networks is highly personalized: they often use informal language and there is even a signature on the postings on the official page, whereas the big parties make this postings completely impersonal, similar to press-releases. A major role in communication is played by the key persons of the party, such as 24-year-old member of the board of the party Marina Weisband or the chairman Sebastian Nerz;
5. Although 'pirates' seek to construct a horizontal and non-hierarchical party structure, they still can't avoid building hierarchies. These hierarchies are based on the unequal distribution of information flaws, where traditional media play a significant role by constantly putting forward the same newsmakers;
6. In their social networks "pirates" often mix personal and public information. They put serious political arguments next to the information about a party they went to yesterday or mentioning that it was cold in the room where a press-conference was held. As result of this merging of public and private spheres, pirates give an impression of being "the guys next door," ordinary citizens, which in turn gives voters more trust in their politics. In the case of conventional politicians as for example Barack Obama in the USA this kind of image is usually being created by PR-people and often gives the impression of being artificial. At the same time similar behavior of the young "Generation Z"-politicians is being perceived as authentic.

5. "Liquid Democracy" and its prospects

In terms of reforming of representative democracy 'pirates' advocate the concept of 'liquid democracy', which nowadays is being developed in many countries. The idea is to give each citizen the possibility to vote on each particular issue: s/he can do it himself or delegate his voice to a person he thinks is more competent in this specific issue. This approach aims to give people more power to really take part in the decision-making process besides going to elections once in four years. This model is however criticized for being inapplicable in huge networks such as the whole nation. Still the Pirate party works on developing this mechanism and is already implementing in their internal decision-making process. On the platform 'liquid feedback' each party member can create a profile where his competencies are shown and can also list the people to whom he delegated his voice on different issues. The chairman of the party is elected by online-voting of all members. In a 'liquid democracy' the decision-making is based on the so-called 'intelligence of the network'.

Some researchers (Zolleis, Prokopf, Strauch, 2010), argue that the Pirate Party functions more as a social network than a political party and consider this to be the weakness of the party structure, which would lead to instability and final collapse. The main problem of managing a network is obviously the fact that one cannot control its content. Consequently it is extremely challenging to use it as a basis for a nationwide decision-making. However, the tools of 'liquid democracy' can in our opinion be successfully used for agenda-building, and for participation of citizens in the framing of political issues.

Thus, the Pirate party can be seen as an ongoing experiment in the field of media democracy. The new generation of politicians is trying to set on the agenda fundamental questions of reforming politics according to the needs of the information society, as the "Green-party" did for the society of 1970s and the 1980s with putting new issues into the public discourse. Political opponents accuse 'pirates' of being "hollow", populist and too technocratic in their approach to democracy (Spitz 2011, Dreier 2011). But even critics acknowledge that "they have already changed the politics" (Gathmann 2011), making another parties also deal more intensively with the challenges of the information age.

References

Castells, M. (1996–1998, revised 2010). The Information Age: Economy, society, and culture. (Vols. 1–3). Oxford: Blackwell.

Castells, M. (2007). Communication, Power and Counter-power in the Network Society. Retrieved October 15, 2011, from http://ijoc.org/ojs/index.php/ijoc/article/view/46/35

Edelman Capital Staffers Index 2011: Digitale Medien sind heute politische Kommunikationsrealität" [online] http://www.edelman-newsroom.de/edelman-studien (accessed on 1 December 2011)

Dreier, C. (2011) . „Was ist von den Piraten im Abgeordnetenhaus zu erwarten?" [online] 22.10.2011 - http://wsws.org/de/2011/sep2011/pira-s22.shtml (accessed on 29.09.2011)

Facebook-Euphorie verflogen – Deutsche Politiker setzen kaum auf Wähleransprache via Facebook" [online] http://www.tu-ilmenau.de/pr/nachrichtenarchiv/einzelnachricht/newsbeitrag/6653/

Gathmann, F. (2011) „Gegenangriff der Möchtegern-Piraten [online] http://www.spiegel.de/politik/deutschland/0,1518,792502,00.html (accessed on 25.11.2011)

Habermas, J. (1989). The Structural Transformation of the Public Sphere: An Inquiry into a Category of Bourgeois Society. Cambridge: Mass, MIT Press.

Hawkins P., Schmidt L. (2008). ‚Gen Z: digital natives'. [online] http://www.essentialkids.com.au/entertaining-kids/games-and-technology/gen-z-digital-natives-20080716-3g5p.html?page (accessed 10.10.2011)

Heimrich, L. (2011) Politische Public Relations in sozialen Online-Netzwerken. Eine inhaltsanalytische Untersuchung zum Einsatz von Facebook-Seiten in der Kommunikation zwischen Politikern und Bürgern, [online] http://www.wolfgang-schweiger.de/download/Studie_Facebook-Euphorie.pdf (accessed on 15.12.2011)

Hofmann, N. (2011) „Programm der Piratenpartei Freiheit, die wir meinen" [online] http://www.sueddeutsche.de/politik/programm-der-piratenpartei-freiheit-die-wir-meinen-1.1146146 (accessed on 30.10.2011)

Merkle, M.-A. (2011) „Wir sind Forscher, keine Ideologen" [online]

Knaut, Annette. Politikvermittlung online: Abgeordneter des Deutschen Bundestages im Web 2.0. // Mediendemokratie. Hrsg.Gerhard Göhler, Annette Knaut, Cornelia Schmalz-Jacobsen, Christian Walther. Frankfurt am Main, 2010. S. 17. http://www.heise.de/tp/artikel/35/35721/1.html (accessed on 30.10.2011)

Piratenpartei klettert auf zehn Prozent // http://www.spiegel.de/politik/deutschland/0,1518,792622,00.html (accessed on 10.11.2011)

Piraten: Partei oder Posse, talk-show „Augstein und Blome" [online] http://www.youtube.com/watch?v=ZR4T5U8A64w (accessed on 15.11.2011)

Prof. Peter Kruse über Kreativität (2007) [online]
http://www.youtube.com/watch?v=oyo_oGUEH-I&feature=youtu.be (accessed
on 09.01.2012)

Sinus Milieus [online] http://www.sinus-institut.de/loesungen/sinus-milieus.html
(accessed on 02.10.2012)

Spitz, M. (2011) „Die Piraten machen es sich leichter", [online]
http://www.spiegel.de/politik/deutschland/0,1518,791683,00.html (accessed
on 11.10.2011)

Schwarzmantel, J. (2008) Ideology and Politics, Sage Publications Ltd, London.

Zolleis U., Prokopf S. and Strauch F. (2010) Die Piratenpartei. Hype oder Herausfor-
derung für die deutsche Parteienlandschaft? Hans-Seidel-Stiftung, München.

Evolution Roadmaps for Smart Cities: Determining Viable Paths

Leonidas Anthopoulos and Panos Fitsilis

Technological Education Institute (TEI) of Larissa, Larissa, Greece

lanthopo@teilar.gr
fitsilis@teilar.gr

Originally published in the Proceedings of the European Conference on e-Government (2013) Eds Walter Castelnovo & Elena Ferrari, ACPIL, pp27-35.

Editorial Commentary

"Smart cities" is an important theme that is becoming more and more popular in public opinion, thanks to the interest of the media. As Anthopoulos and Fitsilis point out in their contribution, "smart cities" involve many important topics such as e-Government service delivery, e-service adoption, smart growth, social networking, living labs. The authors show that behind the appeal of the "smart city" (and related) concepts, there are many complexities affecting their successful development. Based on a review of the literature and using a technology road-mapping technique, the authors identify different typologies of "smart cities" and different evolution paths for "smart cities." Their analysis shows that not all "smart city" approaches are ideal for urban areas, since various parameters could determine the precise direction toward which a particular "smart city" must evolve. Deciding which evolution path to follow is the task of municipal decision makers, which means that city governance should take centre scene, that all too often has been left to technology alone.

Abstract: Smart cities have emerged for more than twenty years from their primary website form to modern ubiquitous and environmental sensitive ones and they encounter an extensive number of representative cases, with an international spread. Today they are considered living labs, areas of smart growth and favorable e-Government environments, while they structure a modern and globalized market with a raising and competitive industry. Various alternative approaches to smart city can be observed, which appeared and have evolved during this timeline. These approaches have attracted various and significant cases, which either evolved to other forms or they later declined. This paper recognizes these different smart city approaches and their evolution, and it seeks to answer the following questions: what different approaches to smart city exist or have existed? How have the smart cities evolved? Do particular evolution roadmaps exist for smart cities? In order to answer these questions, this paper presents a worldwide smart city classification, which describes all the alternative approaches that appear in literature and determines representative city cases together with similarities and differences among these approaches. Literature review is combined with data from an investigation of the official websites of the representative cases, which returns groups of e-services that are being offered by different smart city approaches. These e-service groups are used to identify evolution roadmaps for smart city that can show how smart cities have emerged and to which particular directions are being evolved. The evolution roadmaps are depicted via technology roadmapping tool. Moreover, these roadmaps can become a useful tool for municipal decision makers, who have to choose between evolution forms and smart city projects that secure smart city's viability. Viability is a crucial parameter for every project, especially due to recent financial recession, since smart cities concern extensive and demanding investments, which affect large communities and local life in a significant manner.

Keywords: Smart cities, technology roadmapping, e-Government, digital cities, e-services, geographies, ubiquitous technologies

1. Introduction

Various terms have been used to describe the application of the Information and Communications Technologies (ICT) and the deployment of various e-services in the urban areas (Anthopoulos and Vakali, 2012): *web* or *virtual, broadband, wireless* or *mobile, digital, smart* and *ubiquitous* cities are only some of these terms. Moreover, terms such as *knowledge spaces, virtual* or *digital communities* extend the physical urban limits and describe groups of citizens who distantly share virtual spaces for a common reason.

No commonly agreed "umbrella" term can be found in the literature to describe this "booming" phenomenon of the abovementioned metropolitan ICT environments, while the *digital city* and the *smart city* ones are the most usual. For the purposes of this paper the term *smart city* will be used to describe all these alternative terms. Smart cities are crucial because, they deal with important state-of-the-art topics i.e., e-Government service delivery, e-service adoption, smart growth, social networking, living labs etc.

Various cities around the world have approached the smart city. Each of them usually faced different challenges and prioritized alternative objectives, such as improvement of local everyday life; development of knowledge-based societies; narrowness of the digital divide; and promotion of e-Government locally (Anthopoulos and Vakali, 2012). Others emphasized on the enhancement of e-commerce services and on local growth, while recently the environmental protection has been put first on the objectives' list.

The implementation of a smart city is based on sets of projects, which address these predefined priorities and objectives. However, these various smart city cases did not keep their initial forms and they have updated – even more than once- to different directions and objectives, a fact that questions the strategic purposes, the effectiveness and the viability of a smart city.

This paper tries to answer the following questions: what different approaches to smart city exist or have existed? How have the smart cities evolved? Do particular evolution roadmaps exist for smart cities? The first question sounds simple, but the appearance of so many different terms that describe the same phenomenon can be confused and the similarities and differences have to be specified. The second question is very interesting, since many smart city cases –i.e., Amsterdam and Barcelona- have changed their approaches even more than twice. and questions rise regarding the reasons that lied behind this change. The third question seeks for answers regarding whether the evolution of smart city approaches is logical and based on technological evolution or it concerns strategic choices and priorities' update.

The remaining of this paper is organized as follows: in the following background section 2 a classification of different smart city approaches is performed. Moreover, representative city cases for each approach are extracted and the evolution of these cases is presented. Then, section 3 structures smart city evolution roadmaps according to the provided e-services. In section 4 this paper's questions are discussed according to the extracted outcomes. Finally, in section 5 some conclusions and some future thoughts are given.

2. Background

In this section, a bibliographic review on smart city is performed and many cities appear to follow alternative approaches. Authors combined literature findings with information from the official websites of the extracted cases in order to explore the current condition of the identified cases (Table 1).

According to (Giffinger et al., 2007) the term smart city is not used in a holistic way describing a city with certain attributes, but is used for various aspects which range from mesh metropolitan ICT environments to a city regarding the education (or smartness) of its inhabitants (Giffinger et al., 2007), (Komninos, 2002). Smart city was originally introduced in the Australian cases of Brisbane and Blacksbourg where the ICT supported social participation, narrowness of the digital divide and accessibility to public information and services. Smart City was later evolved to (a) urban spaces for business opportunities, which was followed by the city network of Malta, Dubai and Kochi (www.smartcity.ae); and to (b) ubiquitous technologies installed across the city, which are integrated into everyday objects and activities.

Moreover, smart city has been approached as part of the broader term of digital city by (Anthopoulos and Tsoukalas, 2006), where a generic multi-tier common architecture for digital cities was introduced and assigned smart city to the software and services layer of this architecture. For the purposes of this article, the term *smart city* will refer to all alternative approaches to metropolitan ICT cases.

An investigative literature review returns eight (8) different smart city approaches and 31 representative city cases, which have evolved since the early '90s and faced different challenges. *Web* or *Virtual City* is the primary smart city form with representatives the America-On-Line (AOL) cities (Wang and Wu, 2001), the digital city of Kyoto (Ishida, 2002), (Ishida et al., 2010) and the digital city of Amsterdam (Lieshout, 2001). This approach concerns web environments, which offer local information, online chatting and meeting rooms, and a city's virtual simulation.

The second approach is the *Knowledge Bases*, which was adopted by Copenhagen and then ex-industrial area of Craigmillar (Edinburgh, Scotland) (Van Bastelaer, 1998). Copenhagen developed a public database entitled Copenhagen Base, which had crowd sourcing options, it delivered local information and it was accessible via the Internet and via text-TV. The case of Craigmillar concerns a Community Information Service, which capitalized the ICT to structure groups of citizens who shared knowledge and collaborated to deal with unemployment and with other local needs.

The city of Seoul introduced the third approach entitled *Broadband City/Broadband Metropolis*, where fiber optic backbones were installed in the city and enabled the interconnection of households and of local enterprises to ultra-high speed networks (Townsend, 2007). Last mile connections to the backbone were established with fiber optic channels (Fiber-to-the-Home, FTTH), composing a flourish environment for telecommunication vendors and for private investments in general. Other cities that can be classified in this category is Beijing (China) (Sairamesh et al. 2004), Antwerp (Belgium), Helsinki, Amsterdam and Geneva (Van Bastelaer, 1998). Antwerp and Amsterdam collaborated and interconnected their broadband networks.

Another approach is the *Mobile* or *Wireless* or *Ambient* Cities, with representatives New York City and Atlanta (Ganapati and Schoepp, 2008)-, which installed wireless broadband networks in the city, accessible (with or without charge) by its inhabitants.

Digital City extends the above approaches and older ones (Moon, 2002) and describes a "mesh" metropolitan environment that interconnects virtual and physical spaces in order to deal with local challenges. Anthopoulos and Tsoukalas (2006) define the digital city as the "ICT-based environment whose priorities concern a) the ICT contribution to local needs and transactions, b) the transformation of the local community to a local information society, c) the direct and indirect, official and unofficial information collection, in order to support the sustainable development of the local community". This approach has been followed by various cities such as Hull (UK), Cape Town (South Africa), Tampere (Finland) and Trikala (Greece).

Smart City approach was described above and is currently fully applicable in Dubai, where the "media city" (www.dubaimediacity.com) and the "internet city" (www.dubaiinternetcity.com) offer broadband and media infrastructures to the enterprises. Other smart city representatives are Barcelona, Austin (USA), Tampere (Finland) and European cities (http://smart-cities.eu, http://www.smartcities.info), which recognize several dimensions of intelligence to which the ICT can contribute: economy (Smart Economy), education (Smart People), governance (Smart Governance), transportation (Smart Mobility), sustainability (Smart Environment) and everyday life (Smart Living). Various ICT vendors (e.g., IBM, Microsoft, Hitachi and Oracle) have implemented commercial solutions for the smart city approach.

Ubiquitous City (u-City) concerns the result of broadband costs' minimization and commercialization of large-scale information systems, cloud services and ubiquitous computing in urban spaces. U-city has representatives New Songdo (Hyang-Sook et al., 2007) (South Korea), Manhattan Harbour and Kentucky (U.S.A.), Masdar city (Abu Dhabi) and Osaka (Japan), where information is accessible anytime, from everywhere by anybody via ubiquitous ICT. In many cases (i.e., in South Korea and Abu Dhabi) this approach is accompanied with the construction of new urban spaces where pervasive computing will is included from the scratch in buildings.

Finally, the *Eco-city* or *Green City* approach capitalizes the ICT for sustainable growth and for ecological protection. ICT sensors for environmental measurement and for buildings' energy capacity's evaluation; smart grids produce energy for inhabitants' consumption; encourage smart solutions for renewable energy production are only some of the eco-city services. This approach has been followed by New Songdo and Dongtan (South Korea), Tianjin (Singapore) and Masdar (Abu Dhabi), while it is being followed by others (i.e., Amsterdam).

Except from the above approaches, various cities joined networks of common interests to provide intelligence about their urban spaces or to structure virtual teams of collaborative people. Eurocities network (http://www.eurocities.org), Intelligent Communities (www.intelligentcommunity.org), the World Foundation of Smart Communities (http://www.smartcommunities.org) and Community Networks (e.g. the Seattle Community Network (http://www.scn.org)) are representative cases.

Table 1: The classification and current status of various smart cities

Approach	Cases: Started – Current Condition

Virtual City	- **America-On-Line (AOL) Cities** (1997- today)
	  Today: City Guides for U.S. cities http://www.citysbest.com
	- **Kyoto**, Japan (1996-2001)
	  Web prototype finished its experiments by September 2001
	  http://www.digitalcity.gr.jp
	- **Bristol, U.K.** (1997- today) http://www.digitalbristol.org/
	- **Amsterdam** (1997- today)
	  It evolved to other approaches (broadband, smart, eco-city)
	  http://www.amsterdamsmartcity.com

Knowledge Bases	- **Copenhagen Base** (1989- today)
	  Today it operates as a city portal http://www.kk.dk and Copenhagen evolved to Eco-City
	- **Craigmillar Community Information Service**, Scotland (1994- today)
	  It operates as a community portal http://www.s1craigmillar.com
	- **Blacksburg Knowledge Democracy**, Australia (2001- today)
	  It evolved to the digital city approach

Broadband City / Broadband Metropolis	- **Seoul**, S. Korea (1997- today)
	  Evolves with 84% broadband penetration, it is expected to reach 1GB web connections by 2012, and it provides with Wi-Fi access its public buildings (Engadget, 2011)
	- **Beijing**, China (1999- today)
	  It has been evolved to digital city, which focused on buildings of the Olympic Games 2008 (Gauggel, 2011), (Qi and Shaofu, 2001)
	- **Helsinki** (1995-today)
	  New e-services' deployment on WLAN infrastructure
	  http://www.hel.fi
	- **Geneva-MAN**, Switzerland (1995 – 2012)
	  It exists and offers broadband connectivity to its inhabitants and local enterprises

Wireless / Mobile / Virtual City	- **New York** (1994- today) Exists offers various e-services http://www.nyc.gov/html/doitt/ - **Kista / Stockholm** (2002- today)

231

Approach	Cases: Started – Current Condition
	Kista has become a thriving Science City and a leader in mobile and ICT development http://en.kista.com - **Florence,** Italy (2006- today) Exists and a charter is documented for future similar developments http://senseable.mit.edu/florence/
Smart City	- **Antwerp**, Belgium (1995- today) Started as Broadband City and today interconnected to Brussels and to Amsterdam (Baeyens, 2008). - **Taipei**, Taiwan (2004- today) It exists and it evolves to eco-city - **Tianjin**, China (2007-today) It exists and it evolves to eco-city http://www.tianjinecocity.gov.sg - **Barcelona**, Spain (2000- today) Exists, http://w3.bcn.es, http://www.bcn.es - **Brisbane**, Australia (2004- today) Exists and limited its scope to local e-Government, traffic and parking services, and on waste management http://www.brisbane.qld.gov.au - **Malta** (2007- today) Continues to connect ICT companies especially in the field of healthcare and education http://malta.smartcity.ae/ - **Dubai** (1999- today) Exists and continues to integrate top ICT solutions - **Tampere** (Finland) (2003-today) It began as a thinking tank for innovative ICT applications. Today it occupies more than 1,000 professionals who develop various e-Services http://www.tampere.fi
Digital City	- **Hull**, U.K. (2000- today) Exists and focused on e-Government, on e-learning and on smart TV (http://www.hullcc.gov.uk) - **Cape Town,** South Africa (2000- today) Exists and offers various e-services such as environmental, for tourism, transportation (http://www.capetown.gov.za) - **Trikala**, Greece (2003- today) Exists and limited its scope to tele-care and to metro-Wi-Fi services (www.e-trikala.gr) - **Austin**, U.S.A. (1995- today) Exists and emerges to Eco-City http://www.cityofaustin.org/ - **Knowledge Based Cities**, Portugal (1995- today) Portals of the digital cities do not meet projects' objectives http://www.cidadesdigitais.pt

Approach	Cases: Started – Current Condition
Ubiquitous City	- **New Sondgo**, S. Korea (2008- today) Under development and evolves to eco-city (Jackson et al., 2011) - **Dongtan**, S. Korea (2005- today) Evolves to eco-city http://www.udongtan.or.kr/ - **Osaka**, Japan (2008- today) Under development (Jackson et al., 2011) - **Manhattan Harbour, Kentucky**, U.S.A. (2010- today) Under development. http://www.themanhattanharbour.com - **Masdar**, United Arab Emirates (2008- today) Under development. http://www.masdarcity.ae
Eco-city	- **Dongtan** S. Korea (2005- today) Evolves to eco-city http://www.udongtan.or.kr/ - **Tianjin (Singapore)**, Under development. Public housing project in the Eco-city and Keppel District Heating and Cooling System Plant http://www.tianjinecocity.gov.sg - **Masdar**, United Arab Emirates (2008- today) Under development. http://www.masdarcity.ae

Moreover, this investigation identified the following types of e-services that have or are being offered by the examined cases (Table 2):

- *e-Government services* concern public complaints, administrative procedures at local and at national level, job searches and public procurement (they are faced in Digital, Smart and Ubiquitous approaches).
- *E-democracy services* perform dialogue, consultation, polling and voting about issues of common interests in the city area (they are offered by Virtual, Digital, Smart and Ubiquitous approaches).
- *E-Business services* mainly support business installation, while they enable digital marketplaces and tourist guides (met in Digital and Smart city approaches).
- *E-health and tele-care services* offer distant support to particular groups of citizens such as the elderly, civilians with diseases etc. (appear in Digital and Smart city approaches).
- *E-Security services* support public safety via amber-alert notifications, school monitoring, natural hazard management etc. (only available in Ubiquitous approaches).

- *Environmental services* contain public information about recycling, while they support households and enterprises in waste/energy/water management. Moreover, they deliver data to the State for monitoring and for decision making on environmental conditions such as for microclimate, pollution, noise, traffic etc. (met in Ubiquitous and Eco-city approaches).
- *Intelligent Transportation* supports the improvement of the quality of life in the city, while it offers tools for traffic monitoring, measurement and optimization (delivered in Digital and Smart city approaches).
- *Communication services* such as broadband connectivity, digital TV etc. (offered by Broadband, Mobile, Digital, Smart and Ubiquitous approaches).
- *E-learning and e-education services* (available in Smart and Digital city approaches).

Table 2: e-services that are being offered by smart cities

Case	Started	e-Services
AOL Cities	1997	Online City Guides, Information from local enterprises
Digital City of Kyoto	1996	GIS information about the city, City Guide, Municipal Transportation, Crowd Sourcing, 3D Virtual Tour
Bristol	1997	Advertising spaces, Connection with citizens personal sites, Public information
Amsterdam	1997	Energy Management, Smart Building, Tele-presence Conference Centers, Grid energy solutions, Sustainable Public Spaces, Sustainable Working
Copenhagen	1989	Local e-Government Services, National e-Government Services, City Guide, e-parking services, Guides for entrepreneurship
Craigmillar	1994	Self-recycle Services, Local online news, Job opportunities in the city, Marketplace for cars and property
Blacksburg	2001	GIS services, Crowd sourcing, MAN, 3D Virtual City model with crowd sourcing options, Broadband services, Online guides and training for entrepreneurs
Seoul	1997	Wired and Wireless broadband internet services, Digital Mobile TV
Beijing	1999	Wired and Wireless Broadband Services, Smart Olympic Buildings

Case	Started	e-Services
Helsinki	1995	Regional Map Service, WLAN hot spots, e-health cards
Geneva	1994	Wired and Wireless Broadband Services, Public Information and public service guides, Tourist Guides, Job Opportunities, (http://www.ville-geneve.ch)
Antwerp	1995	e-Government services (e-Counter), Online Tourist Guide, e-Booking Property Database, environmental information and guides for entrepreneurs
New York	2004	Wireless broadband services, e-Government portal (www.nyc.gov), GIS city information (http://gis.nyc.gov/doitt/nycitymap/)
Stockholm (Kista)	2002	residential parking permits, e-Government services, elderly care treatment
Taipei	2004	Intelligent transportation, e-parking, 3D website for virtual tours, public e-services, E-Future Classroom
Dongtan	2005	Eco services like smart grids, energy/water/waste smart management, green buildings
Tianjin	2007	Eco services like smart grids, energy, water and waste smart management, green buildings
Barcelona	2000	e-Government services, mobile services, Online city guide, guides for entrepreneurs (https://w30.bcn.cat), Intelligent transportation, Open data from city Council
Hull	2000	e-Government information and e-services, GIS maps
Trikala	2003	Tele-care services, Intelligent Transportation, Wireless broadband services
Brisbane	2004	e-parking, e-Government services, mobile services, e-procurement services via national portal, virtual communities
Malta	2007	Smart grids
Dubai	1999	Media services, e-Education, e-commerce, Develops business services
New Songdo	2008	Intelligent Buildings, Ubiquitous computing, Local information (http://www.songdo.com)
Osaka	2008	Tourist guides, Public information(http://www.city.osaka.lg.jp), Guides for entrepreneurs (http://www.investosaka.jp)
Manhattan Harbour, Kentucky	2010	Intelligent Buildings, Ubiquitous computing

Case	Started	e-Services
Masdar	2008	Renewable resources and smart energy management
Cape Town	2000	Environmental services, tourist guides, intelligent transportation
Knowledge based cities	1998	Broadband and telecommunications services, Online city guides, Public information

3. Visualizing smart city evolution

The above investigation identified the existence of various alternative smart city forms, with representative cases that concern large scale projects, most of which have been evolved for more than ten years. Additionally, these projects can be recognized as ongoing since they have redefined their scope and objectives, even more than once. Furthermore, this classification and analysis illustrates how the examined cases followed the alternative categories; it is determined which of them and when they changed to other smart city approaches and which of the approaches have been the most popular since the smart city introduction (Figure 1).

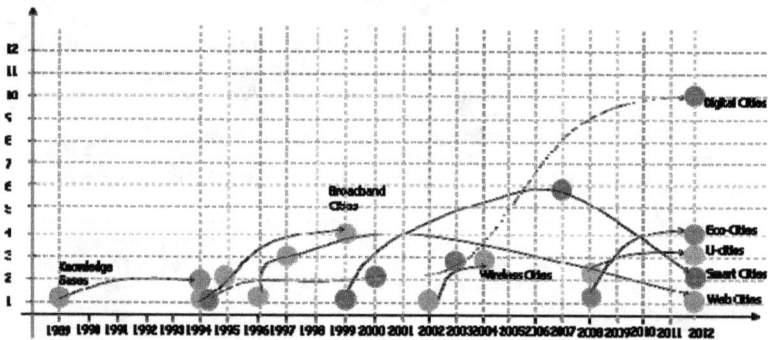

Figure 1: Smart city evolution

(Figure 1) illustrates that (a) knowledge bases appeared first and they updated to digital cities. (b) Broadband cities were next on the timeline and they mostly evolve to smart cities. (c) A relative evolution path is followed by the wireless cities. (d) Today, not all of the approaches are available, but the digital, smart, ubiquitous, eco-cities and web cities. Additionally, the evolution path of each alternative approach can be observed. For instance, digital cities appeared in 1994, they are still active and today, they account twelve of the examined cases.

In order to answer the third question of this paper regarding smart city evolution roadmaps, technology roadmapping is used, which is a powerful and flexible technique that is widely used within industry to support strategic and long-range planning (Phaal et al., 2003). Roadmapping provides structured means for exploring and communicating the relationships between technological resources, organizational objectives and the changing environment. Moreover, the path-dependent roadmap (Li et al., 2009; Li and Wang, 2011) that is based on the technology roadmapping has been used to demonstrate several formula changes over time and to interpret how these changes depended on its own past.

In this context, data from investigative analysis that concern the types of e-Services that each of the examined case offers together which of them were adopted by smart cities' updates (Table 2) can be applied on technology roadmapping. The information of (Table 2) generates e-service groups according to their end-users (Table 3). The values that are contained on the year column concern the earliest year, when a smart city case appears and offers e-services from the e-service group; the frequency column enumerates the cases that match each e-service group.

Table 3: E-service groups structured by the examined cases

Service Group	e-Services	Year	Freq.	Cases
SGroup1	e-business, city guides, urban virtualization	1989	6	AOL cities, Bristol, Copenhagen Base, Craigmillar, Osaka, Blacksburg, Amsterdam
SGroup2	e-Government, e-Democracy, e-learning	1994	9	Bristol, e-Trikala, Antwerp, Stockholm (Kista), Taipei, Barcelona, Hull, Brisbane, New York
SGroup3	Broadband communications services	1994	14	Craigmillar, Blacksburg, Seoul, Beijing, Helsinki, New York, e-Trikala, Dubai, New Songdo, Knowledge based cities, Geneva, Barcelona, Amsterdam, Cape Town
SGroup4	E-health and tele-care services, e-security	1995	3	Helsinki, e-Trikala, Stockholm (Kista)

Service Group	e-Services	Year	Freq.	Cases
SGroup5	Intelligent Transportation, e-parking	2002	6	Stockholm (Kista), Taipei, e-Trikala, Brisbane, Amsterdam, Cape Town
SGroup6	Ubiquitous ser-vices, communi-cations services	2008	4	Osaka, New Songdo, Masdar, Man-hattan Harbour
SGroup7	Eco-services, smart grids, waste/recycle management	2005	7	Amsterdam, Craigmillar, Malta, Masdar, Tianjin, Dongtan, Cape Town

Data from (Table 3) extract the path-dependent roadmap (Li et al., 2009) of (Figure 2), which demonstrates smart city approaches changes and how each change depends on its own past. Path dependency can explain smart city evolution on the basis of the e-service provision, while paths do not illustrate co-existences of cases in more than one groups (i.e., e-Trikala simultaneously belonged to SGroup1, SGroup2 and SGroup3). Some fur-ther findings show that SGroup1 and SGroup2 are root nodes in these paths, while SGroup7 is an end-node, illustrating that this smart city cate-gory has not evolved to a different approach yet.

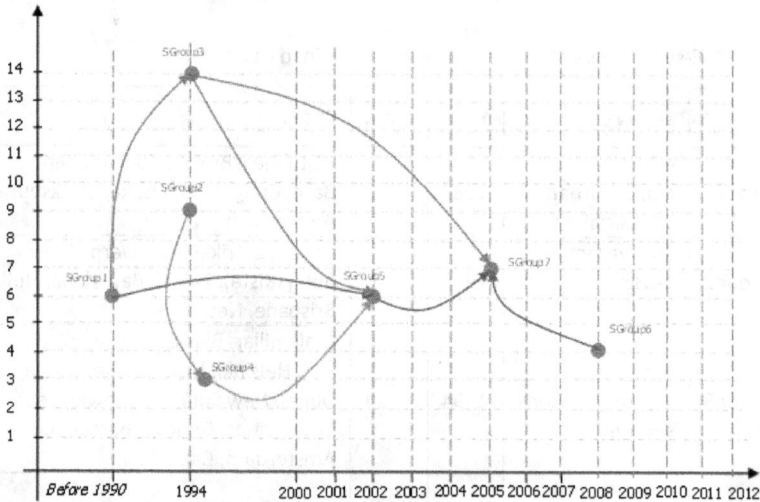

Figure 2: Path-dependent roadmaps for smart city evolution

4. Discussion

The investigation that was previously presented was performed on a 31 smart cities and returned important findings that answer the questions 1 and 2 of this paper. The term smart city does not describe a city with some particular attributes, but various types of municipal ICT environments. Some researchers have used this term to calculate the intelligence that is produced in urban spaces, while others to depict urban areas that offer smart e-services or encourage the generation of intelligence. The identified alternative approaches generates eight classification groups for smart cities. Another finding confirms that most cases did not retain their initial approach, but they have been updated to other(s). (Figure 1) illustrates the evolution timeline of the smart cities, where five of the smart city categories still exist.

In order to answer the third question of this paper regarding smart city evolution roadmaps, the provided e-services are combined in eight e-service groups (Table 3). Technology roadmapping for these e-service groups shows that smart cities have not evolved to all particular approaches, but five path-dependent roadmaps can be observed (Figure 2). This final finding can be interpreted in the following hypotheses: (a) not all smart city approaches are suitable to be followed by all urban areas, but various parameters could determine to which direction a smart city must evolve. However, it is beyond the purpose of this paper to determine these variants. (b) Not all approaches have attracted smart city evolution, but environmental e-service provision appears the "peak" in recent evolution, while smart cities that provide e-business, broadband and transportation services have also been popular.

These two hypotheses, when they will be confirmed could provide answers regarding smart city viability. Viability stands as "capability of successful operation" (Oxford Dictionary, 2012). This can be interpreted as the "feasibility and the operational continuity of an organization, a business, a facility or a project's outcome in political, social, legal, environmental, economical, and financial terms" (Salman et al., 2007). Viability should not be confused with sustainability, which can be defined as "the development that meets the needs of the present without compromising the ability of future generations to meet their own needs" (United Nations, 1987). Smart city viability is questioned and is not secured, although the project finishes in time, on budget and aligned to its requirements.

Viability has become crucial for municipal decision makers; San Francisco and Chicago mobile cities have been questioned for their feasibility (New Millennium Research Council, 2007); Iowa Communications Network and California CALNET system have failed to secure incomes; Trikala has shortened its scope; or have changed their priorities in order to sustain (i.e., Amsterdam). In Tampere, decision makers prioritized outsourcing for infrastructure deployment and for e-service delivery in order to sustain, promoted only the self-sustained e-services, while the smart city occupies a significant amount of ICT professionals and researchers in order to secure viability via innovation.

From the viability point of view, various determinants have to be considered (Salman et al., 2007): geographical, financial, legal, cultural, technological, social and environmental are crucial for projects' viability and various indices have to be determined for each of these variants. In this context, the five path-dependent roadmaps that were extracted in this paper align to technological determinants and could support decision makers in dealing with smart city's prospect. Moreover, although five different smart city approaches exist today (Figure 1), the eco-city has mostly attracted the evolution.

5. Conclusions – Future Thoughts

This paper confirmed that smart city is a "booming" phenomenon, while the term smart city is confusing. An investigative review of 31 cities identified eight classification approaches, five of which are still active, while most of the investigated cases have experienced updates from their initial approach.

Furthermore, technology roadmapping on the examined cases returned interesting outcomes, such as five path-dependent roadmaps for smart city evolution. This paper did not try to recognize the reasons lying behind these paths, but it hypothesized the requirement for viability. Since viability is influenced by a number a parameters, these path-dependent roadmaps can be useful for municipal decision makers in determining their smart city prospect. Some future thoughts concern exploration of the variants that influence smart city evolution and of the factors that make eco-city the most popular, and the determination of viability indices for smart city.

Acknowledgments

This paper is supported by the "Enterprise Architecture for Digital Cities (EADIC)" research project, which is being developed between 2012 and 2014, and funded by the Greek General Secretary for Research and Development (ARCHIMEDES III program).

References

Anthopoulos, L. and Tsoukalas, I. A. (2006) "The implementation model of a Digital City. The case study of the first Digital City in Greece: e-Trikala". *Journal of e-Government*, Vol.2, Issue 2, 2006.
Anthopoulos, L. and Vakali, A. (2012) Urban Planning and Smart Cities: Interrelations and Reciprocities. In the Alvarez, F. et al., (Eds.), *Future Internet Assembly 2012: From Promises to Reality, 4th FIA book* - LNCS 7281, Springer.
Baeyens, H. (2008) A Multipolar World of Smart City-Regions. In Pr. zb. pod red. Antoniego Kuklińskiego i Krzysztofa Pawłowskiego (Ed.), *The Atlantic Community - The Titanic of the XXI Century* (pp. 172-181). REUPUS publishing, 2008.
Engadget (2011) "South Koreans could see 1Gbps web connections by 2012", [online], retrieved December 7, 2011, from http://www.engadget.com/2009/02/02/south-koreans-could-see-1gbps-web-connections-by- today/
Ganapati, S. and Schoepp, C. F. (2008) "The Wireless City". *International Journal of Electronic Government Research* 4 (4), 54-68, 2008, IGI Global.
Gauggel, A. (2011) "Digital Beijing", [online], retrieved, December 8, 2011, from http://www.daapspace.daap.uc.edu/~larsongr/Larsonline/BldgIndx+76_files/Digital%20Beijing%20Gauggel.pdf
Giffinger, R., Fertner, C., Kramar, H., Meijers, E. and Pichler-Milanovic, N. (2007) "Smart Cities: Ranking of European medium-sized cities", [online], retrieved, July 2012 from http://www.smart-cities.eu/download/smart_cities_final_report.pdf
Hyang-Sook, C., Byung-Sun, C. and Woong-Hee, P. (2007) "Ubiquitous-City Business Strategies: The Case of South Korea", In the proceedings of the Management of Engineering and Technology (PICMET 2007), IEEE.
Ishida, T. (2002) "Digital City Kyoto". *Communications of the ACM*, vol.45, No.7, July 2002.
Ishida, T., Aurigi, A. and Yasuoka, M. (2010) The Advancement of World Digital Cities. In Nakashima, H., Aghajan, H. and J.C. Augusto (Ed) *Handbook on Ambient Intelligence and Smart Environments*, Springer.

Jackson, M., Gardner, Z. and Wainwright, T. (2011) "Location-awareness and Ubiquitous Cities A report to the U-City Research Institute", [online], Yonsei University, S. Korea, retrieved December 7, 2011 from
http://elogeo.nottingham.ac.uk/xmlui/handle/url/59

Komninos, N. (2002) Intelligent Cities: Innovation, Knowledge Systems and Digital Spaces, 1st. ed. London: Routledge , 2002.

Li, Y. R., Wang, L. H. and Hong, C. F. (2009) "Extracting the significant-rare keywords for patent analysis", *Expert Systems with Applications*, vol. 36, pp.5200-5204, April 2009.

Li Y.R. and Wang, L.H. (2011) "Exploring the evolutional roadmapping of technological trajectory: Case study of Shimano", in the Proceedings of the Interaction Sciences (ICIS), 2011 4th International Conference, 16-18 Aug. 2011 (IEEE).

Lieshout, V. (2001), "Configuring the digital city of Amsterdam". *New Media & Technology*, vol. 3(1), p. 27-52. SAGE Publications.

Moon, M. J. (2002) "The evolution of e-Government among Municipalities: Rhetoric or Reality?" *Public Administration Review*, Blackwell Science Ltd., July/August 2002, Vol. 62, No. 4.

New Millennium Research Council (2007), Not In The Public Interest – The Myth of Municipal Wi-Fi Networks.

Phaal, R. Farrukh, C. J. and Probert, D. R. (2003) "Technology roadmapping - A planning framework for evolution and revolution", *Technological Forecasting and Social Change*, vol. 71, pp. 5-26, January 2003.

Oxford Dictionary (2012), Definition for Viable, [online],
http://oxforddictionaries.com/ definition/viable

Qi, L. and Shaofu, L. (2001) "Research on digital city framework architecture". In Info-tech and Info-net, 2001, International Conferences (pp. 30-36, vol. 1), IEEE.

Sairamesh, J., Lee, A. and Anania, L., (2004) "Information Cities". *Communications of the ACM*, vol. 47, No.2, February 2004.

Salman, A. F. M., Skibniewski, M. J. and Basha, I. (2007) "BOT viability model for large-scale infrastructure projects", *Journal of Construction Engineering and Management*, 133 (1), 50-63, 2007.

Townsend, A. (2007) "Seoul: Birth of a Broadband Metropolis". *Environment and Planning B: Planning and Design*, vol. 34(3), pp. 396-413, 2007.

United Nations (1987) "Report of the World Commission on Environment and Development: Our Common Future", [online],
http://conspect.nl/pdf/Our_Common_Future-Brundtland_Report_1987.pdf

Van Bastelaer, B. (1998) "Digital Cities and transferability of results", in the proceedings of the 4th EDC Conference on Digital Cities, Salzburg, October 29-30, pp. 61-70.

Wang, L., and H., Wu, (2001) "A Framework of Integrating Digital City and Eco-city", School of Business, Hubei University, Wuhan, China, [online],
www.hku.hk/cupem/asiagis/fall03/Full_Paper/Wang_Lu.pdf

Should Governments Move to the Cloud? Requirement Considerations

Birgit Oberer[1] and Alptekin Erkollar[2]

[1]Kadir Has University, Istanbul, Turkey
[2]Halic University, Istanbul, Turkey

birgit.oberer@khas.edu.tr
erkollar@etcop.com

Originally published in the Proceedings of the Eropean Conference on e-Government (2012) Ed. Mila Gascó, ACPIL, pp555-562.

Editorial Commentary

There are new and interesting web-based technologies that are being introduced on a regular basis. One such technology that has caught the interest of government is "cloud-computing."Oberer and Erkollar investigate some of the important requirements for cloud-based e-Government applications. They further outline some of the specific issues that impact government ICT initiatives. The authors propose a special tool that can help support civil servants in better understanding how to approach "cloud computing" initiatives.

Abstract: Cloud computing is a model for enabling ubiquitous, on demand network access to a shared pool of configurable computing resources that can be rapidly provisioned and released with minimal management effort or service provider interaction, using different deployment models, such as 'software as a service' (SaaS), 'platform as a service' (PaaS), and 'infrastructure as a service' (IaaS), with public, private community, and hybrid clouds as deployment models. In general, cloud computing can be defined by considering its characteristic attributes, such as multi-tenancy, scalability, elasticity, pay as you go, and self provisioning of resources. Governments around the world are actively looking into cloud computing as a means of increasing efficiency and reducing cost. Apart from the potential benefits, such as increased flexibility, cost reduction, elastic scalability, and service quality that cloud computing could offer governments, different concerns, such as security, performance, availability, ability to customise, investment or regulatory requirements also have to be taken into consideration. In this study, first the cloud computing attributes that are needed for government use, such as governance, legal requirements, risk management, outsourcing, and security issues, and the requirements for e-Government applications that are used in clouds were analysed, and second e-Government use cases were analysed and categorised according to their fit to the cloud deployment models and then the GOV.Cloud Dashboard is introduced. The results of the study revealed that parameters, such as security management by vendors, security architecture, user, access, and identity management, are key success factors for clouds being used for governments. Apart from that, government applications themselves have to fulfil special requirements to be included in clouds, such as availability, authenticity, transparency, and interoperability.

Keywords: application, cloud computing, e-Government, government, success factor

1. Introduction

For being competitive in global markets and to meet the needs of being competitive in an increasing area of globalisation, public authorities must think about how to make their services more competitive. One aspect of becoming more competitive is investing in emerging technologies such as cloud computing. Cloud computing challenges traditional approaches to enterprise application design and management, and promises cost savings combined with an increased agility of IT. At the core of cloud computing there is the need for having specific requirements incorporated into a well-defined strategy on cloud computing, where the cloud roadmap has to consider all the government aspects, such as performance, control, availability, legal framework and, among the most important, security. In general, it is considered critical that governments start to adopt this technology because of complex economic constraints. Security, legal framework, and interoperability are some major barriers for a broad adoption of the cloud technology among governments. Different delivery models, such as public meplatform, or infrastructure provision in a cloud. The basis for government cloud delivery decisions is the analysis of government applications. Governments have to evaluate specific applications, factor in mainly security, legal, and compliance considerations, and to decide what applications are appropriate for a private cloud, which could be included in a public one (Schultz 2011).

To answer our research question 'what are requirements for governments moving to the cloud and how can requirement management be implemented for governments?' we did a requirements analysis for e-Government cloud applications

To answer our research question 'what are requirements for governments moving to the cloud and how can requirement management be implemented for governments?' we divided our analysis in three parts. Firstly, we did a requirements analysis for e-Government cloud applications by considering the different cloud computing models and their influence on governments., showing the theoretical base for our analysis. Secondly, ased on the findings of several cloud computing related projects conducted by the European Union government requirement for cloud computing were derived, followed by an analysis of tipical government related use cases and their ability to be offered in the cloud. Finally, we developed a tool for requirements management, the GOV.Cloud Dashboard, which can be used by government to track their activities on moving their services to the cloud.

2. Literature review

Electronic government is the use of information and communication technologies for providing and improving governmental services by enabling electronic information provision, communication, and transactions for administrations and their customers, which are citizens, businesses, as well as governments or administrative authorities themselves. Electronic government includes all administration measures at all levels (federal, state, as well as regional) to improve the citizen satisfaction (qualitative improvements in spheres of life), businesses and for governments to improve internal processes and procedures and to force structural changes (Aichholzer and Strau 2010). An electronic government strategy is a fundamental element of the modernisation process in administrations. Electronic government activities worldwide are driven by a need for higher efficiency, effectiveness, and the accessibility of public services for the administration's customers. Most governments follow certain strategies for electronic government or launched projects in this area to ensure a web presence of the administration, to offer communication methods, and on a higher level to offer transactional services for the government's customers (Ebrahim and Irani 2005, Burn and Robin 2003, Chesher et al. 2003. Information and communication technologies evolve into complex, globally oriented networks, and governments are under pressure offering reliable, efficient, and effective services to their customers including, apart from citizens' services trade and travel security, social service delivery and support for military services (Haselbeck 2011, Simon 2005).). Governments produce, manage, and use huge amounts of data that become more valuable the easier the customers, which are citizens, businesses, and governmental authorities themselves, access these data. The main challenges for e-Government are the processing of citizen related business processes and IT based document management. Newer projects in governments work on the combination of the consumer side of the used web applications and the traditional Internet appearance of governments and its agencies. This combination is the key issue for talking about cloud computing for governments. The main question to be answered is how cloud computing can support the service provision in e-Government (Haselbeck 2011).

Cloud computing is a 'model for enabling convenient, on-demand network access to a shared pool of configurable computing resources (e.g., networks, servers, storage, applications, and services) that can be rapidly provisioned and released with minimal management effort or service provider interaction' (NIST 2010). For cloud computing, three delivery models are relevant, which are 'Software as a Service' (SaaS), 'Platform as a Service' (PaaS), and 'Infrastructure as a service' (IaaS) (Pütter 2011, Rössler 2011, Jackson 2009). For 'Software as a Service' the consumer uses an application, but does not control the operating system, hardware, or network infrastructure on which it is running. For 'Platform as a Service' the consumer uses a hosting environment for their applications, controls the applications that run in the environment but does not control the operating system, hardware, or network infrastructure on which they are running. For 'Infrastructure as a Service' the consumer uses fundamental computing resources, such as processing power, storage, networking components, or middleware, and can control the operating system, storage, deployed applications, and possibly networking components, such as firewalls and load balancers, but not the cloud infrastructure beneath them (Rössler 2011, Jackson 2009).

Table 1: Cloud computing basics (Rössler 2011, NIST 2010, Jackson 2009)

Cloud computing basics	
Cloud Computing models	
Delivery models	Software as a Service SaaS
	Platform as a Service PaaS
	Infrastructure as a Service IaaS
Deployment models	Public Cloud
	Private Cloud
	Hybrid Cloud
Cloud computing (dis) advantages	
Cloud benefits	Cloud concerns
Cost reduction	Security
Increased flexibility	Legal framework
Elastic scalability	Availability
Easy to implement	Performance
Service quality	Ability to customize
Access anywhere	Availability of suppliers
Cloud computing characteristics	
Characteristic	Description
Rapid elasticity	Ability to scale resources up and down as needed
On-demand self service	The customer can use cloud services as needed without cloud provider interaction.
Ubiquitous network access	Capabilities of the cloud provider are available over the network.
Resource pooling	A cloud provider uses a multi-tenant model, assigning and re-assigning physical and virtual resources according to customer demand.
Measured services	Some cloud service parts are controlled and monitored by the cloud provider.

The user and cloud provider have better control over the cloud infrastructure, in turn improving the security gap because of restricted access (PriceWaterhouseCoopers 2010, Jackson 2009). Hybrid clouds are a combination between a public cloud and a private cloud, which are interoperating. Non-critical data can be processed on a public cloud while business critical data are processed in a private one. Deployment models for clouds of interest for governments are public, private, and hybrid clouds. For public clouds, cloud services are characterised as being available to clients from a third party service provider via the Internet. What a private cloud offers is elastic and service based, such as a public cloud, but processes and data are management within the organisation and do not have restrictions for security issues, network bandwidth, or legal requirements.

3. Governments and cloud computing

3.1 Requirements for cloud based e-Government applications

Service models offered by cloud computing providers have a significant influence on the possible cloud e-Government applications. The outsourcing of an internal IT infrastructure offers an economic advantage for organisations, whereas for infrastructure as a service (IaaS) options, the operating system and operating environment and an increasing organisational effort have to be considered. Existing applications can be implemented easily in a cloud with an IaaS model, focusing on a deployment hosted in an internal or a trusted third party data centre instead of one hosted in the cloud.

New applications should be designable in a cloud but the increased administrative burden remains a parameter harming governments' enthusiasm of a cloud based future for its services. Security issues are a key factor to be considered by developers, because not only common data protection and security issues but also other factors, such as the operating system in use, have an influence on the success of a cloud based e-Government approach (Brunette and Mogull, 2009, Weichert 2011, Haselbeck 2011). In comparison to that, the development of an application based on the platform as a service (PaaS) model seems to offer more advantages, for instance scalability does not have to be considered because of data processing resources are not rare in the cloud. The administrative burden is not that significant because the operating system and operating environment are offered outside the organisation. Existing applications need to be prepared for a migration into the cloud environment but, in comparison to that, new applications can fully take advantage of the cloud functionalities. Considering the administrative burden as a key indicator for deciding on a cloud model, the software as a service (SaaS) approach offers the most attractive approach for governments. In contrast to this advantage, the SaaS approach is limited because, currently, cloud providers offer only basic functionalities, and customising the services regarding government needs is time and cost intensive. Currently, mainly email systems and basic office applications are offered by cloud providers. This missing ability to customise the service is a tremendous disadvantage for governments, its services are quite special and they mostly need to be adapted to common government needs, legal requirements, and agency related requirements (Pfneiszl 2011). Because of that, complete e-Government applications will not be offered by public cloud providers in the nearest future, but maybe by third parties, using the PaaS model of the public cloud provider as their own SaaS model. Considering the requirements and limitations mentioned above, SaaS and PaaS seem to fit for governments' requirements on cloud computing: with PaaS, applications can, based on being interfaced to cloud providers, best be developed considering the existing resources; the same for SaaS, in case the development or migration of applications has to be outsourced (Zwattendorfer 2011, Platform Digital Austria 2011, Felser 2011).

Having strong fixed and mobile networks, governments have three main areas to work on, which are a legal framework for cloud computing, technical and commercial fundamentals, and the market (Kroes 2011): Within the legal framework, data protection and security are of significant importance, with the need for clear rules for the allocation of jurisdiction, responsibility and liability, and stakeholder protection. Technical standardisation of Application Programming Interfaces and data formats are needed to enhance interoperability and competition between cloud providers. One example for a standardisation project Kroes (2011) names is the 'SIENA project', the 'Standards and Interoperability for eInfrastructure Implementation Initiative, which is funded by the European Commission under Framework Programme 7 (2007-2013), available online at <http://www.sienainitiative.eu/>. According to Kroes (2011), pilot projects must be scaled up and public sector has to be pushed to really make use of the potential that cloud computing offers.Apart from the legal framework and technical issues, the market itself is a key factor for the successful use of cloud computing for governments.

Table 2: e-Government requirements

Government requirements for cloud services	
Requirement	Description
Confidentiality	No data should be accessible for cloud providers or third parties.
	Valid for data stored in the cloud and transferred within the network
	Key management: date encryption needed
	Data need to be confident during their whole life cycle within the cloud. After data are used, they must be deleted from the cloud.
Integrity / Reliability	The system needs to work properly.
	Data are not allowed to be modified in the system.
	Data integrity, software integrity, message integrity and configuration integrity must be considered.
Availability	Standardised interfaces
	Redundancy possible (one applications can be deployed by different cloud providers). This can reduce the risk of a total breakdown of the system.
	Protection against hacker attacks, intrusion detection systems in use
Authenticity / authentication	The authenticity of sensitive data processed in e-Government applications is needed.
	Authenticity for processed data and the cloud itself
	Use of digital signature
	Authentication management for users
Transparency	For application development: Standardised interfaces
	For user: The functionality of the system should be transparent for users
Migration Interoperability	Standards for migration and system portability are needed (how to transfer applications from one cloud provider to another.
	Standards are needed for cloud communication as well.

Government requirements for cloud services	
Requirement	Description
Dependence	Service oriented architectures for cloud applications. A dependence on other services needs to be considered (within one cloud [intra-cloud dependence] or between clouds [inter-cloud dependence]). Hybrid clouds are one example for such dependence. A concept is needed to handle dependence.
Scalability	Cloud providers are responsible for ensuring the scalability of the cloud.
Auditing / Logging	Systematic recording and controlling of processes and system attributes. In general, log files are stored in a data centre. For cloud computing, log files can be stored worldwide and, apart from an administrator, a cloud provider could access and read the stored data. Although in log files sensitive data should not be stored, sometimes because of legal requirements or for traceability issues, sensitive data are stored in a clouds' log files. e-Government applications need to ensure that only the needed data are stored in the clouds' log files and that privilege classes for accessing these data are developed.
requirement	description
Compliance	National legal requirements for e-Government and cloud computing need to be defined, such as data protection, public procurement, IT contracting, liability and warranty, EU regulations, or international ones.
Data protection	Because data are stored in the systems of the cloud provider, which can be spread throughout the whole world, this does not match most national data protection regulations. Currently, there are no technical solutions to overcome these data protection issues. In general, the needed data protection is organised by contract with the cloud provider, such as a regulation that a specific type of data is only allowed to be stored in pre-defined countries (mostly defined in service level agreements (SLAs) between a government and the cloud provider (Wiehr 2011).
Governance	Internal regulations and strategies must be observed. Close related to compliance issues which focus on external regulations. Government strategies must have the highest priority when migrating systems to a cloud provider.

Government requirements for cloud services	
Requirement	Description
User friendliness	User friendliness for government applications is important because the systems are accessed not only by government employees but also by citizens and businesses as well. Therefore, user friendliness regarding the navigation, readability, and design of the application must be ensured. The higher the user friendliness the higher the interactions (citizen/business and government) undertaken electronically.
Efficiency	Economic criteria, such as return on investment, are important for all the systems implemented. This holds for governments and newly designed applications are also migrated.

3.2   e-Government use case analysis

For governments, the usability of cloud systems must be evaluated systematically. In general, e-Government applications must process user related data, which should not be accessible to third parties. Considering the three cloud computing deployment models, which are public clouds, hybrid clouds, and private ones, none of these models have to be sorted out, as all of them can be suitable for government use. Nevertheless, data protection and data security issues must be considered, not only for public and hybrid clouds, which share resources and services with other users in public networks. Private clouds seem to be the easiest way to handle person-related data. Considering the main delivery models for cloud computing, which are SaaS, PaaS, and IaaS, in relation with the cloud deployment models, different use cases are possible (Zwattendorfer 2011, Platform Digital Austria 2011, Asendorpf 2011).

Table 3: Use cases

Government cloud use cases		
Delivery model	Use case	Deployment models*
Software as a service (SaaS)	Desktop software for governments offered as a cloud based office application (user access office applications via a thin client)	P Pu H
	Collaboration suite	P Pu H

Government cloud use cases		
Delivery model	Use case	Deployment models*
	Identity management as a service: citizen card application offered as a cloud service	P H
	Security as a service: mail filter offered as a cloud service	Pu
Platform as a sevice (PaaS)	Platform for designing: - government internal processes - citizen related processes	Pu H
	eForms	P H
	government cloud use cases	Deployment model
Delivery model	Use Case	
Infrastructure as a service (IaaS)	Data storage	P H
	Data backup	
	Virtual server	

P... private   *Pu... public*   *H... hybrid [cloud]*

3.3   GOV.Cloud Dashboard

To support governments during their journey into the GovCloud, a GOV.Cloud Dashboard was designed by the authors of this study. Using our knowledge on incident management from former studies in governmental authorities and private companies, we designed a template for government requirement management. The dashboard offers different views on GovCloud issues, such as the business view, development view, or process view. In the business view, business, such as government agencies, commissions, or departments, can prioritise issues that come along with the move to one or more clouds. It is proposed that the involved departments, authorities, developers, cloud providers, and other professionals meet in dashboard meetings regularly, to review business priority for issues, define development milestones, discuss challenges, and ensure that the business driven changes fit the government strategy and implemented processes. In addition, task forces should be formed for specific topics, as part of the move project or defined challenges. During the move to the cloud, incidents could occur. Possible incidents could include an unexpected technical impact on the system or organisational challenges. Incidents should be added to the dashboard list and linked with the main business issues defined. One or a team, such as an incident manager, should be responsible for tracking incidents, adding them to a separate incident list as well and working on solving these incidents together with selected experts and professionals. For every main business issue and incident, two owners must be named, which could be a person or a team, one for the business issue and one for the corresponding technical development or implementation, or incident management. In case a workflow system is used for managing the move to the cloud, the system could be used to dispatch workflow items to queues, defined for solving specific technical issues. A user acceptance test (UAT) team could be formed to test whether implemented systems or parts of them work properly, in turn meeting business requirements in a technical sufficient way. To get an overview on the progress within the project, the owner status could be defined for every single business issue or incident, using states such as 'intake', 'analysis', 'in progress', or 'on-hold'. After a UAT test, business has to validate the implemented system or functionalities in a 'business validation (BV)' routine.

Business Priority	Main Business Issue	Detailed Business Issue	Incident	Main Focus	Queue/Owner	Owner/Status	UAI	Patch	UAI	BV	Action/Comments
1	Oder Entry	Only wrong PR status after	1144/h	Heing	AM	Solving	18 01 17	13 Y_148			CLY 322 NOK on
1		During a move, if you add and	CR 38604 (138609)	Billing							resulting from packs
3		Parent for pack data fixes	130852	Billing	HAS	Intake					will be closed when the last child case is
4		PR stick on "ready to	144211	billing				CLY_193	OK	NOK	157045 solving HV
5		CL_upsell during a move out of AS - second approach	157045	Billing	AM	CR/PF in progress					only after giving BV NOK for 144211 a misunderstan
6		HAS C goes wrong	176151	Billing	BST	Intake					
7		header is HGS	176538		AM	CR/PF in progress	10.01.12				
8		CLAR pack	176655		AM	Intake					
9	Part	Products	130564		AM	Solving		CLY 112			

Figure 1: GOV.Cloud Dashboard: prioritised business view

Review Status	Case #	Updated Status	Title	P?	Owner	Case Status	Business Impacts	Actions / Comments	Status	When in radar	Expected Actions by...
1. In Radar	85854	Closed	AT_ITS_MH Status mismatch between SIC and ARTUS	P4	?	Closed		up: Volker + Christian (76996) => Claudia Based on inputs from Volker it is...	Amber	April 22	
1. In Radar	63003	BV	Telephony: Telephony usage displayed twice after up-/downgrade	P2		Closed	AM	Not possible to rate the usage of upgraded /	Amber	April 21	Nina
1. In Radar	77073	Closed	All Services: Missing print request for some WO and Contracts	P2	AM	Closed		No Business impact - Some work orders are lost between...		April 16	
1. In Radar	73655	Closed	All Services (PR): CPE installation failed	P2	BST	Closed		Around 20 discrepancies between the CPE network status and...		April 16	
1. In Radar	80688	Closed	TFD (PR): Data Synchronisation	P2	AM	Closed		Around 120 Telephony customers are...		April 16	

Figure 2: GOV.Cloud Dashboard: solution team view

4. Conclusion

Cloud computing is a novelty that will influence governments. In the shorter run, a data centre will switch to cloud similar structures using international cooperation. If these data centres are used for electronic government, cloud computing must also be considered for government services. Territorially limited private clouds could be used for e-Government platforms, such as electronic internal workflow systems (offered as SaaS) or web forms (offered as PaaS). Especially for smaller governments, these solutions could allow them to offer their services cheaper without the explicit need of an internal deeper technical knowledge. Governments could use common workflow systems and customised e-Government forms as cloud services. In combining delivery and deployment models for cloud services, different use cases were defined, which could be offered as a cloud service; such as citizen card application as SaaS or design of government internal processes as PaaS. A GOV.Cloud Dashboard was introduced to support governments in their journey to cloud based services. This dashboard could support government management and agencies in defining their needs for cloud based services, track the process of its implementation, and ensure that developers consider the business needs when implementing cloud based services.

Cloud computing could help governments connect with citizens, businesses, and other stakeholders, improve transparency while addressing the government goals of scalable and interactive portals for stakeholders, and collaborate more easily across organisations. The challenges to be considered mainly focus on security issues, legal frameworks, and interoperability.

References

Aichholzer G. and Strau, B.S (2010) The Austrian case: multi-card concept and the relationship between citizen ID and social security cards, Identity in the Information Society, Netherlands: Springer.

Asendorpf, D. (2011) Ab in die Wolken. Zeit Online [online]. Available at: < http://www.zeit.de/2011/08/Cloud-Computing> [Accessed 30 December 2011].

Brunette, G. and Mogull, R. (2009). Security Guidance for Critical Areas of Focus in Cloud Computing. [pdf]: Cloud Security Alliance, Available at: <https://cloudsecurityalliance.org/csaguide.pdf> [Accessed 02 January 2012].

Burn, J. and Robins, G. (2003) Moving towards e-Government: a case study of organizational change processes, Logistics Information Management, 16(1), pp.25-35.

Chesher, M., Kaura, R. and Linton, P. (2003) Electronic Business & Commerce, London: Springer.

Ebrahim, Z. and Irani, Z. (2005) e-Government adoption: architecture and barriers, Business Process Management Journal, 11(5), pp.589-611.

Felser, R. (2011) Government Cloud für Österreich. Computerwelt [online] 06 July. Available at: < http://www.computerwelt.at/detailArticle.asp?a=135614&n=2> [Accessed 03 January 2012].

Haselbeck, S. (2011). Neue Wege im Government. Vom e-Government zum Cloud-Government? FabaSoft eGov-Suite [blog] March 13. Available at: <http://blog.egov-suite.com/de/2011/03/vom-e-Government-zum-cloud-government/> [Accessed 02 January 2012].

Jackson, K (2009) Government Cloud Computing [online] Dataline. Available at: <http://www.dataline.com> [Accessed 03 January 2012].

Kroes, N. (2011) The clear role of public authorities in cloud computing. Neelie Kroes Blog [blog] 04 April. Available at: <http://blogs.ec.europa.eu/neelie-kroes/public-authorities-and-cloud/> [Accessed 02 January 2012].

National Institute of Standards and Technology (NIST) (2010). NIST Cloud Computing Program. [online] Available at: < http://www.nist.gov/itl/cloud/> [Accessed 30 December 2011].

Pfneiszl, H. (2011) Ratlos in die Cloud?. Economyaustria [online] 18 November. Available at: < http://www.economyaustria.at/technologie/ratlos-die-cloud> [Accessed 03 January 2012].

Platform Digital Austria (2011). Cloud computing. Position paper. Vienna: Platform Digital Austria

PriceWaterhouseCoopers (2010). 10 Minuten Cloud Computing [online]. PriceWaterhouseCoopers. Available at: < http://www.pwc.de/de/prozessoptimierung/assets/CloudComputing.pdf> [Accessed 30 December 2011].

Pütter, Ch. (2011) 3 Megatrends und die Folgen. Das Daten-Management von morgen. CIO [online] 04 March. Available at:

<http://www.cio.de/strategien/2264118/index2.html> [Accessed 02 January 2012].

Rössler, Th. (2011) Anforderungen für e-Government und Cloud Computing. Graz: e-Government Innovationszentrum EGIZ.

Schultz, B. (2011) Public Cloud vs. Private Cloud: Why not Both?. Network World [online] 4 April. Available at: < http://www.networkworld.com/supp/2011/enterprise2/040411-ecs-cloud.html> [Accessed 03 January 2012].

Simon, K.D. (2005) The value of open standards and open-source software in government environments, IBM Systems Journal, 44(2), pp.227-238.

Weichert, T. (2011). Cloud Computing and Data Privacy. In: The Sedona Conference. Working Group Series (wgs). Working Group on International Electronic Information Management, Discovery & Disclosure (WG6). Phoenix: The Sedona Conference.

Wiehr, H. (2011) Forrester-Ratschläge. Die 10 Fallen bei Virtualisierung und Cloud. CIO [online] 13 March. Available at: < http://www.cio.de/knowledgecenter/server/alles_zu_virtualisierung/hintergrund/2267615/> [Accessed 02 January 2012].

Zwattendorfer, B. (2011) Anforderungen für e-Government Anwendungen in der Cloud. Graz: e-Government Innovationszentrum EGIZ.

A Conceptual Model of Critical Success Factors for an e-Government Crowdsourcing Solution

Kevin Cupido and Jacques Ophoff

Dept. of Information Systems, University of Cape Town, South Africa

kevin.cupido@gmail.com
jacques.ophoff@uct.ac.za

Originally published in the Proceedings of the European Conference on e-Government (2014) Ed. Alexandru Ionas, ACPIL, pp77-84.

Editorial Commentary

There is a general level of apathy amongst citizens to activity engage with government, engagement only appears to occur then there is a crisis and the citizen requires assistance from government. Governments have attempted unsuccessfully to use e-Government systems as an approach to interact with citizens on a more meaningful level. Cupido and Ophoff argue that one approach that could be used to foster meaning communication is "crowdsourcing." However, "crowd-sourcing" in the e-Government space is not well understood and they propose a conceptual model of critical success factors in e-Government "crowd-sourcing."

Abstract: Most e-Government implementations have resulted in failures with many implementations being one-way (government-to-citizen) and mainly informational (Dada, 2006; Cloete, 2012). However, advances in technology provide governments with the opportunity to engage with citizens using new methods, such as crowdsourcing. Successful commercial and open source software implementations of crowdsourcing have sparked interest in its potential use in the public sector. Brabham (2009) advocated for the use of crowdsourcing in the public sector to increase public participation and for governments to access citizens as a source of ideas and solutions. However, crowdsourcing lacks a theoretical and conceptual foundation (Geiger, et al., 2011; Pedersen, et al., 2013). Within e-Government there is also a lack of knowledge regarding the implementation of crowdsourcing platforms (Koch & Brunswicker, 2011). The main research questions is: How are crowdsourcing initiatives able to motivate citizen participation in e-Government? A conceptual model of critical success factors for an e-Government crowdsourcing solution is presented, based on a comprehensive review of relevant literature. The model uses Self-Determination Theory as a basis to examine citizen motivation and the influence of incentives or rewards. The model also addresses system factors such as task clarity and types, management, and feedback. The model examines behavioural intention to use crowdsourcing through the Unified Theory of Acceptance and Use of Technology. In order to explore this model a sequential explanatory mixed-method approach will be adopted with a quantitative survey, followed by qualitative semi-structured interviews to add richness to the quantitative data. This research benefits future work by building a conceptual foundation for a potential e-Government crowdsourcing solution.

Keywords: crowdsourcing, e-Government, critical success factors, conceptual model, self-determination theory, citizen participation, democracy, mixed methods

1. Introduction

Involving all citizens in decision-making has eluded governments around the world (Brücher & Baumberger, 2003). For many citizens participation amounts to voting, with few partaking in government public participation initiatives, creating the general belief in citizen apathy. However, apathy is not the reason for low participation – rather citizen participation has changed in that citizens participate in different ways and on their own terms (Bang, 2009).

One of the ways is to leverage advances in web technologies such as Web 2.0, which allowed for greater user-generated context and, combined with the widespread availability of internet-enabled mobile technologies, have made it even easier for people to connect and collaborate. Realising this potential, businesses have used these technologies to tap into 'crowds' of people as a source of ideas, and for problem solving (Howe, 2006). Crowdsourcing using web technologies accesses the potential of a large network of people who respond to calls towards the completion of tasks, or offer ideas and solutions to problems posed (Geiger, et al., 2011). Different crowdsourcing systems use incentives as motivation, whereas others are driven by individual, social, or personal values and principles. The aim of this research is to determine what factors would influence public-sector crowdsourcing initiatives for citizen participation in government. This re-search will attempt to answer the question: What are the critical success factors for an e-Government crowdsourcing solution?

This paper proceeds with a discussion of e-Government and technology, before looking at crowdsourcing as a concept. It then examines various factors that could influence a crowdsourcing solution including motivation, rewards, tasks and management. Next the conceptual model is presented which draws the factors together. Finally some concluding remarks end the paper.

2. Citizen participation in government

Uncertainty of how to contend with the increased complexity in modern-day governing has led governments to exclude citizens from the delibera-tion process (Li & Marsh, 2008). The political scientist Henrik Bang de-scribes the emergence of two political identities, the 'expert citizens' and 'everyday makers' as a response to this exclusion. Expert citizens are in-volved and interested in politics and often speak on behalf of the everyday makers, many of whom are less privileged (Marsh, 2011). Williams (2006, p. 197) equates community participation to "spectator politics, where ordinary people have mostly become endorcees of pre-designed planning programmes". A possible way to address the above issues is the use of technology through e-Government.

2.1   e-Government and technology

e-Government refers to the use of technology to deliver information and services and enable digital interactions between government and other parties, such as citizens. Unfortunately many e-Government implementa-tions have been total or partial failures, either abandoned or not achieving their intended goals. Many implementations are still one-way, govern-ment-to-citizen (G2C) in nature and mainly informational (Cloete, 2012).

According to Dada (2006, p. 4) there is a need for the public sector to "change and reengineer" its processes to the new technology and culture of e-Government system functions; one reason for e-Government failure is a "mismatch between the current reality and the design of the future e-Government system". Brabham (2009) also viewed the web as a means to reduce the constraints placed on citizen participation in democracies. Citizens have embraced the 'democratised' web offered by Web 2.0, which allowed for user-generated content, where consumers also became producers and publishers.

Citizens are already utilising technology to engage in 'alternative' ways through blogs, forums and on social networks (Bang, 2009). Some extreme uses of technology has led to the unseating of the Egyptian president, through extensive use of Facebook and Twitter for citizen reporting and the coordination of efforts (Cloete, 2012). Similarly, citizens have used the short message service (SMS) to organise demonstrations in the Philippines and Syria, and Blackberry messaging (BBM) has been used to coordinate riots in the United Kingdom. During the 2008 Obama election drive in the United States of America (USA) citizens interacted via social networks including the raising of election funds. What these examples illustrate is that technologies have allowed for a vast number of people to be mobilised.

As technology is a facilitator between government and citizens it is expected that advances in information and communication technologies (ICT) would increase the potential of crowdsourcing initiatives. The successful use of crowdsourcing concepts to engage large groups of people has ignited interest in its potential to mobilise citizens, and Brabham (2009) has advocated the use of crowdsourcing concepts in the public sector to not only increase public participation, but also for governments to access citizens as a source of ideas and solutions.

2.2   Crowdsourcing

As a concept crowdsourcing is not new – the term was coined by Howe (2006) and described as a means to outsource a function, previously performed by someone internal to an organisation, to a larger network of people in the form of an 'open call'. The primary components of crowdsourcing are that of the organisation, the crowd itself, and a platform to "link the two together and to provide a host for the activity throughout its lifecycle" (Zhao & Zhu, 2012, as in Seltzer & Mahmoudi, 2012, p. 194). The organisation component in this context is government, the crowd component refers to citizens as part of an online community, and the platform is the technology which plays a vital role as facilitator.

Estellés-Arolas & González-Ladrón-de-Guevara (2012) list forty different definitions, and even the word 'crowdsourcing' itself is sometimes used in the same breath as many others such as 'co-creation', 'open innovation', and 'citizen-sourcing'. One definition that is a good fit for the use of crowdsourcing in a public participation context is that, "It involves an organisation-user relationship whereby an organisation executes a top-down, managed process that seeks the bottom-up, open, creative input of users in an online community", and it is this management that makes it "productive and full of potential to do good" (Brabham, 2013, p. 127). Charalabidis et al. (2012) and Bani (2012) mention the use of an unstructured approach, such as the use of social networking tools by citizens in Iceland to craft their constitution. However, the use of social networking can generate unanticipated outcomes and serve to disrupt participation by others, as well as a loss of control over the process (Cobo, 2012). This definition then distinguishes a government-based crowdsourcing as being a more deliberate process, and may have greater appeal to governments, being bureaucratic and more process-driven.

Crowdsourcing types range from *crowd rating* (a simple voting system) akin to a poll or Facebook Like, and *crowd processing* (micro tasks motivated by a financial reward), to the more complex types of *crowd solving* and *crowd creation* which require idea generation and collaborative problem-solving. Depending on the application the four types often appear in various combinations. The options within a government context would range from gauging sentiment through a simple opinion poll (crowd rating), distributed task processing (crowd processing), to knowledge gathering and creation (crowd solving and crowd creation), or combinations thereof. A process of idea generation through crowd solving followed by crowd rating would accommodate different 'levels' of citizens, but more importantly by being inclusive it would also assist in gaining buy-in and legitimacy. However, current government implementations of crowdsourcing just give a "semblance of participation but does not promote collaboration" (Warner, 2011).

While crowdsourcing has emerged as a low effort and low cost way of eliciting ideas from a vast number of people (Leimeister, et al., 2009), the initial problem is how to 'kick-start' the crowd as well as how to grow a vibrant community (Brabham, 2009). Understanding the motivations for participation in crowdsourcing systems is key to the development of "best practices for governments and non-profits hoping to take the genius of crowdsourcing further into the service of the public good" (Brabham, 2010). However, there is a lack of knowledge as to the implementation of a government crowdsourcing platform and the motivation for individual par-ticipation (Koch & Brunswicker, 2011).

3. Self-determination theory and motivation

Ryan & Deci (2000, p. 54) state that "to be motivated means to be moved to do something", or moved into 'action'. Self-Determination Theory (SDT), defines different types of motivation (see Figure 1). It ranges from unwill-ingness manifested in amotivation, extrinsic motivation which is related to passive compliance, and personal commitment in the form of intrinsic mo-tivation. The continuum is also an indication of levels of internalisation increasing from left to right, which is the process of adopting a value or regulation, and the degree to which this has been integrated to be a part of the self (Ryan & Deci, 2000).

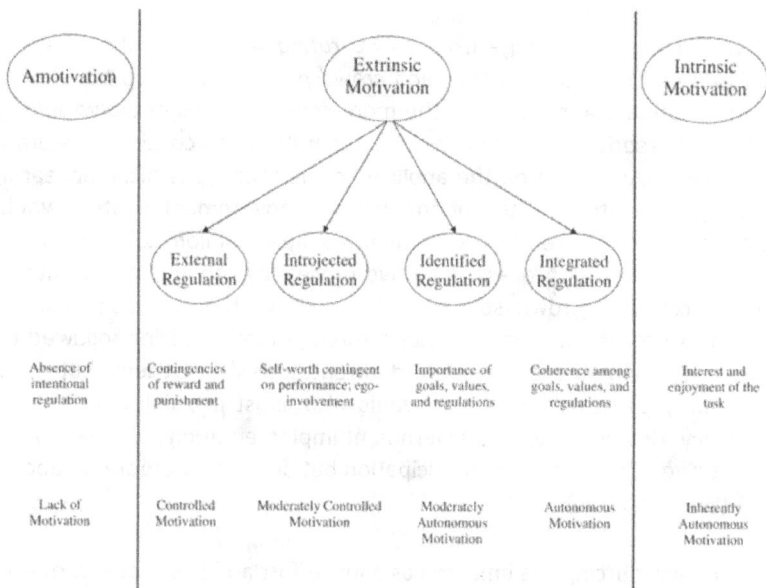

Amotivation	Extrinsic Motivation				Intrinsic Motivation
	External Regulation	Introjected Regulation	Identified Regulation	Integrated Regulation	
Absence of intentional regulation	Contingencies of reward and punishment	Self-worth contingent on performance; ego-involvement	Importance of goals, values, and regulations	Coherence among goals, values, and regulations	Interest and enjoyment of the task
Lack of Motivation	Controlled Motivation	Moderately Controlled Motivation	Moderately Autonomous Motivation	Autonomous Motivation	Inherently Autonomous Motivation

Kevin Cupido and Jacques Ophoff

Figure 1: Self-determination continuum (Gagne & Deci, 2005)

Amotivation is the least self-determined, and is associated with a lack of intention to act. This comes about as a result of not valuing an activity, not feeling competent to do it, or not believing it would amount to anything (Ryan & Deci, 2000). On the other end of the scale, intrinsic motivation refers to being driven internally or from the 'inside', where autonomy and internalisation are at their peak and relates to an individual drive to do something because of enjoyment or satisfaction. For an individual, autonomy denotes choice and therefore being in control.

Extrinsic motivation is divided into types of behaviour regulation, being that of external, introjected, identified, and integrated. An example of external regulation would be the need for incentives or reward as 'encouragement' to perform a task (Kauffmann & Schulze, 2011). Internalisation of behaviour regulation occurs when external regulation of behaviours and their associated values no longer require the external stimulus. Introjected regulation is, "internalised extrinsic motivation" (Gagne & Deci, 2005, p. 334), where a behaviour regulation is taken in but is not accepted as one's own (Ryan & Deci, 2000). This would lead someone to take action because of internal pressure based on ego or the desire to increase self-worth. Identified regulation is when more autonomy is perceived even though an activity may not be intrinsically motivating. This is a sense that the activity resonates with internal values and goals, an understanding and attached importance to performing an activity. With integrated regulation this association with values and goals goes deeper, beyond just awareness and importance of the behaviour to it being perceived as a reflection of the self, or 'who you are'. Extrinsic motivation reduces autonomy, but as extrinsically motivated behaviours are internalised, they become more self-determined, and being more self-determined equates to a feeling of being 'in control', and greater feelings of autonomy (Ryan & Deci, 2000). Internalisation also increases with feelings of competence, or the ability to perform, and relatedness which is the individual association with a group or community.

Within a crowdsourcing system, some tasks may be both intrinsically and extrinsically motivated. Different crowdsourcing systems use incentives as motivation, whereas others are driven by individual, social, or personal values and principles.

265

4. Rewards

Batson, Ahmed & Tsang (2002) presents a 'rewards' perspective divided into *self, social, or material*. This would include upholding of self-esteem, recognition, status, praise and payment or prizes. Batson et al. (2002) notes that these are not exclusive categorisations as even though individuals may be driven by self-interest, the result of their actions could also have some 'unintended' benefits for the group or community.

4.1   Self

Some individuals are driven by self-interest, whether that is for pure enjoyment, recognition or financial gain. Batson et al. (2002) argue that individuals exhibit other motives such as altruism, collectivism and principlism, with principlism relating to aspects such as juctice. Altruism is described as the motivation to assist others more broadly, on an individal level, whereas collectivism is characterised by a greater preference for a particular in-group. However, altruism is seen a means to gain an internal rather than external reward, by feeling good about oneself, or to avoid negative feelings such as guilt. Vassileva (2003) mentions that the use of emotions such as guilt, a sense of belonging and relatedness, or owing, could help to kindle feelings of altruism which can drive an individual to action. However, the intentions for altruism are not always clear and as such can encompass both self and social rewards.

4.2   Social

Henn et al. (2007) suggest that a strong positive relationship exists between social capital and civic attitudes. Strong or weak ties between individuals create trust networks, described using social capital (Putnam, 2000). Stronger ties are bonding relationships between homogenous groups, typically between family or close friends, characterised by frequent contact and high levels of trust. Bridging relationships on the other hand are between heterogeneous groups where there is less contact and consequently lower trust. Power relationships or linking social capital are vertical connections such as those between different socio-economic groups, or a link from citizens to government. The motivation to participate is greater if 'significant others' highlight the importance of an activity. Hence participants seek approval and in addition it promotes a 'sense of belonging', or 'sense of relatedness' in SDT terms and facilitates internalisation (Ryan & Deci, 2000). These significant others are those with whom there are close relationships and would include family members, friends, or other close members within the online community (Leimeister et al., 2009; Vassileva, 2003).

It should be noted that self and social motivations are not mutually exclusive as, "the decision to participate in politics may be motivated by both a desire to make things better for everyone (altruism) and a desire to specifically acquire as many benefits as possible for an ingroup (social identification)" (Fowler & Kam, 2007, p. 816).

4.3   Material

A common crowdsourcing process would be to put out a call for ideas or solutions to a stated problem with the motivation to participate being a bounty or prize. "The crowd-sourcing model is faced with a question that has long concerned economists, psychologists, and management theorists; that is, whether and how financial incentives can be used to motivate workplace performance" (Mason & Watts, 2010, p. 100). Leimeister et al. (2009) mention that motivation to participate comes about with the right mix of incentives. Bayus (2013) notes that in the case of financial incentives one large prize would attract those who were prepared to put in the most effort, which typically turns out to be those who were more skilled. On the other hand those who were less-skilled put in more effort when there were several smaller prizes. Yet, the creativity of submissions was not affected by the size of the prize at all, and despite a large number of entries, a single large prize resulted in fewer creative ideas.

Lakhani & Wolf (2005) note that both intrinsic and extrinsic motivations appear to be balanced within OSS projects. Pedersen (2013) also reports a study in which a purely intrinsic-driven crowdsourcing initiative resulted in only 35% of tasks being completed, concluding that some form of extrinsic motivation (external regulation) may still be required. Whereas the other 'internalised' extrinsic motivators besides external regulation may be more desirable, financial rewards cannot be ruled out as a mechanism to drive participation.

5. Task purpose and type

As indicated in SDT, a goal is only internalised when it is both understood and the person has the necessary ability or competence in order to achieve it (Ryan & Deci, 2000). According to Brabham (2008) and Pedersen et al. (2013), the success of crowdsourcing solutions are dependent on the clarity of tasks or activities, and even extrinsic motivations would fail to drive participation if tasks or activities were poorly designed (Skinner, 2009). Leimeister et al. (2009) indicate that design plays an important part in the successful implementation of a crowdsourcing competition or challenge. Pedersen et al. (2013, p. 7) mention that "a positive user experience is a strong predictor of continued involvement" for participants in a crowdsourcing system.

Design refers to aesthetics as well as the design of the challenge or campaign and of external incentives which can have an effect on motivation (Kauffmann & Schulze, 2011). Design considerations that would support this include planned processes with clear descriptions of purpose and tasks. A process consists of steps that have to be taken in order to arrive at a certain outcome or result (Pedersen et al., 2013). These can range from simple tasks such as idea gathering to more complex collaborative activities. Failure to implement clearly defined processes can lead to confusion or a perception that the system is not useful and could lead to amotivation. Citizens also need tasks that they feel comfortable and competent at performing, otherwise it could also result in amotivation (Elliot & Dweck, 2005).

Poetz & Schreier (2012) distinguish between needs-based and solutions-based enquiry. Needs-based would be in the form of a request for a list of problems or issues which may not have been addressed. A crowd-rating stage may follow, to identify the most pressing or popular items, and the solution itself may then still be left up to government. Conversly, tasks or challenges that request solutions may require a citizen with a different level of knowledge. Some commercial crowdsourcing solutions restrict the more collaborative types such as crowd-creation to 'expert' citizen, who are believed to have specific domain knowledge. This may be sensitive within a public participation context as it could be seen to mirror the kind of exclusion that exists in real-world participation alluded to by Bang (2009).

For some citizens participation would mean being part of a collaborative process. Some may be content with posting ideas while for others participation would be the means by which they can cast their vote on issues. A crowdsourcing system therefore needs to cater for different levels, or grading, of tasks so that it is as inclusive as possible, empowering a wide spectrum of citizens in the process.

6. Management and feedback

Although excessive control is not desirable, a lack of governance can make the system uncontrollable. Jain (2010) advises that appropriate mechanisms be put in place to 'steer' the crowd, helping to maintain focus towards the completion of tasks. In this regard, some lessons can be learned from Communities of Practice (COP), which are voluntary associations between individuals with a common interest. In COP individuals feel that they could derive some value from association with others and therefore share learning. For an organisation COP are to be supported as it helps individuals perform better. However, as it is not a formal structure it is better facilitated than managed or controlled, otherwise "they lose their unique identity and cease to function as self-organising COP" (Grant, Hackney & Edgar, 2010, p. 227). As with the experience of COP, a balance is needed that allows for freedom of expression while maintaining a certain level of control. Agreed rules and policies also facilitate trust between participants as well as in the system (Leimeister et al., 2009; Preece & Shneiderman, 2009). Failure to implement these would "destabilize an online community and interfere with the problem solving abilities of the crowd" (Brabham, 2009, p. 257). Effective stewardship would allow the crowdsourcing initiative to proceed with a purpose so as to achieve the desired outcomes.

Continued future participation has been related to the feedback provided to participant contributions and motivation is driven by the desire for recognition and status (Halavais, 2011). Wanting recognition is an important motivator for indivuduals (Lampel & Bhalla, 2007). Other motivators would include community visibility of contributions and recognition for the quality and quantity of individual contributions (Preece & Shneiderman, 2009). This underlines the importance of system features and mechanisms that allow for feedback and recognition. An effective mechanism would not only facilitate individual self-esteem and confidence but also social visibility. Besides direct individual feedback the motivation to continue in a public participation crowdsourcing initiative would be negatively affected if results or benefits were not reflected in the real-world (Warner, 2011; Lampel & Bhalla, 2007).

7. Conceptual model

The topics discussed above are combined in a conceptual model, presented in Figure 2. The model presents the critical success factors for an e-Government crowdsourcing solution and shows the relationship between factors. The factors of intrinsic motivation, extrinsic motivation, and task were derived from the reviewed literature.

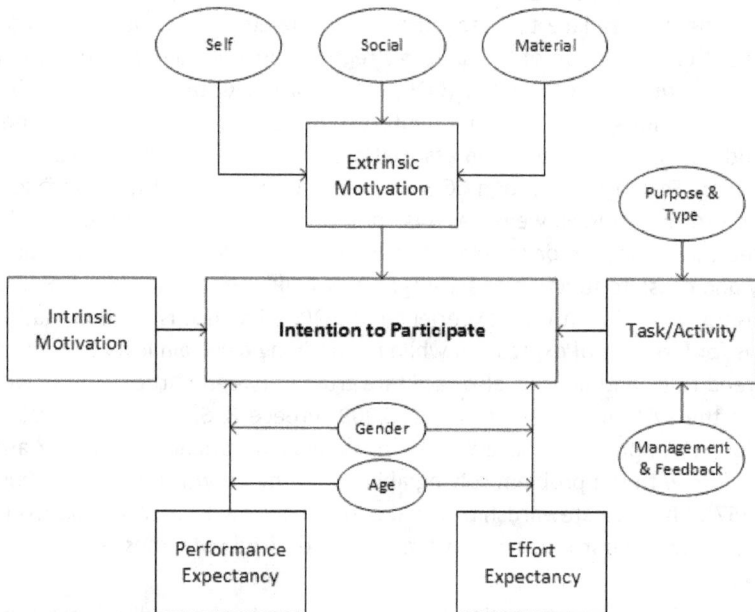

Figure 2: Conceptual model of critical success factors for an e-Government crowdsourcing solution

Two additional factors, performance expectancy and effort expectancy, are derived from the Universal Theory of Adoption and Use of technology (UTAUT). Performance expectancy refers broadly to perceived usefulness and the degree to which a person believes the system will be beneficial. In the UTAUT it is considered to be the strongest predictor of intention to use a technology (Venkatesh, et al., 2003). Effort expectancy is the "degree of ease associated with the use of the system" (Venkatesh, et al., 2003, p. 450).

It is noted that both performance expectancy and effort expectancy will be moderated by gender and age (Venkatesh, et al., 2003). Within the UTAUT these are both predicted drivers of behavioural intention, which is referred to as 'Intention to Participate' in the model.

8. Conclusion

Successful implementations of crowdsourcing within the non-government space has managed to mobilise large numbers of people and thus it offers the possibility of addressing citizen 'apathy' and tapping citizen ingenuity. Although there has been some experimentation, the lack of government use of crowdsourcing could in part be the result of a lack of management and skills to correctly implement e-Government initiatives. Another reason could be the lack of a suitable platforms either because they are inaccessible to the majority of citizens, or because they are not suitable for crowdsourcing initiatives. Although it may at first seem an obvious choice, social networking platforms such as Facebook, which is privately owned and unregulated, would have to address issues around control and privacy as well as other system-related issues such as workflow, tasks, management, and mechanisms for incentives and feedback (Cobo, 2012).

This research assimilates prior research on crowdsourcing-related issues into a conceptual model, proposing critical success factors for a potential e-Government crowdsourcing solution. While information systems are typically envisaged to support operations, provide structure, or manage processes, this research highlights the importance of including mechanisms to facilitate and increase motivation. A quantitative study would assist with a broad understanding, though it cannot answer deeper 'why' questions. Brabham (2010, p. 1128) calls for more crowdsourcing cases to add "rich qualitative data... to the stable of research on the crowdsourcing model, all with the intent to develop best practices and core findings for use in government". A mixed-methods sequential explanatory design is suggested going forward.

A citizen shift from a 'once-off' election mind-set to one of 'on-going' participation would require changes in government employee mind-set and skills, as well as changes to existing structures and processes. This highlights a limitation of this research in that it is wholly focused on the mechanisms to increase citizen participation and does not explore the impact of crowdsourcing on government structures. Future research should address the government perspective, as it would require a shift from traditional bureaucratic processes and require government officials with different skillsets. A proposed model could assist by providing guidelines for conducting a crowdsourcing initiative implemented on existing platforms, or highlight system features required in a new system build.

References

Bagui, L., Sigwejo, A. & Bytheway, A. (2011). Public participation in government: assessing m-Participation inSouth Africa and Tanzania. Johannesburg, Cape Peninsula University of Technology, pp. 5-26.

Bang, H. P. (2009). 'Yes we can': identity politics and project politics for a late-modern world. Urban Research & Practice, April, 2(2), pp. 117-137.

Bani, M. (2012). Crowdsourcing Democracy: The Case of Icelandic Social Constitutionalism. Politics and Policy in the Information Age, pp. 1-19.

Batson, D. S., Ahmed, N. & Tsang, J.-A. (2002). Four Motives for Community Involvement. Journal of Social Issues, 58(3), pp. 429-445.

Bayus, B. (2013). Crowdsourcing: Fresh Thinking or Online Fad?. [online] Available at: http://www.kenan-flagler.unc.edu/faculty/roi-magazine/spring-2013/crowdsourcing-fresh-thinking-or-online-fad

Brabham, D. (2010). Moving the Crowd at Threadless. Information, Communication & Society, 17 August, 13(8), pp. 1122-1145.

Brabham, D. C. (2009). Crowdsourcing the Public Participation Process for Planning Projects. Planning Theory, 8(3), pp. 242-262.

Brabham, D. C. (2012). Motivations for Participation in a Crowdsourcing Application to Improve Public Engagement in Transit Planning. Journal of Applied Communication research, 40(3), pp. 307-328.

Brücher, H. & Baumberger, P. (2003). Using Mobile Technology to Support eDemocracy. Hawaii, Hawaii International Conference on System Sciences, p. 144b.

Charalabidis, Y., Triantafillou, A., Karkaletsis, V. & Loukis, E. (2012). Public Policy Formulation through Non Moderated Crowdsourcing in Social Media. Kristiansand, Norway, Springer Berlin Heidelberg, pp. 156-169.

Cloete, F. (2012). e-Government lessons From South Africa 2001 - 2011: Institutions, State of progress and Measurement. The African Journal of Information and Communication, pp. 128-142.

Cobo, C. (2012). Networks for citizen consultation and citizen sourcing of expertise. Contemporary Social Science, 7(3), pp. 283-304.

Dada, D. (2006). The failure of e-Government in Developing Countries : A Literature Review. The Electronic Journal of Information Systems in Developing Countries, 26(7), pp. 1-10.

Elliot, A. J. & Dweck, C. S. eds. (2005). Handbook of Competence and Motivation. Newy York: Guidlford Press.

Estellés-Arolas, E. & González-Ladrón-de-Guevara, F. (2012). Towards an integrated Crowdsourcing Definition. Journal of Information Science, 38(2), pp. 189-200.

Fowler, J. T. & Kam, C. D. (2007). Beyond the Self: Social Identity, Altruism, and Political Participation. The Journal of Politics, 69(3), pp. 813-827.

Gagne, M. & Deci, E. L. (2005). Self-determination Theory and Work Motivation. Journal of Organizational Behaviour, 26(1), pp. 331-362.

Geiger, D., Rosemann, M. & Fielt, E. (2011). Crowdsourcing Information Systems – A Systems Theory Perspective. Sydney, s.n.

Halavais, A. (2011). Do Dugg Diggers Digg Diligently. Information, Communication & Society, pp. 444-459.

Henn, M., Weinstein, M. & Hodgkinson, S. (2007). Social Capital and Political Participation: Understanding the Dynamics of Young People's Political Disengagement in Contemporary Britain. Social Policy & Society, 6(4), pp. 467-479.

Howe, J. (2006). The Rise of Crowdsourcing. June, 14(6), pp. 1-5.

Kauffmann, N. & Schulze, T. (2011). More than fun and money. Worker Motivation in Crowdsourcing – A Study on Mechanical Turk. Detroit, s.n.

Koch, G. F. J. & Brunswicker, S. (2011). Online Crowdsourcing in the Public Sector: How to Design Open Government Platforms. Orlando, Florida, Springer Berlin Heidelberg, pp. 203-212.

Lakhani, K. R. & Wolf, R. G. (2005). Why Hackers Do What They Do: Understanding Motivation and Effort in Free/Open Source Software Projects. In Perspectives on Free and Open Source Software, MIT Press..

Lampel, J. & Bhalla, A. (2007). The Role of Status Seeking in Online Communities: Giving the Gift of Experience. Journal of Computer-Mediated Communication, 12(2), pp. 434-455.

Leimeister, J. m., Huber, M., Bretschneider, U. & Krcmar, A. H. (2009). Leveraging Crowdsourcing: Activation-Supporting Components for IT-Based Ideas Competition. Journal of Management Information Systems, 26(1), pp. 197-224.

Li, Y. & Marsh, D. (2008). New Forms of Political Participation: Searching for Expert Citizens and Everyday Makers. British journal of Political Science, Volume 38, pp. 247-272.

Marsh, D. (2011). Late Modernity and the Changing Nature of Politics: Two Cheers for Henrik Bang. Critical Policy Studies, 5(1), pp. 73-89.

Mason, W. & Watts, D. J. (2010). Financial incentives and the performance of crowds. ACM SigKDD Explorations Newsletter, pp. 100-108.

Pedersen, J., Kocsis, D., Tripathi, A., Tarrell, A., Weerakoon, A., Tahmasbi, N., Jie Xiong, Wei Deng, Onook Oh & de Vreede, G.-J. (2013). Conceptual Foundations of Crowdsourcing: A Review of IS Research. 46th Hawaii International Conference on System Sciences (HICSS), pp. 579-588.

Poetz, M. K. & Schreier, M. (2012). The value of crowdsourcing: can users really compete with professionals in generating new product ideas?. Journal of Product Innovation Management, 29(2), pp. 245-256.

Preece, J. & Shneiderman, B. (2009). The Reader-to-Leader Framework: Motivating Technology-Mediated Social Participation. AIS Transactions on Human-Computer Interaction , March, 1(1), pp. 13-32.

Ryan, R. M. & Deci, E. L. (2000). Self-Determination Theory and the Facilitation of Intrinsic Motivation Social Development and Well-Being. Amercian Psychologist, January, 55(1), pp. 68-78.

Seltzer, E. & Mahmoudi, D. (2012). Citizen Participation, Open Innovation, and Crowdsourcing Challenges and Opportunities for Planning. Journal of Planning Literature, 28(1), pp. 3-18.

Vassileva, J. (2003). Motivating Participation in Peer to Peer Communities. Madrid, Spain, Spinger Berlin Heidelberg, pp. 141-155.

Venkatesh, V., Morris, M. G., Davis, G. B. & Davis, F. D. (2003). User Acceptance of Information Technology: Toward a Unified View. MIS Quarterly, 27(3), pp. 425-478.

Warner, J. (2011). Next Steps in e-Government Crowdsourcing. Maryland, USA, ACM, pp. 177-181.

Williams, J. J. (2006). Community Participation : Lessons from post-apartheid South Africa. Policy Studies, 27(3), pp. 197-217.